"Vine Deloria—that giant oak tree of a man—accomplishes what I would have thought impossible. It is the best book he wrote. Its virtues begin with its conception. Instead of summarizing what the visionaries of his people saw and understood, he draws on his vast data bank—vaster than that of anyone else's of our time, and very likely any time—to let them speak for themselves. … This is a veritable library between two covers. Its conception, its scope, and its eloquence make it, in my judgement, the best single book on Native Americans that has been written. Novices and pundits will gain from it equally.

This book is a priceless addition to the history of humankind."

—Huston Smith, author of *The World's Religions*

The World We Used to Live In

The World We Used to Live In
Remembering the Powers of the Medicine Men

Vine Deloria Jr.

Fulcrum Publishing
Golden, Colorado

Library of Congress Cataloging-in-Publication Data

Deloria, Vine.
  The world we used to live in : remembering the powers of the
  medicine men / Vine Deloria Jr.
        p. cm.
    Includes bibliographical references.
    ISBN-13: 978-1-55591-564-3 (pbk.)
    ISBN-10: 1-55591-564-7
    1. Shamans—North America. 2. Indians of North America
—Medicine. 3. Indians of North America—Religion. 4. Indians of
North America—Rites and ceremonies.   I. Title.
    E98.M4D45 2006
    299.7—dc22

                                                              2006000100

ISBN-13: 978-1-55591-564-3

Printed in the United States of America
0 9 8 7 6

Editorial: Sam Scinta, Katie Raymond
Cover and interior design: Jack Lenzo
Cover image courtesy of Sam English

Fulcrum Publishing
4690 Table Mountain Drive, Suite 100
Golden, Colorado 80403
800-992-2908 • 303-277-1623
www.fulcrumbooks.com

CONTENTS

✶ ✶ ✶ ✶ ✶ ✶ ✶ ✶ ✶ ✶ ✶ ✶ ✶

Chapter Three

Continuing Communications 83

Chapter Six

Chapter Seven

PREFACE

✳ ✳ ✳ ✳ ✳ ✳ ✳ ✳ ✳ ✳ ✳ ✳ ✳ ✳

Vine Deloria Jr., like all human beings, was a man of complications and contradictions. Unlike most, his complexities were sometimes lived out under public scrutiny. Nowhere was this more the case than in his understanding of faith, tradition, and spiritual practice. Some have wondered how he squared his work in politics and law—which required a national vision and a profound secularism—with his equally vehement insistence on the power and validity of indigenous (and, indeed, all) spiritual experience. Given this insistence, they ask, why was he not a more active participant in the spiritual life of Indian people? These are not unfair questions, and the book you hold in your hands offers at least some sense of his understanding.

Tracing Vine Deloria Jr.'s career, one might follow a trajectory that runs from his initial engagement with Indian policy and politics as executive director of the National Congress of American Indians (NCAI), to the literary and legal activism that followed the 1969 publication of *Custer Died for Your Sins*, to later engagements with theology, philosophy, and metaphysics, to the critique of the politics of scientific knowledge that characterized his last years. Such a peri-odization—entirely reasonable, by the way—would, however, sepa-rate out long-lasting and overlapping interests. His career was as much a layering of these things as it was a progression from one to another. It would also ignore a curious and vital part of his life—an intellectual bedrock that developed in relation to western philosophy and theology.

Vine Deloria Jr. graduated from Iowa State University in 1958. At the time, Iowa State was a college rather than a university, and it offered only the bachelor of science degree. He majored in general science, which meant a broad background in social and natural sciences. His formative intellectual experiences, however, came out of encounters with the theological and philosophical classics. Wishing to pursue these fields further, he entered the Lutheran School of Theology in February 1959, graduating, after a couple of detours, in 1963. He had, in other words, a long and sustained interest in questions of spirituality, faith, knowledge, and practice. Though that interest would later prove well suited to bridging indigenous and Western traditions, the possibility of such bridging was latent and undeveloped in the mid-1960s.

His experiences at NCAI and the publication of *Custer Died for Your Sins* changed everything. Vine Deloria Jr. rapidly developed his political and rhetorical talents in a national arena, which required an orientation to big pictures and strategic contexts. He cultivated what would become an unparalleled expertise in the legal and political situations of hundreds of tribes across the country. He trained himself in history, law, politics, and education, and he learned the ways of the American academy. All of these things he did to advance the place of Indian people in the world. In celebrating this overriding, unwavering purpose, it is critical to understand that his seemingly "secular" actions originated in a spiritual history, one that, as he has recounted in the book *Singing for a Spirit*, stemmed from a four-generation family vision of broad, cross-cultural leadership. His political and intellectual path—which had both spiritual origins and spiritual consequences—pointed him away from a specific, intimate engagement with any home community. And if there was one essential of which he was convinced, it was that indigenous spiritual practice relied decisively upon the unity and presence of a human-scale community. He found himself arguing for the power and legitimacy of indigenous spirituality then, without engaging substantially in its practice. This disengagement had no small measure of irony, perhaps, but it should also be read as a measure of his understanding of and respect for that practice.

Vine Deloria Jr. passed to the spirit world on November 13, 2005. Only days before, he finished the final revisions of this manuscript. An apparently simple and straightforward book, it can also be seen as a complex kind of coming home, a weaving together of the many strands of his life and work. At the broadest level, this project returned him to his oldest interests in theology and experience and led him to decry the gross secularism that has devalued *all* spiritual tradition. Writing as a historian, he insists that old accounts of spiritual power be read not in terms of magical trickery or performance, but as real manifestations of the permeating reality of indigenous spiritual power. He speaks, as always, directly to Indian people, calling forth what has been lost and raising the possibility that contemporary ceremonies are simply "walk-throughs" that have little effect on participants. Given the importance of ceremonial life to Native people today, the critique has the potential to be a devastating one. Optimistic to the core, however—and in the spirit of the critiques he willingly launched at tribal politics, leadership, and education—Vine Deloria Jr. did not fail to offer an indigenous alternative.

Not surprisingly, he uses logic to make an argument about faith. Reshuffle the categories that have been used to sort hundreds and hundreds of reports of indigenous spiritual power, he tells us, and you will find that what has been easily read as anomalous should, in fact, be taken as representative of a different and better world. Real power, in other words, exists in and on this earth. That argument is then linked to his critique in order to provide a road map for the future. If we can but see the possibilities that our ancestors experienced, he argues, we can recapture the reality of spiritual power for Indian people today. His own words, as usual, express his desire better than any others: "A collection of these stories, placed in a philosophical framework, might demonstrate to the present and coming generations the sense of humility, the reliance on the spirits, and the immense powers that characterized our people in the old days. It might also inspire people to treat their ceremonies with more respect and to seek out the great powers that are always available to people who look first to the spirits and then to their own resources."

The legacy of Vine Deloria Jr. is rich and complex, bridging multiple kinds of knowledge, multiple sets of people, and multiple visions of the future. This book offers a fitting capstone to his career, for it encapsulates those multiplicities, while also returning to the root, the core, the bedrock—his own faith in the powers that exist in the world and in the ability of Indian people to draw upon them as resources for Indian futures. It is, in many ways, the work of an elder, a label my father resisted for a very long time. This fall, as he struggled with his health, it came to seem, to me at least, that he passed into a new kind of intellectual experience. He had perceived the virtues of an elder's wisdom—a deep, reflective, and meditative sensibility—and he had embraced those virtues. This book, which is so much about listening to the old ways, marks not simply his passing, but a loss that we have only glimpsed. The world has known Vine Deloria Jr. in the spring, summer, and autumn of his life. We can only imagine the things he would have been able to say as an elder, during a wintertime of reflection. This book stands, then, as a taste of that which we will never know.

—Philip J. Deloria

PROLOGUE

* * * * * * * * * * * * * * *

TRADITIONAL RELIGION TODAY

Sweat lodges conducted for $50, peyote meetings for $1,500, medicine drums for $300, weekend workshops and vision quests for $500, two do-it-yourself practitioners smothered in their own sweat lodge—the interest in American Indian spirituality only seems to grow and manifests itself in increasingly bizarre behavior—by both Indians and non-Indians. Manifestos have been issued, lists of people no longer welcome on the reservations have been compiled, and biographies of proven fraudulent medicine men have been publicized. Yet nothing seems to stem the tide of abuse and misuse of Indian ceremonies. Indeed, some sweat lodges in the suburbs at times seem like the opening move in a scenario of seduction of naive but beautiful women who are encouraged to play the role of "Mother Earth" in bogus ceremonies.

Even on the most traditional reservations, the erosion of the old ways is so profound that many people are willing to cast aside ceremonies that stood them in good stead for thousands of years and live in increasing and meaningless secularity. The consumer society is indeed consuming everything in its path. It is fair to say that the overwhelming majority of Indian people today have little understanding or remembrance of the powers once possessed by the spiritual leaders of their communities. What we do today is often simply a "walk-through" of a once-potent ceremony that now has little visible

effect on the participants. The exercise of spiritual powers still continues in some places but lacks the definitive intensity of the old days.
Like the Christian sacraments, the mystery is largely gone, and in its
place is the perfunctory recitation of good thoughts not unlike the
mantras of self-improvement books and videos that remind us we are
our own best friends.

The secularity of the society in which we live must share considerable blame in the erosion of spiritual powers of all traditions,
since our society has become a parody of social interaction lacking
even an aspect of civility. Believing in nothing, we have preempted
the role of the higher spiritual forces by acknowledging no greater
good than what we can feel and touch. The change of living conditions
experienced by Indian people in the last century also has a great deal
to do with the erosion of our spiritual powers. Wrenched from a free
life where the natural order had to be understood and obeyed, confined within a foreign educational system where memorization and
recital substitute for learning and knowledge, each generation of
Indians has been moved farther and farther away from the substance of
the spiritual energy that once directed our lives. We no longer have
the testimony of eyewitnesses who saw the spectacular feats of our
spiritual leaders and understood that there were much larger boundaries than the life of accumulating goods. We no longer depend on
the presence and wisdom of elders who can consult with the spirits
and give us their counsel when making important decisions. Most of
us cannot even fathom how living in that manner would be.

The society in which we live tends to isolate the facts of experience and then to accept only those facts that support already popular beliefs and dogmas. People discredit or discard facts that call into
question the socially acceptable explanations of phenomena. So it has
been with the stories of the exercise of spiritual powers of medicine
men and spiritual leaders. There are hundreds of reports from eyewitnesses or unimpeachable sources hidden in diaries, biographies,
commentaries, and scholarly writings that reveal a world wholly different from the one in which we live. But each account has been kept
in isolation so that, by itself, it is merely a strange story that can easily

be dismissed as a quirk in which the narrator admits a clever magician fooled him or her. We come to believe that things were not much different a century ago than they are today. This uncritical acceptance of modernism has prevented us from seeing that higher spiritual powers are still active in the world. We cannot, for the most part, believe that a firm relationship with them can be cultivated today. We need to glimpse the old spiritual world that helped, healed, and honored us with its presence and companionship. We need to see where we have been before we see where we should go, we need to know how to get there, and we need to have help on our journey.

Growing up in Bennett County, South Dakota, and listening to stories of the old days and learning, from time to time, of the unusual things that were still being done by spiritual leaders, I have never emotionally or intellectually questioned the veracity of the old accounts. Over the years, I have listened to stories told by others or accidentally come across accounts of incidents in which amazing spiritual powers were displayed. Our ancestors invoked the assistance of higher spiritual entities to solve pressing practical problems, such as finding game, making predictions of the future, learning about medicines, participating in healings, conversing with other creatures, finding lost objects, and changing the course of physical events through a relationship with the higher spirits who controlled the winds, the clouds, the mountains, the thunders, and other phenomena of the natural world. Knowing how little superstition exists in Indian communities, I have always considered these accounts as truthful remembrances of past events. Medicine men, for the most part, performed their healings and predictions in front of large Indian audiences that were saying, "Show Me" long before Missouri adopted that slogan for itself.

In regard to the veracity of these accounts, many skeptics abound. People reject the stories and claim (in self-protection) that the demonstration of spiritual powers was delusional or coincidental, that it involved trickery or sleight of hand, that it was not properly reported in the first place. Or they argue that the original story was greatly elaborated to make it sound supernatural. Thus they can easily excuse each story or anecdote describing the exercise of spiritual powers. Many accounts have been lost because the non-Indians who heard the stories tended to treat them as fables made up to entertain children or scare them into behaving.

Over the years, as I found these stories, I began to xerox and file them as against some future time when they might be useful. But what would they really illustrate, except the presence of spiritual powers in the old days and the glaring lack of such powers today? Then I came across a statement by an Eagle power medicine man reported by Thomas Lewis in his book *The Medicine Men*: "It would be helpful to return to the old religions in a new form. It would help the Indian people and give them a sort of spiritual strength they need to be able to move on to a less destructive life without such things as liquor, accidents, and people begging and walking the highways asking for rides."[1]

It then occurred to me that a collection of these stories, placed in a philosophical framework, might demonstrate to the present and coming generations the sense of humility, the reliance of the spirits, and the immense powers that characterized our people in the old days. It might also inspire people to treat their ceremonies with more respect and to seek out the great powers that are always available to people who look first to the spirits and then to their own resources. As the collection of stories grew and the reality behind the events became more obvious, I could see many connections between the practices and beliefs of our ancestors and some of the thoughts of contemporary non-Indian thinkers. Reading the non-Indian materials reassured me that there was wholeness in the manner in which our ancestors related to the world that transcended the popular beliefs of today and had a place in human understanding alongside other great spiritual and philosophical traditions.

This collection is hardly complete. It is more a sketch of a vast field of inquiry. It represents those accounts I was fortunate enough to find. A thorough search of the old literature would produce much more additional material that could further illuminate the relationships that are possible with the spiritual world and its entities. In gathering materials, I found a strange but not unexpected fact: there are very few accounts of the powers of medicine men from tribes east of the Mississippi, although their contact with Europeans was both profound and quite lengthy. Both the Catholic and Protestant missionaries in early colonial days observed the wonderful feats of the medicine men but interpreted them as works of the devil. So in such sources as *The Jesuit Relations*, many times Indian ceremonies are hinted at, but rarely are they described. Only when a missionary had a reasonably open mind and was stunned by the experience were stories recorded with some degree of accuracy.

Not only that, but there are hardly any accounts of Indian spiritual feats to be found in the literature of the Southwest, these tribes generally being wise enough not to allow strangers into their ceremonies who might write down what they experienced. The southwestern tribes are to be congratulated for their protection of sacred ceremonies and for their continued use of the ceremonies to help their communities. While some dances and ceremonies have been open to the public, for the most part there remains a reservoir of spiritual power in the traditional people of those tribes. One need only view a picture of Frank Cushing, the anthropologist who studied the Zuni, in his Indian costume to see how insidious have been the efforts to uncover the secrets of the religious practitioners of those tribes.

In the northern Plains, not unexpectedly, we can find a substantial number of stories recounting the exercise of spiritual powers of the people. Very few of these stories originate in the missionaries' literature, such as diaries and monthly reports to their superiors. Indeed, most accounts come from people such as trappers and traders who would not ordinarily be associated with spiritual matters. Biographers, travelers, and longtime residents also recorded the unique things they had experienced, and they generally gave an accurate and objective account without a frightened, defensive, theological commentary. Perhaps the best source of accounts of spiritual feats is Frances Densmore's *Teton Sioux Music and Culture*, which recounts her visit to the Standing Rock Reservation in the early part of the last century. Densmore faithfully recorded what the old men told her, and her book is a treasure-house of material, demonstrating how rich was the way the people lived and how dependant they were on the spiritual world for assistance. Indeed, reading her book and encountering the wide variety of unusual events represented by a few of the tribal elders demonstrates quite clearly that they were a uniquely spiritual people who had important stories to tell. Sadly, one wishes that Densmore or people like her had visited every tribe and written down their stories, for each tribe had its special relationship with the higher powers and could have contributed many marvelous stories to this collection.

Introduction

✶ ✶ ✶ ✶ ✶ ✶ ✶ ✶ ✶ ✶ ✶ ✶ ✶ ✶ ✶

The Universe of Spirits

Every Indian tribe has a spiritual heritage that distinguishes them from all other people. Indeed, in the past, recognizing their unique relationship to the world and its creatures, most tribes described themselves as "the people" or "the original people." Regarding themselves as unique, they rigorously followed the commands of the spirits as they had experienced them over uncounted generations and recognized that other peoples had the same rights and status as themselves. So the idea of quarreling over the traditions by which they lived was felt to be absurd. Religious wars, then, were simply inconceivable, and while they may have fought ferociously over hunting and fishing grounds or launched hostilities in vengeance, the closest they came to combat over beliefs and practices was to find medicines—powers—that could negate the medicine and power possessed by other peoples.

Many avenues of spiritual expression seem to have been shared by tribes. Many tribes practiced the sun dance, the spirit lodge, the vision quest, the sweat lodge, use of sacred stones, and other rituals, with slight variations in format, that originated in the past. Certain birds and animals offered their help to people with some degree of uniformity. The bear, wolf, eagle, buffalo, and snake lent their powers to people of many tribes, although their functions, such as healing, making prophecies, or offering protection against dangers, were often similar. Some animals, such as the bear, seem to appear in almost every tribal heritage as healers or providers of medicines. It should not be surprising, therefore, to find that the helpful animal spirit appears in many roles in the history of many tribes.

In order to understand the scope and intensity of the spiritual powers possessed by our ancestors, I have arranged the stories of their exploits in a somewhat developmental fashion. I begin with the apprehension of the natural world and the life force within, behind, and directing it. We then move to an examination of the communications received in dreams and to the unusual encounters with the sacred that led people to devise ways to open themselves to the high powers. The vision quest seems to have been nearly universal and represented a human effort to establish a relationship with whatever spiritual powers agreed to assist people. Then come, in no particular order, the reports of the exercise of unusual powers by various spiritual leaders in a variety of circumstances. Some of these examples will be familiar to people, others will come as a surprise, and some will cause embarrassment—did I really read that book and miss this incident? For the convenience of the student and scholar, I reproduce the accounts exactly as I found them. They are set off clearly as extracts or in quotation marks, with the sources documented, so that if the reader wants a copy of the original story, he or she need only to reproduce the page to make them available. Where I interject my own voice within the extracts, the material is italicized. The final chapters of the book try to relate these materials to some of the current thinking in several interesting fields.

THE PATHS OF SPIRITUAL EXPERIENCE

In order to understand the spiritual/intellectual journey of the Indian elders, we must start where they began their quest for understanding. There were two paths that led them to make sense of their world: empirical observation of the physical world and the continuing but sporadic intrusion of higher powers in their lives, manifested in unusual events and dreams. From observing the world around them, they could see orderly processes that marked the way organic life behaved. From the obvious motions of the sun and moon to the effects of periodic winds, rains, and snows, the regularity of nature suggested some greater power that guaranteed enough stability to be reliable and within which lives had meaning. By observing the behavior and growth of other organic forms of life, they could see that a benign personal energy flowed through everything and undergirded the physical world. They understood that their task was to fit into the physical world in the most constructive manner and to establish relationships with the higher power, or powers, that created and sustained the universe. They sought to learn a way of living that would most efficiently accomplish these tasks. This posture was not unique to any tribe; it was generally the way Indians of all tribes described the mysterious reality that affected their lives.[1]

Observations, however, were not enough. People had dreams in which aspects of the living universe came forward to urge them to take certain well-defined paths of behavior. Often in dreams, a bird, animal, or stone would speak to them, offer its friendship and advice, or reveal the future, information they could not possibly derive from the most intense observation of the physical world. The people had no good reason to doubt these dreams, because their content was always later empirically verified in their daily lives—things they dreamt about happened. If a plant told them how to harvest it and prepare it for food or use as a medicine, they followed the plant's directions, and they always found the message to be true. From generations of experience, then, people learned to have confidence in the content of dreams and followed their instructions faithfully.

Once having intuited the regularity of the physical world, young people would consult with a spiritual leader for advice on how they could best live in the world. Over the generations, they had come to recognize that certain individuals had experiences, insights, and powers that could not be denied when searching for answers to basic questions. Today, we call these people medicine men and women, but technically, these terms should be restricted to describing those people who had medicinal powers to heal. A much better description would be the holy ones, people who had lived a more rigorous and disciplined life because they had been in contact with the higher powers. However, since the majority of sources refer to the medicine men, I have decided to use that term when talking about the holy ones of each tribe. Let us examine two examples of how the people began their spiritual journeys to get their knowledge of the living universe.

Brave Buffalo, a Teton Sioux Elder— Learning Knowledge from Dreams

> When I was 10 years of age I looked at the land and the rivers, the sky above, and the animals around me and could not fail to realize that they were made by some great power. I was so anxious to understand this power that I questioned the trees and the bushes. It seemed as though the flowers were staring at me, and I wanted to ask them: "Who made you?" I looked at the moss-covered stones; some of them seemed to have the features of a man, but they could not answer me. Then I had a dream, and in my dream one of these small stones appeared to me and told me that the maker of all was Wakan tanka, and that in order to honor him I must honor his works in nature. The stone said that by my search I had shown myself worthy of supernatural help. It said that if I were curing a sick person I might ask its assistance, and that all the forces of nature would help me work a cure."[2]

It was unusual for a ten-year-old boy to receive a stone, but this dream must have set him aside early to do great things. Generally, people would receive help to cure certain diseases and not others. We do not know if this limitation applied to Brave Buffalo's stone, but tradition would suggest that it did. Lone Man, another Teton Sioux from the same community as Brave Buffalo, solicited the assistance of a spiritual leader to get answers to the same question. The inquiry each man made is answered in a manner that would be most satisfactory to him.

Lone Man, a Teton Sioux Elder

When I was a young man I went to a medicine man for advice concerning my future. The medicine man said: "I have not much to tell you except to help you understand this earth on which you live. If a man is to succeed on the hunt of the warpath, he must not be governed by his inclination, but by an understanding of the ways of animals and of his natural surroundings, gained through close observation. The earth is large, and on it live many animals. This earth is under the protection of something which at times becomes visible to the eye. One would think this would be at the center of the earth, but its representations appear everywhere, in large and small forms—they are the sacred stones. The presence of a sacred stone will protect you from misfortune."

He then gave me a sacred stone which he himself had worn. I kept it with me wherever I went and was helped by it. He also told me where I might find one for myself. Wakan tanka tells the sacred stones many things which may happen to people. The medicine man told me to observe my natural surroundings, and after my talk with him I observed them closely. I watched the changes of the weather, the habits of animals, and all things by which I might be guided in the future, and I stored this knowledge in my mind.

Shooter

Another Sioux Elder, Shooter, saw the world in two ways: one was the clever design originating in Wakan tanka's wisdom, and the other was noting the changes that occur when the place of other creatures was disturbed. His perspective could easily be incorporated in both philosophy and biology courses as a spiritual statement of what we feel when we observe the world and its offspring that leads us to believe there is indeed a purpose to life.

The reason Wakan tanka does not make two birds, or animals, or human beings exactly alike is because each is placed here by Wakan tanka to be an independent individual and to rely on itself. Some animals are made to live in the ground. The stones and the minerals are placed in the ground by Wakan tanka, some stones being more exposed than others. When a medicine man says that he talks with the sacred stones, it is because of all the substance in the ground these are the ones which most often appear in dreams and are able to communicate with men.

All animals have not the same disposition. The horse, dog, bear, and buffalo all have their own characteristics. This is also true of the fowls of the air, the living creatures in the water, and even the insects, they all have their own ways. Thus a man may enjoy the singing of all the birds and yet have a preference for the melodies of certain kinds of birds. Or he may like all animals and yet have a favorite among them.

From my boyhood I have observed leaves, trees, and grass, and I have never found two alike. They may have a general likeness, but on examination I have found that they differ slightly. Plants are of different families, each being adapted to growth in a certain locality. It is the same with animals; they are widely scattered, and yet each will be found in the environment to which it is best adapted. It is the same with human beings, there is some place which is best adapted to each. The seeds of the plants are blown about by the wind until they reach the place where they will grow best—where the action of the sun and the presence of moisture are most favorable to them, and there they take root and grow. All living creatures and all plants are a benefit to something.

Certain animals fulfill their purpose by definite acts. The crows, buzzards, and flies are somewhat similar in their use, and even the snakes have a purpose in being. In the early days the animals probably roamed over a very wide country until they found their proper place. An animal depends a great deal on the natural conditions around it. If the buffalo were here today, I think they would be different from the buffalo of the old days because all the natural conditions have changed. They would not find the same food nor the same surroundings.

We see the change in our ponies. In the old days they could stand great hardship and travel long distances without water. They lived on certain kinds of food and drank pure water. Now our horses require a mixture of food; they have less endurance and must have constant care. It is the same with the Indians; they have less freedom and they fall an easy prey to disease. In the old days they were rugged and healthy, drinking pure water and eating the meat of the buffalo, which had a wide range, not being shut up like cattle of the present day. The water of the Missouri River is not pure, as it used to be, and many of the creeks are no longer good for us to drink.[3]

Shooter felt the goal in life was to seek the genuine and to avoid, insofar as it was possible, the artificial. Each living entity had its own particular body form, a unique set of talents peculiar to its kind, and the intelligence to make decisions based upon what knowledge it had been given to live on the earth. The task of each individual of that kind was to fulfill, as much as possible, its inherent possibilities through physical real-life experiences. Birds and animals were true to their breed, and while different birds made different nests, birds as a group were restricted to using a certain general pattern in creating a dwelling place and raising their offspring. This belief in the orderliness of things, regardless of the apparent chaos, represents the spiritual side of life—how spirit manifests itself in the physical world. This belief is not inconsistent with the findings of contemporary evolutionists who admit that species are found in complete form when they first appear in strata and change very little thereafter. Physical forms, as a rule, did not change, but animal behavior, adapted by experience, created a body of wisdom that eventually produced relationships with humans.

One might argue that the changes Shooter saw in the water,

plants, and horses were an Indian recognition of evolution. It can be equally well argued that species do not change, but simply adjust to the environment around them. As the environment and/or diet changes, all forms of life change slightly in physical form or move elsewhere, if possible, but they do not change into other species. More importantly, Shooter conceived of a primordial time when all creatures sought to find their place. Given the nature of the physical world, the proper place designed for each species maximized the contribution the environment could make to the maturity and happiness of the respective creatures. Once the proper place was found, the entity was free to develop its potential as best it could. Changes in the environment, unfortunately, more often forecast death and extinction in the physical world and a loss of spirit rather than prolonging physical life.

Lame Deer, a modern Lakota medicine man, explained this belief of the inherent talents of creatures—indeed, of the fate of every creature—in this way: Wakan tanka "only sketches out the path of life roughly for all the creatures on earth, shows them where to go, where to arrive at, but leaves them to find their own way according to their nature, to the urges in each of them."[4] Eventually, a biosphere operating at its maximum positive potential should produce a fruitful and fulfilled planet if every creature does its best to fulfill all its possibilities. We are then, in a real sense, cocreators with the ultimate powers of the universe because in striving to fulfill our destiny, we make the changes that help spiritual ideas become incarnate in the flesh. In the spirit world, there might be a wonderland of possibilities, but until an idea takes on flesh and demonstrates its significance, the universe does not appear at all.

THE HIERARCHY OF INQUIRY

By analogy, the preliminary efforts by Indians to gain knowledge of the physical world through observation and inquiry may be understood as the aboriginal equivalent of high school and college education. People come to know a great deal by observation. Add to that body of data the knowledge that was passed down in the stories told by the elders describing their experiences—the habits and practices of the other creatures or their knowledge of reading the clouds and winds. At least with respect to their own environment, these people had considerably more knowledge than we do today.

All this information certainly provided a sufficient framework to enable people to live nicely wherever their place might be, no matter how desolate the landscape. Thus, animals adjusted to different lands and the tribes adjusted to their lands also. Rupert Sheldrake commented that "knowledge gained through experience or plants and animals is not an inferior substitute for proper scientific knowledge: it is the real thing. Direct experience is the only way to build up an understanding that is not only intellectual but intuitive and practical, involving the senses and the heart as well as the rational mind."[5] The analogy is therefore appropriate. But is there a "graduate and post doctoral" level to this kind of Indian education?

Every indication we have about traditional Indian life suggests that they never stopped learning and gathering insights into the operation of the natural world. Indeed, Luther Standing Bear noted that the Indians were tuned in to the almost indiscernible rhythms of nature. "The earth was full of sounds which the old-time Indian could hear, sometimes putting his ear to it so as to hear more clearly. The forefathers of the Lakotas had done this for long ages until there had come to them real understanding of earthways. It was almost as if the man were still a part of the earth as he was in the beginning, according to the legend of the tribe."[6] And he explained how the old people continued to learn from the earth. They "came literally to love the soil and they sat or reclined on the ground with a feeling of being close to a mothering power. It was good for the skin to touch the earth and the old people liked to remove their moccasins and walk with bare feet on the sacred earth."[7] Morris Opler, in *An Apache Lifeway*, quoted an old Apache regarding the feeling toward the earth, and the sentiment is similar to that expressed by Standing Bear. "Some say that the earth talks to them. They get their ceremony from that. Some say the wind has life. Some say the mountains, like the San Andreas, have life. Anyone who gets power from it says, 'That mountain talks to me.' The old people tell stories that show that all things have life—trees, rock, the wind, mountains. One believes that there is a cliff where the Mountain People stay and they open the cliff and talk to him."[8]

CHAPTER ONE

DREAMS—THE APPROACH OF THE SACRED

* * * * * * * * * * * * *

Initial and unexpected contact with the Great Mysterious power must have come prior to the development of ceremonies and rituals for seeking a relationship with the spirits. We can imagine the surprise of the first person having an unusual, and perhaps prophetic, dream and then discovering that it accurately described an event that came to pass in his or her daily life. Surely, here was reliable information, but from an unknown source that could not be summoned at one's pleasure. How eagerly people must have yearned for similar dreams that would guide them in their daily lives!

Today, we place special emphasis on the experiences of the vision quest, but surely dreams must have preceded this ritual. That the experiences of the vision quest had a close relationship with dreams is certain, since many tribes refer to the vision quest encounters as "dreaming." This nomenclature, of course, makes it nearly impossible a century later to distinguish between the ceremonial and ritual experiences and the messages received in dreams that come to us at night. Sometimes, an elder, relating his dream, would emphasize that a vision appeared to him while he was in a waking state; other times, there was no clarification. Thus, when we are reading the old accounts of unusual happenings, unless there is qualification, we simply have to guess how the experience came about.

Not unexpectedly, dreams represent a significant percentage of the materials we will examine and lead us to conclude that in the old days, the ordinary person had as much opportunity to receive special messages as did the people who sought out the experience in visions. One common thread of the people interviewed seems to be that having received some powers in a dream, the benevolent spirit would continue to provide information and songs that would enhance the individual's capability. A person might well be told in dreams that it would be necessary for him to undertake a vision quest to expand his knowledge and receive more powers. Let us look at some of the messages received in dreams by our ancestors.

EAGLE SHIELD'S DREAM

A man appeared to me in a dream, showed me a plant, and said, "My friend, remember this plant well. Be sure to get the right one, as this is good." It was a badger who appeared to me in the form of a man and said this. It was the first time that the badger came to me, but afterwards he brought me other herbs. There were no songs with any of the herbs which the badger brought me. In return for the kindness of the badger I took tobacco, cut it up fine, and dug a hole in the ground. I buried the tobacco and said, "Badger, I give you this in return for what you have told me. When the badger is alive he eats this herb. Whatever herb the badger introduces is especially good. Some consider his medicine stronger than that of the bear, as he digs deeper and farther into the ground. Eagle Shield said that he buried a little tobacco as an offering to the badger whenever he dug any of these roots.[1]

How would the average person respond to this kind of dream? Familiarity through observation with the behavior of the badger would not necessarily lead one to conclude that any plant the badger used was anything more than his natural food. That the badger would or could transmit its particular knowledge of the natural world to a human being and recommend food that would be useful to people would not necessarily follow from observation. The little additional information provided by the badger in the dream changes completely the human's ability to confront the natural world. The dreamer now has a first insight into the real nature of the world and its interlocking set of relationships.

Some dreams had considerably more complexity when it came to establishing a relationship between humans and the higher powers as mediated through other creatures. These dreams often provided the dreamer with powers that could not have been imagined or developed as a spiritual exercise. It is important to note that the animal and not the human takes the initiative, although the moral profile of the human seems to be the determining factor that caused the animals to choose this individual. The animals observe the human, and if he or she treats other animals kindly, they want a friendship with the human also.

BRAVE BUFFALO'S DREAM ABOUT THE ELKS

The dream came to me when I was asleep in a tent. Some one came to the door of the tent. He said he had come for me, and I arose and followed him. It was a long and difficult journey, but at last he led me to a beautiful lodge. All the surroundings were beautiful. The lodge was painted yellow outside, and the door faced the southeast. On entering the lodge I saw drawings on the walls. At the right of the entrance was a drawing of a crane holding a pipe with the stem upward, and at the left was a drawing of a crow holding a pipe with the stem downward. I could see that the occupants of the lodge were living happily and luxuriously. I was escorted to the seat of honor opposite the entrance and reached it with difficulty, as the lodge was filled with brush, and I was not accustomed to making my way through thickets. *[At this point, the occupants of the lodge seem to have been recognized as elks.]*

The elks in the lodge watched me with interest and encouraged me to go on, saying they had something they

3

wished to tell me. At last I managed to reach the seat assigned me, and when I was seated the elks rose and said they had heard that I was a great friend of the buffalo, and that they wanted me to be their friend also. They said they had tested me by requiring me to reach this difficult place, and as I had succeeded in doing so they were glad to receive me. They then said that they were going to sing a song and wished me to learn it."[2]

At this point, Frances Densmore becomes the narrator, summing up the consequences of the dream.

After teaching Brave Buffalo this song the elks gave him numerous instructions. He noticed that every elk had a downy white eagle feather tied on its right horn to indicate that it could run as fast as the eagle flies. He was told to wear a similar feather on his head, and at the time of giving this narrative he had a downy eagle plume fastened on the right side of his felt hat. The elks told him to paint his tipi in a manner similar to theirs, yellow outside with drawings of the crane and the crow on its inner walls, saying that these birds would protect him. This manner of painting the tipi he faithfully followed. The elks told him further that before he would be entitled to request help from them he must conduct a Performance which he himself should devise, by which he would show the people that he was acting under their patronage.

On reaching home Brave Buffalo made a mask of elk hide, using for this purpose the skin of the head with the horns. He then painted himself yellow and held in each hand a hoop wound with elk hide and decorated with an herb which is much liked by the elks. ... The young men chiefly on account of its fragrance used this. Eagle Shield used another variety of the "elk herb" in his practice of medicine. Brave Buffalo made also a hoop which he said was similar to the one he carried when enacting his dream. As the flowers of the "elk herb" were not then in season, he used flowers resembling them as nearly as possible, and also such fur as was available.

Brave Buffalo related that after arraying himself as described he went around the camp, passing close to the tents. Two virgins preceded him, carrying his pipe. As he was making this circuit and imitating the actions of the elk a thought occurred to him: "Now I have done everything as I was directed to do it, and I wish I might show these people that I have the power of the elk. There is a spot of damp ground before me. I wish that when I step on this damp ground I may leave the footprints of an elk."

A crowd of people followed him, and after he had passed over this spot they saw the footprints of an elk instead of those of a man.[3]

One suspects that this dream was not Brave Buffalo's first encounter with spiritual things. His power was certainly unique, and the use of the watered ground in which to imprint the elk's feet indicates that he had given considerable thought to how he could demonstrate the acquisition of these special powers and decided that the tactic he chose would demonstrate beyond doubt the validity of his dream.

BLACK ELK'S DREAM/VISION

Readers familiar with the great vision of Black Elk will remember that his initial vision occurred when he was a small boy and stricken with a mysterious illness. His experience could therefore be classified as either a vision or a nighttime dream, depending on how one interpreted the substance of the experience. Black Elk felt he had glimpsed a different world because, on waking to consciousness, he remembered: "As I lay there thinking about the wonderful place where I had been and all that I had seen, I was very sad; for it seemed to me that everybody ought to know about it, but I was afraid to tell, because I knew that nobody would believe me, little as I was, for I was only nine years old."[4] The power of his vision manifested itself in his response. He noted: "everything around me seemed strange and as though it were far away. I remember that for twelve days after that I wanted to be alone, and it seemed like I did not belong to my people."[5]

This vision could also be classified as a near death experience, and considering that he was in a comalike state for twelve days, there would be merit in arguing that it was simply a near death experience. However, his subsequent remembrance of the details in a highly complex experience suggests the experience be included as a vision.

Most unusual was the experience of Two Leggings, the Crow war chief. He seems to have fallen asleep during the night of his fifth day on his vision quest. He dreams until a little bit of rain awakens him and then steps directly into a vision in which his medicine person sorts through the possible gifts he could be given.

THE DANGERS OF DAYDREAMING

As much as possible, the Sioux elders tried to discourage people from taking naps during the daytime. They felt that people became inordinately vulnerable to the Heyokas and other spirits that might require them to do shameful and embarrassing things. There was an uncompromising mischievous aspect of the Thunder powers, and if a person did not do as they instructed, there were often dire consequences. A mixed blood named George Schmidt became a victim of daydreaming and found himself torn between obeying the Thunders' commands and listening to his white father, who soundly rejected the tribal traditions.

GEORGE SCHMIDT'S DAYDREAM

> In the precepts of the old men, they preached saying, "Day-dreaming is bad; keep awake; instead of reclining, go walking about to rouse yourselves! As certain as anything, the sun will set in due time, and then at last is the time when man sleeps!" I have myself through personal experience, knowledge that that practice is a bad thing. Once I napped in the daytime, I had a dream, and it was like this:

A dark cloud appeared across the west, and it was drawing near. And out of that cloud, I heard the shouts of a scout. And then a little distance away I realized here was a man, so I fixed my attention upon him for a better view, and saw as I lay gazing, that it was someone painted up in fantastic designs, who was walking away from me, entirely nude. And then someone whispered close to my ear, saying to me, "That is you!" And with that, there suddenly came over me the knowledge of what was implied in all this, even in my sleep and as this happened, I got this thought: "Alas, alas, and if I do not do as they want (appear as I see the man in the dream) I shall be killed by lightning!" and a panic overtook me and woke me up.

I had been lying face downward, so now I rolled over on my back, and, just to be doing, I glanced towards the west, and, there, lo and behold, a dark cloud lay across the west! The Thunders were really returning, so I grew very sad, and kept always within close range of where my father sat until in time the storm passed on. Because my father was a white man, I was reticent about telling him about it; because I knew he would instantly dismiss it as of no account, in a few words. But then, on the other hand, because he didn't believe in the thunders I found it comfortable to keep near him all the time. They went on past but it did seem that they repeatedly sent their bolts round our home, and it took them forever to go on.

And from then on I was always secretly in fear of the thunders, but I also feared my father because he ridiculed that sort of thing, and so between the two, I went about dodging; and because of fear of my father I never let myself enter into the Heyoka-woze ceremony. Thus I lived on until after I attained manhood; and then one day the thunders did strike me, and burned me in odd designs, but I recovered. If only I had obeyed in the first place when I was ordered to carry out the ceremony to the Heyoka, from then on I should not have been so unhappy."[6]

SHARED DREAMS

People had ordinary dreams, ordinary people had extraordinary dreams, but, as far as I can determine, the dream images found in the Western context did not appear. Instead, the dreams were pretty much the same as the conscious life the people were leading. But Luther Standing Bear reported an instance where a dream or vision was apparently shared by several people, and I thought it had some relevance in this topic. It was, by all accounts, an unusual event and suggests that the sacred sometimes uses unusual ways to get a message to humans. Let us examine Standing Bear's narrative. At the time, he was responsible for recruiting Indians to go with Buffalo Bill on one of the Wild West tours.

> I was loading my wagon and making all preparations to go to Ruschville [the departure station], there to take charge of the band of Sioux for the Buffalo Bill Wild West Show. Wakan Hunska came to me, and solemnly shaking hands, said: "Nephew, I don't see why you are going with the others and I ask you not to go. You may know why I say this to you."
>
> While making ready, two young men, who had been with me on the previous trip to England, came and asked if I would consent to let them off and get two other men in their places. I inquired why the change of mind, since most young men were keen about the trip, and they explained that one night just before reaching Rushville they had made camp and gone to sleep in the tipi. About midnight, both had been suddenly awakened by a deafening crash and screams of terrified people. Rushing outside, they found the night perfectly calm and still, and they then and there understood what was bound to happen to those who took the journey.
>
> Just before we reached Chicago the disaster occurred. Our train while stopped for a few moments, was crashed into by a swift traveling one, and a passenger car filled with Lakota braves was torn to splinters, and human bodies crushed in among the wrecked steel and timbers. When I returned home,

recovering from what seemed fatal injuries, Wakan Hunska came to see me. "Nephew," he said, "what I saw came to pass!"[7]

This warning dream/experience apparently happened to Wakan Hunska and the two young men. But Standing Bear himself had no dream event to warn him of the immediate future disaster. Had he been too civilized to pick up on the warning? Did Wakan Hunska have the same experience as the two young men? At what point does a dream/vision merge with ordinary life events? This account I believe stands between the power dream and the real-life intrusions of the sacred that have great clarity and are easily identified as the initiative of the sacred spiritual powers.

THE SACRED INTRUSION

The dream was not the only means by which the higher powers revealed themselves to people. Equally important were those intrusions of the sacred into people's everyday lives in ways that startled them. Being keen observers of the natural world, the people could quickly tell when something was amiss from the response of birds and animals to disturbances or the sudden changes of weather patterns. When an anticipated activity did not take place, people thought carefully that they might be dealing with some aspect of the supernatural. Instead of showing fear, they demonstrated curiosity and waited for the situation to unfold. In this manner, they were able to respond in the proper way to an approach by the higher powers. Goose reported a good example of this kind of event. While hunting, he suddenly found himself standing in a sacred place where ordinary expectations did not apply. He was given medicines and a mission to heal people of certain kinds of physical ailments. His experience is typical of the kinds of encounters with the sacred in the old days.

GOOSE'S EXPERIENCE

When I was a young man I was an excellent marksman with bow and arrows. After coming in contact with the Army I was given a rifle and cartridges and never missed aim. One morning I arose before daybreak to go on a hunting trip. As I went around a butte I saw an antelope, which came toward me and stood still a short distance away from me. The antelope looked at me and then began to graze. I took my rifle and fired several shots with no effect. I fired 16 cartridges and wondered what could be the matter. I put in four more cartridges and fired again, but with no effect whatever. Then the animal stopped grazing and began to move slowly away.

Then I heard a voice speaking three times, then a fourth time, and the voice said it was going to sing something, and I must listen. The voice was above me and commanded me to look at the sun. I looked and saw that the rising sun had the face of a man and was commanding all the animals and trees and everything in nature to look up.

In the air, in front of the sun, was a booth made of boughs. In front of the booth was a very bright object and between this and the booth was a man, painted and wearing an eagle-down feather, while around him flew all kinds of birds. The bright object was a sacred stone, and it was heated red hot. After seeing this I heard another voice telling me to look and receive what would be given me. Something in the form of a bird came down, and where it touched the ground an herb sprang up. This occurred three times. The voice above me said that I was to use these three herbs in the cure of the sick. The fourth time the descending object started in the voice of a bird, but a human skeleton came to the ground.

Then the voice above me told me to observe the structure of the human body. I then saw blood run into the skeleton, and a buffalo horn appeared on the back, between the shoulders, and drew the blood out of the skeleton. The voice above me said this was a sign that I would have power more than any other to cure diseases of the blood. The voice came from the sacred stone and said I must use the buffalo horn in curing diseases of the blood, a practice which I have followed ever since. *I do not consider that I dreamed this as one dreams in sleep; it appeared to me when I was early on the chase.*[8] (Emphasis added)

We will encounter the phenomenon of the willfully invulnerable animal later and learn more about Goose, who played a prominent role in helping Densmore collect these materials. More important are the circumstances in which Goose found himself. I suspect that events such as this were a transitional step between depending on dreams and seeking a vision, since they gave proof that the sacred realm was relevant to human physical existence. If one could have this kind of revelatory experience while performing a perfunctory task such as hunting, could not one invoke the presence of the sacred by making oneself available for this kind of experience by finding an isolated spot and appealing to the higher powers to recognize the effort?

There are some reports of visions that seem to have been triggered by the desperation of the supplicant. They are not exactly forcing the spirits to respond, nor do they represent the traditional experience in which, during the four or more days in the ritual, spirits willingly come to people. We have found two cases in which people had reached a level of frustration so depressing that they sought to do away with themselves. During this crisis, the spirits responded. While not strictly an intrusion, these visions could certainly be described as an intervention. Edward Goodbird relates the story of Bush and how he was saved from death by buffalo spirits.

BUSH'S BUFFALO SPIRITS

Many years ago when our villages were on Knife River a man named Bush went out to find his god. He sought a vision from the buffalo spirits; and he thought to make himself suffer so that the spirits might pity him. He tied four buffalo skulls in a train, one behind another, and as Bush walked he dragged the train of skulls behind him.

He made his way painfully up the Missouri, mourning and crying to the gods. The banks of the Missouri are much cut up in ravines, and Bush suffered greatly as he dragged the heavy skulls over this rough country. Fifty miles north of the villages, he came to the Little Missouri, a shallow stream, but subject to sudden freshlets; he found the river flooded, and rising.

He stood on the bank and cried: "O gods, I am poor and I suffer! I want to find my god. Other men have suffered and found their gods. Now I suffer much, but no god answers me. I am going to plunge into this torrent. I think I shall die, yet I will plunge in. O gods, if you are going to answer me, do it now and save me! He waded in dragging the heavy skulls after him. The water grew deeper. He could no longer wade, he had to swim; he struck out.

He wondered that he no longer felt the weight of the skulls, and that he did not sink. Then he heard something behind him cry, "Whoo-oo-ooh!" He looked around. The four buffalo skulls were swimming about him, buoying him up; but they were no longer skulls! Flesh and woolly hair covered them; they had big blue eyes; they had red tongues. They were alive!⁹

The reference to "gods" here reflects Goodbird's acceptance of the Western notion of gods and a mistranslation or deliberate changing of words to convey the meaning of the experience. In the Indian context, of course, we are talking about spirits.

The famous Oglala medicine man Horn Chips had a similar experience, and he was thought to be the greatest medicine man of his generation. His descendants are today among the most prominent and powerful practitioners of the old powers in the Sioux tribe.

HORN CHIPS'S BLESSING

> On his way to a lonely spot to end his life, he heard a voice
> who said it was that of the Great Spirit. The voice told Horn
> Chips not to kill himself, that he was destined to become a
> great man. Horn Chips was told to go to a high mountain, dig
> a hole four feet deep, cover it with boughs, and stay there four
> days with no food or drink. Horn Chips followed directions.
> When he was in the pit, he had a vision. A snake came to him
> from the Great Spirit and gave him his instructions.[10]

THE NATURE OF THE MEDICINE MAN

Black Elk has wished that everyone could have shared his experience, but it stood to reason that not everyone was destined to go
beyond the physical world into the deep mysteries of the cosmos.
Most people, even though they went on vision quests, simply
expected to live their lives to the fullest with some protection from
the spirits. Others sought to obtain powers that would enhance their
capabilities. As a rule, however, people avoided confrontations with
the sacred because the gift of powers always imposed additional
responsibilities on them.

They were set aside in the tribe or band because of their knowledge and power and often must have felt much as Black Elk did
when ordinary life became strange. Although they had special powers and enjoyed alliances with other creatures, this status meant they
were "on call" to perform tasks given them by the spirits and/or
requested by the people. Thus, while anyone might have a spiritual
experience and come to the intellectual understanding that Wakan
tanka was in everything, only certain people, it seems, were called to
enter into a knowledge of the deeper mysteries.

The successful demonstration of powers that occurred over a
significant period of time would seem to be the best indication that
an individual was a medicine man; however, many people had several
powers and yet were not regarded as standing outside the camp as

specially chosen. Skill in healing would certainly count for a great deal in evaluating a person. Lame Deer offered a combination of factors that made him a successful spiritual leader. "I am a medicine man because a dream told me to be one, because I am commanded to be one, because the old holy men—Chest, Thunderhawk, Chips, Good Lance—helped me to be one."[11] So mere anointment in a dream or vision only opens the path for most people. They also need the approval and support of the older medicine men of the tribe.

Lee Irwin suggested that being a medicine man actually involved a search for truth that in other societies is granted most often from wealthy patrons or achieved through the stubborn rejection of social values by rebellious intellectuals. Thus, he argued: "While power could be sought as a means to an explicitly and socially conceived end, the shaman's calling is most frequently associated with the search for knowledge. A recognition of the reality and profound significance of the sacred character of the religious world, the inner impulses of a questioning mind, and the determination to delve ever more deeply into the mystery and meaning of life are intrinsic to the shaman's search."[12] Lame Deer probably said it more concisely: "I believe that being a medicine man, more than anything else, is a state of mind, a way of looking at and understanding this earth, a sense of what it is all about."[13]

One aspect of the life of the medicine man that is rarely even mentioned is the necessity of having a stable home life. The medicine man must have a compatible spouse who can understand the nature of his calling, withstand and compensate for the constant expenditures of energy by the medicine man, share the secret intimate information that such a life produces, and anticipate how events will unfold as her husband performs his rituals. George Bird Grinnell understood this requirement and commented: "A man cannot become a doctor by himself; when he receives the power, his wife— who afterward is his assistant—must also be taught and receive certain secrets. … If the wife of the man who is receiving the power does not wish to become a doctor, the man must find another woman to act with him. A man may become a doctor through a dream, thus receiving spiritual power directly from above, but even in this case he must have a woman to help him."[14]

Sword explained the mystery of the vision to James R. Walker, illustrating the wide variety of possibilities that this experience made possible. "Hanble (a vision) is a communication from the Wakantanka or a spirit to one of mankind. It may come at any time or in any manner to anyone. It may be relative to the one that receives it, or to another. It may be communicated in Lakota *[or any tribal language]* or handloglaka (language of the spirits). Or it may be only by sights and sounds not of a language. It may come directly from the one giving it, or it may be sent by an akicita (messenger). It may come unsought or it may come by seeking it."[15]

Yet there appears to be a specific purpose in who gets chosen to be a medicine man and who doesn't. Morris Opler cited an Apache elder who understood the nature of becoming a spiritual leader. "It seems that these powers select for themselves. Perhaps you want to be a shaman of a certain kind, but the power doesn't speak to you. It seems that, before the power wants to work through you, you've got to be just so, as in the original time. You've got to believe in things as in the old days and carry everything out."[16] Lone Man recognized this difference in people's fates and seemed to imply that being chosen by the spirits opened up a much larger arena of experience. In a sense, the person was set aside from ordinary individuals and actually lived an isolated life in which higher invisible powers controlled much of what the person did. Thus a medicine man may be sitting in a congenial social atmosphere and yet be receiving information he hears perfectly but is inaudible to anyone else in the group.

LONE MAN—TETON SIOUX

Ever since I have known the old Indians and their customs, I have seen that in any great undertaking it is not enough for a man to depend simply upon himself. Most people place their dependence on the medicine men, who understand this life and all its surroundings and are able to predict what will come

15

to pass. They have the right to make these predictions. *If as we sit here we should hear a voice speaking from above, it would be because we had the light to hear what others could not hear, or we might see what others had not the right to see because they were not properly qualified.* (Emphasis added)

Such are some of the rights and privileges of the medicine-men, and those who desire to know mysterious things must seek their aid. If a man desires success in war or the hunt, or if he wishes to make the greatest of all requests, which is the request for long life, he should make it through a medicine-man, who will give him a charm, probably a root or herb wrapped in buckskin, and he will wear this charm. It is not enough for a man to make his request. There is a way which it has been found best to follow, and that is to make an offering with the request.[17]

Communication with the higher powers has its limitations, as we can see. The spirits do not confer powers on anyone, but seem to recognize that certain people are chosen to fulfill certain tasks and missions. There seems to be an aspect of predestination inherent in the recognition of a medicine man. The voices people hear in a dream or vision are addressed specifically to them and their situation and lead one to conclude that each individual has already received an outline for his or her life and need only to realize their unique inherent possibilities. This belief comes from the observation of many generations of people and is not so much a doctrine as a psychological fact. It fits nicely with some of the pioneer work being done in near death experience and reincarnation studies of recent years.

MEN'S VISION QUEST EXPERIENCES

Deeper knowledge than what had been originally allotted to human beings was possible only if the spirits, through the mediation of other creatures, shared some of their knowledge with us. Thus there came about a ritual in which humans set aside time from their routine lives and opened themselves up to the possibility of establishing relationships with spirits and other creatures. This ritual was the vision quest, a time and means for seeking communications from nonhuman sources. The vision quest differs from dreams or daytime sacred events in that it is almost wholly dependent on the initiative of the human, whereas the other two means of establishing a relationship occur because of the initiative of higher powers. So what was the basic form of this ritual?

A person would go to an isolated location and fast and pray for a number of days (usually four) or until there had been some contact with another entity. The motivation was twofold. Some people were called to do this quest by hearing voices or having dreams in which they were instructed to make themselves available. Saswe, the Yankton Sioux medicine man, heard a voice calling him for three consecutive years before he did the vision quest. Elmer Running, a modern medicine man, had a series of calls over a period of years before he underwent this ritual.

More generally, young people, under the supervision of an older spiritual leader, would perform the ceremony asking for pity and hoping for some kind of recognition by the spirits. Usually, no one was disappointed, although the messages some people received were simple acknowledgments of their efforts, a voice saying the spirits were pleased. Even if the four days were spent without earthshaking results, people would report that a bird or insect had come before them, stating simply that their efforts had not gone unnoticed. Often, they would be told they would be successful in life or that they would have a long life. They might also receive a message concerning their diets. They would be encouraged to eat some foods, or warned against eating other kinds of foods. Whatever the particular case, people not destined to become medicine men were nevertheless encouraged to live a positive and productive life.

In his youth, Siya'ka, a Hunkpapa medicine man, had dreamed of a crow and an owl. He later determined that he would do the vision quest based on what he had experienced with these two birds. His narrative as given here reveals the manner in which Siya'ka believed that his dreams were leading to the need to do the vision quest. The account is instructive in that it demonstrates one of the many motivations for performing this ritual.

SIYA'KA EXPLAINING THE VISION QUEST

All classes of people know that when human power falls they must look to a higher power for the fulfillment of their desires. There are many ways in which the request for help from this higher power can be made. This depends on the person. Some like to be quiet, and others want to do everything in public. Some like to go alone, away from the crowd, to meditate upon many things. In order to secure a fulfillment of his desire a man must qualify himself to make his request. Lack of preparation would mean failure to secure a response to his petition. Therefore when a man makes up his mind to ask a favor of Wakantanka he makes due preparation.

It is not fitting that a man should suddenly go out and make a request of Wakantanka. When a man shuts his eyes, he sees a great deal. He then enters his own mind, and things become clear to him, but objects passing before his eyes would distract him. For that reason a dreamer makes known his request through what he sees when his eyes are closed. It has long been his intention to make his request of Wakantanka, and he resolves to seek seclusion on the top of a butte or other high place.

When at last he goes there he closes his eyes, and his mind is upon Wakantanka and his work. The man who does this usually has in mind some animal which he would like for protection and help. No man can succeed in life alone, and he can not get the help he wants from men; therefore he seeks help through some bird or animal which Wakantanka sends for his assistance. Many animals have ways from which a man can learn a great deal, even from the fact that horses are restless before a storm.[18]

When non-Indians first began to learn about this ritual, they explained away the experiences by noting that going without food or water for several days could lead to hallucinations. This belief came from well-fed scholars observing equally well-fed civilized people who were not accustomed to hardships. Indians, on the other hand, had been trained from their earliest youth to withstand all the rigors of nature and, consequently, could easily go without food and water for long periods of time. A mere four days would not affect a well-raised Indian. There are accounts of non-Indians, scouts, and mountain men who also went days without food and water and had no hallucinations (but no visions either). The explanation of delusion cannot hold because, in some instances, people received messages on the first or second day of their ritual, before any physical deprivation of their body, such as a lack of food, could become a serious threat to their ability to perceive the environment around them. Moreover, people who do extensive fasting will affirm that they actually feel stronger and can think with greater clarity when engaging in this practice.

Indians recognized that this state of weakness and vulnerability could lead to hallucinations and so made efforts to distinguish between visions and accurate information obtained in the ritual from fantasy. After people had finished a vision quest, they participated in a sweat lodge during or after which the elder who supervised them would discuss their experiences. The real criterion that defined the valid experience of the spirits from simple hallucinations was the requirement that any powers or insights received by a person in a vision or dream had to be demonstrated before the whole community sometime in the future. Lest anyone think that this experience is an exciting extension of our daily activities, or that it is performed in a perfunctory manner, let us share what Lame Deer said about his experiences.

LAME DEER, A BRULE SIOUX MEDICINE MAN, EXPLAINING THE VISION QUEST

> Imagine a darkness so intense, and so complete that it is almost solid, flowing around you like ink, covering you like a velvet blanket. A blackness which cuts you off from the everyday world, which forces you to withdraw deep into yourself, which makes you see with your heart instead of your eyes. You can't see, but your eyes are opened. You are isolated, but you know that you are part of the Great Spirit, united with all living beings.[19]

Recognition of the unity of all beings is the preliminary intellectual response to the intense darkness, but much more follows. Lame Deer said, "The real vision ... is not a dream; it is very real. It hits you sharp and clear like an electric shock. You are wide awake and, suddenly, there is a person standing next to you who you know can't be there at all. ... Yet you are not dreaming; your eyes are wide open. You have to work for this, empty your mind for it."[20]

So during the vision quest, the physical world recedes into the background and the seeker is not concerned with the distractions that plague the everyday life. Indeed, they do not seem to exist in the face of this tremendous enveloping of a different environment that pierces into the very heart of the person. Then unusual things begin to happen, but through the events of the experience, one is able to see that the unity with all living beings transcends ordinary time and space.

LAME DEER'S EXPERIENCE

> I shook the rattle and it made a soothing sound, like rain falling on rock. It was talking to me, but it did not calm my fears. I took the sacred pipe in my other hand and began to sing and pray: "Tunkashila, grandfather spirit help me." I don't know what got into me, but I was no longer myself. I started to cry. Crying, even my voice was different. I sounded like an

older man. I couldn't even recognize this strange voice. I used long-ago words in my prayer, words no longer used nowadays.[21]

Surely, the intensity of this kind of experience is not standard fare in most of today's ceremonies. During the course of a lifetime, a person may have one or many of these experiences with the intensity described by Lame Deer. Here we have a physical encounter with the fact of the unity of existence that transcends abstract thought and perfunctory behavior. Encountering a deeper aspect of the cosmos is a necessary part of reaching a more adequate understanding of life.

In reading accounts of the vision quest, we should keep in mind the power of Lame Deer's description so that we do not assume that a mere recognition of a change of physical conditions is the climax of the experience. We can now examine the various stories of the experiences of the vision quest and understand the reception of powers by the medicine men. We begin with a rare account from the eastern Indian traditions from *The Jesuit Relations* of 1642. You will note that the man's name is not mentioned, since the Jesuits did not wish to give credence to this ritual, preferring to label it as a work of the devil rather than to understand it.

THE JESUIT ACCOUNT OF THE VISION QUEST

A certain man, who urges us to Baptize him had, when but fifteen or sixteen years of age, retired into the woods to prepare himself by fasting for the apparition of some Demon. *(After having fasted sixteen days without eating anything, and drinking water only)* he suddenly heard this utterance that came from the Sky: "Take care of this man, and let him end his fast." At the same time, he saw an aged man of rare beauty who came down from the Sky, and approached him, and, looking kindly at him, said: "Have courage, I will take care of thy life. It is a fortunate thing for thee, to have taken me for thy Master. None of the Demons who haunt these countries shall have any power to harm thee. One day thou wilt see thy hair as white as mine. Thou wilt have four children; the first two and the last will be males, and the third will be a girl; after that, thy wife will hold the relation of a sister to thee.

As he concluded these words, he held out to him a piece of human flesh, quite raw. The youth in horror turned away his head. "Eat this," said the old man, presenting him with a piece of bear's fat. When he had eaten it the Demon withdrew, ascending toward the Sky, whence he had come. After that, he often appeared to him and promised to assist him. Nearly all that he predicted to him has happened. This man has had four children the third of whom was a girl; after which a certain infirmity compelled him to the continence that the Devil asked of him. Apart from that, he is in excellent health, and although he is approaching old age, he has been exposed to many contagious diseases without having been attacked by them.

He was always very fortunate in the chase; thus, while in the woods, whenever he heard a certain number of cries from the Sky, they were signs that he would take so many bears. At other times, when he alone saw a number of stags and does entering the Cabin, he would inform others of it, and they would really find in their snares on the following day the same number of animals that he had told them. He attributes this excellent fortune that he has always had in the chase, to the pieces of bear's fat that the Demon made him eat; and he judges from this that he would have equal success in war, had he eaten the piece of human flesh that he refused.[22]

What can we make of this selection? Surely, it must have been discomforting to the Jesuits to know that the predictions made by the "demon" had come true over the man's lifetime. There were perhaps more specific predictions that had also come true, but were not mentioned in this brief summary. Did he go without food, but with water, for sixteen days? It has been done before, but on extremely rare occasions. Did the man conform his life to the predictions, or did the spirit informing him of the markers on the road ahead know this man's future already? We will discuss this possibility later.

Another account from the eastern United States comes from the Micmacs of Maine. Although the articulation of the ritual shows an appalling lack of understanding of the Indian practice, the selection does help demonstrate that seeking assistance from the spirits was a general practice all over the country. As Frederick Johnson reported: "the novice must keep his object a secret while camping alone in the woods with an outfit for two, the other, an invisible companion. A being will finally appear, it is thought, who will give him the gift of magic, the power to assume animal shapes, to walk through fire unharmed, through water without being drowned, to translate himself through the air with the quickness of thought, to control the elements, to walk on water and the like. This is the only reference to the presence of a fast-vigil among the Micmac which has come to hand."[23]

As we have already seen, Siya'ka, the Hunkpapa spiritual leader, discussed his motivation for undertaking the vision quest even though he had already received powers from the crow and the owl. Here is an account of his vision that reinforced the spiritual knowledge he had previously been given. This account is one of a few written descriptions of the vision quest from start to finish.

SIYA'KA'S VISION

> When I was a young man I wanted a dream through which I could know what to depend upon for help. Having this desire, I went to a medicine-man and told him about it. He instructed me what to do, and I followed his instructions in everything. He told me to get four well-tanned robes, with one for my own use, also a decorated pipe and offerings of tobacco, and to appear before him on a certain day prepared to seek my vision. I prepared the articles as he directed and went to him on that day. He painted my face white, and before leaving him we went together into the sweat lodge, and while we were there he told me of his own dream and gave me an idea of

what a dream was like. I had already selected a hill on which to await my dream, and after leaving him I went to this hilltop to follow his instructions.

I was not required to fast before seeking the vision but of course took no food with me when I went to the hilltop. In the middle of this hilltop I dug a hollow about 2 feet deep and large enough so that I could crouch against its side when weary with standing. At each of the four points of the compass I placed one of the robes and some of the tobacco. These offerings were to show that I desired messages from the directions of the four winds and was waiting anxiously to hear the voice of some bird or animal speaking to me in a dream.

Having placed these offerings in position, and according to the advice of the medicine-man, I stood facing the west and watched the sun disappear. As soon as the sun was out of sight I closed my eyes and turned my face toward the east, standing thus for a while, then facing the north and the south. So I stood, wrapped in a buffalo robe. I was not exactly singing, but more nearly lamenting, like a child asking for something. In the crying or lamenting of a young man seeking a vision two things are especially desired: First, that he may have long life, and second, that he may succeed in taking horses from the enemy.

Beside me, at the north, was placed a buffalo skull, the face of which was painted with blue stripes. The openings of the skull were filled with fresh sage, and it was laid on a bed of sage. The skull was placed with its face toward the south. The reason for this was that when the buffalo come from the north, traveling toward the south, they bring news that Wakantanka has provided food for the Indians and there will not be a famine. During part of the time I rested my pipe against the buffalo skull, with the stem pointing toward the north. Part of the time I held the pipe in my hands, with the stem away from me. The pipe was filled, but not to be lighted until I returned to the medicine-man after my dream.

As I still faced the west, after the sun had set and when it was almost dark, I heard a sound like the flying of a bird around my head, and I heard a voice saying, "Young man, you are recognized by Wakantanka." This was all the voice said.

All night I stood with my eyes closed. Just before daybreak I saw a bright light coming toward me from the east. It was a man. His head was tied up and he held a tomahawk in his hand. He said, "Follow me," and in an instant he changed into a crow. In my dream I followed the crow to a village. He entered the largest tent. When he entered the tent he changed to a man again. Opposite the entrance sat a young man, painted red, who welcomed me. When I was thus received I felt highly honored, for, as that was the largest tent I knew it must be the tent of the chief. The young man said he was pleased to see me there. He said, further, that all the animals and birds were his friends, and that he wished me to follow the way he had used to secure their friend-ship. He told me to lift my head. I did this and saw dragonflies, butterflies, and all kinds of small insects, while above them flew all kinds of birds. As soon as I cast down my eyes again and looked at the young man and at the man who had brought me thither, I saw that the young man had become transformed into an owl, and that my escort had changed again into a crow.[24]

TWO LEGGINGS'S VISION

Two Leggings was a Crow medicine man who had a long and complex vision that enabled him to exercise a variety of powers. His vision reveals the boundaries placed on the exercise of powers as well as demonstrating the close relationship between dreams and visions because, after he had considered his experience, he realized that he had received instructions from two sources that operated as a unity. This experience was extremely rare and therefore deserves to be examined in its entirety.

I fasted in the same place four times, staying four days each time. But it was not until the last of these fasts that I met my medicine father. Early the fifth morning a person rose above the horizon until I saw his entire body. As he walked toward me, fires burst out where he stepped. At last he stood next to me and delivered the message that Bird Going Up was coming to me.

He was wearing strange moccasins, the left upper made from a silver fox's head, the right from a coyote's head. The ears had been left and scalp locks were tied around the moccasins' edges. The right heel was painted black and the left red. The man wore a beautiful war shirt trimmed with scalp locks along the arms, and his leggings were decorated with horsehair scalp locks from the manes of different colored horses.

A little rain woke me and my dream became a real vision. My dream person was standing next to me when I heard the little coyote head on his moccasin bark, flames blew from its mouth. I kept trying to see if this man's face was painted but it was hidden. He carried a coup stick with a raven sitting on it. This raven tried to teach me the language of the birds but the man stopped it. Suddenly I heard a loud thunderclap. I seemed to be picked up and dropped whole. My blanket was thrown in the opposite direction. Landing unhurt on the mountain slope with my head downhill, I saw a bird's big tail and large claws, but could not see the body. Red streaks of lightning shot from each claw, leaving trails on the rocks. I noticed hailstones on the bird's spread-out tail.

As the rain turned into fog I tried to see the bird's head but lightning flashed cross in front of it. My dream person told me that this bird was great, that the noise from its throat sounded like thunder. The raven on the coup stick said that I was to have had many visions but that the messenger prevented him from giving them. It meant my dream person, the real messenger from Bird Going Up who was giving me all these visions. Then the raven disappeared and I looked again at my dream person. A large red circle was painted on his face, broken by two other circles scratched into the red paint. The raven returned to its perch on the coup stick and my dream person told me that Bird Going Up had told him not to let the ravens teach me the language of the birds. Instead, he said, he would teach me some of his medicine songs and sang the first one: "The bird is saying this: 'Wherever we are, nothing may be in our way.'"

After each song he blew several times on an eagle-bone whistle. The second song was: "The bird is gone. I will let him return and watch over you."

The third song went: "I am letting him stay. I am letting him stay."

He sang the fourth song: "I am going toward human beings and they are weak."

His fifth song: "The bird from the sky will take care of you."

He sang this sixth song: "Wherever I am going, I say this: 'I am the Bird of the world.'"

His last song went: "My child, I am living among the clouds and there is nothing impossible for me."[25]

Here we have a unique situation in that Bird Going Up did not want the dream person to instruct Two Leggings in the language of the birds. Nevertheless, the dream person gave Two Leggings seven songs used by the birds that will assist him in life. Moreover, it is obvious that the dream person, with his strange moccasins, had powers approaching those of Bird Going Up. Rarely do we have any sign of the deliberations of the higher spirits in measuring which of their powers they will impart to humans. We do have accounts in which one animal spirit, moved by the concern of another spirit, joins in the giving of power and also bestows some of his power to the person seeking a spiritual relationship.

Many vision accounts seem to emphasize benefits for the man or woman who is granted powers as if the ultimate goal was the enhancement of the individual. In the vision of Blows Down, a Crow elder, the benefits were undoubtedly intended for the Crow people as a whole. While Blows Down did receive certain powers, the primary purpose of the gift of Morning Star was a means by which the people could protect themselves from enemies. As a comparatively smaller nation, the Crow were caught between the Sioux and the Blackfeet, and these two powerful and numerous nations saw them as primary foes. Although this is again a longer story, it does encompass the wide variety of powers granted to Blows Down, and thereby is an important account.

BLOWS DOWN'S VISION

Once again, during the dark-face period:

> Just before dawn he awoke. He was wide awake and was gazing toward the east when the first faint streaks of dawn began to color the horizon. Then suddenly, in the clouds overhanging the sky, a man appeared. He came nearer and nearer. Finally he appeared to step out of a cloud upon the toes of Blows Down. Yet Blows Down did not feel any weight. The man then stepped down beside his couch. As his feet touched the ground a blaze of fire issued from the points of contact. The earth seemed to be aflame and a column of smoke ascended skyward.
>
> Then the man spoke. "My child, arise from your bed of torture. I have come to adopt you as my son." He grasped Blows Down by the hand and said, "On you I will bestow my power." Then, apparently from nowhere he produced a hoop. Holding it in front of Blows Down he told him to look through it. When Blows Down did so he saw all the enemy tribes just as if they were close to him. The spirit man then told Blows Down that he was the Morning Star, that he had pitied him for a long time, and had finally decided to come to him, adopt him, and give him his medicine. It would become, in time, one of the most powerful medicines among the Crows.
>
> Morning Star told Blows Down to make a hoop medicine for himself. Furthermore, he might make three copies of this

medicine, but no more than four should ever be in existence among the Crows. He told Blows Down that whenever any enemy war party approached the camp in which he was staying, this medicine would warn him of their coming before their arrival. This medicine would also help Blows Down to see the enemy's location and the strength of their attacking force.

Finally Morning Star told Blows Down, "If you will pray to me, your people [The Crows] will increase in numbers. Go home now. Upon your arrival have the members of the camp build you four sweat-lodges, each with the opening west toward the rising sun. You enter the last of the four, and while you are inside tell those who are with you of the visit and the instructions which I, the Morning Star have just given you."[26]

SMOKING STAR'S NAME

Clark Wissler reported a vision quest in which the young man was simply required to take the name of his special spirit to gain power. Compared with some of the complexity that we find in other vision accounts, it seems likely that this person was predestined to bear the name during his time on earth.

> At last all was ready and old Medicine-Bear left me alone on a high hill to fast, dance, and pray. Each evening and morning he came and, standing afar off, exhorted me to greater efforts. By the third day I was too exhausted to stand. That night I lay on my back looking up at the sky. Then I saw Smoking-star. And as I gazed it came nearer and nearer. Then I heard a voice, "My son, why do you cry here?" Then I saw a fine warrior sitting on the ground before me, smoking my pipe. At last he said, "I will give you power. You are to take my name. You must never change it. Always pray to me and I will help you."[27]

29

Francis Parkman recorded another unique vision in his book *The Oregon Trail*. In this vision, a young man was told to avoid warfare and devote his life to seeking ways to reduce tensions and quarrels within the tribe and to seeking peace with other tribes. This vision coincides with Charles Eastman's statement that the Sioux were beginning to adopt peaceful ways just prior to the onset of the wars against them. According to Eastman, the Sioux mothers began to encourage their boys to seek to bring peace instead of emphasizing war. Le Borgne's vision may be an illustration of what was happening to these people in the 1850s.

LE BORGNE'S VISION

He was one of a powerful family, renowned for warlike exploits. When a very young man, he submitted to the singular rite to which most of the tribe subjected themselves before entering upon life. He painted his face black; then seeking out a cavern in a sequestered part of the Black Hills, he lay for several days, fasting and praying to the spirits. In the dreams and visions produced by his weakened and excited state, he fancied, like all Indians, that he saw supernatural revelations. Again and again the form of an antelope appeared before him. The antelope is the graceful peace spirit of the Ogillallah; but seldom is it that such a gentle visitor presents itself during the initiatory fasts of their young men.

The terrible grizzly bear, the divinity of war, usually appears to fire them with martial ardor and thirst for renown. At length the antelope spoke. It told the young dreamer that he was not to follow the path of war; that a life of peace and tranquility was marked out for him; that thenceforward he was to guide the people by his counsels, and protect them from the evils of their own feuds and dissensions. Others were to gain renown by fighting the enemy; but greatness of a different kind was in store for him.

The visions beheld during the period of this fast usually

determine the whole course of the dreamer's life. From that time, Le Borgne, which was the only name by which we knew him, abandoned all thoughts of war, and devoted himself to the labors of peace. He told his vision to the people. They honored his commission and respected him in his novel capacity.[28]

WOMEN'S VISION QUEST EXPERIENCES

The eastern woodlands tribes seemed to have a much more rigorous vision quest than did the Plains Indians, since we have accounts in which they fast for a significant period of time before they complete the ritual. In Henry R. Schoolcraft's collection of writings on the indigenous peoples, we have a notable narrative by an Indian woman of the fast required of young women experiencing the onset of puberty. I know of no other statement by a woman who had undergone this ritual that is as complete or gives more information. Since most scholars, frontiersmen, and travelers paid almost exclusive attention to Indian men, this account is one of very few that records a woman's experience.

CATHERINE WABOSE'S VISION

When I was a girl of about twelve or thirteen years of age, my mother told me to look out for something that would happen to me. Accordingly, one morning early, in the middle of winter, I found an unusual sign, and ran off as far from the lodge as I could, and remained there until my mother came and found me out. She knew what was the matter, and brought me nearer to the family lodge, and bade me help her in making a small lodge of branches of the spruce tree. She told me to remain there, and keep away from every one, and as a diversion, to keep myself employed in chopping wood, and that she would bring me plenty of prepared basswood bark to twist into twine.

She told me she would come to see me in two days, and that, in the mean time, I must not even taste snow. I did as directed. At the end of two days she came to see me. I thought she would surely bring me something to eat, but, to my disappointment, she brought nothing. I suffered more from thirst than hunger, though I felt my stomach gnawing. My mother sat quietly down and said, (after ascertaining that I had not tasted anything, as she directed) "My child, you are the youngest of your sisters, and none are now left me of all my sons and children but you four," alluding to her two elder sisters, herself, and a little son, still a mere lad. "Who," she continued, "will take care of us poor women? Now, my daughter, listen to me, and try to obey. Blacken your face and fast really, that the Master of Life may have pity on you and me, and on us all. Do not in the least deviate from my counsels, and in two days more I will come to you. He will help you, if you are determined to do what is right, and tell me whether you are favored or not, by the true Great Spirit; and if your visions are not good, reject them." So saying, she departed.

I took my little hatchet and cut plenty of wood, and twisted the cord that was to be used in sewing ap-puh-way-oon-un, or mats, for the use of the family. Gradually I began to feel less appetite, but my thirst continued; still I was fearful of touching the snow to allay it, by sucking it, as my mother had told me that if I did so, though secretly, the Great Spirit would see me, and the lesser spirits also, and that my fasting would be of no use. So I continued to fast till, the fourth day, when my mother came with a little tin dish, and filling it with snow, she came to my lodge, and was well pleased to find that I had followed her instructions.

She melted the snow, and told me to drink it. I did so, and felt refreshed, but had a desire for more, which she told me would not do, and I contented myself with what she had given me. She again told me to get and follow a good vision; a vision that might not only do us good, but also benefit mankind, if I could. She then left me, and for two days she did not come near me, nor any human being, and I was left to my own reflections. The night of the sixth day I fancied a voice called to me, and said, "Poor child! I pity your condition; come, you are invited this way;" and I thought the voice proceeded from a certain distance from my lodge. I obeyed the summons, and, going to the spot from which the voice came, found a thin shining path, like a silver cord, which I followed. It led straightforward, and it seemed, upward. After going a short distance, I stood still, and saw on my right hand the new moon, with a flame rising from the top like a candle, which threw around a board light.

I went on, and I beheld on my right the face of Kau-ge-gay-be-qua, or the everlasting standing woman, who told me her name, and said to me, "I give you my name, and you may give it to another. I also give you that which I have, life everlasting. I give you long life on the earth, and skill in saving life in others. Go, you are called on high." I went on, and saw a man standing, with a large circular body, and rays from his head, like horns. He said, "Fear not; my name is Monido-Wininees, or the Little Man-spirit. I give this name to your first son. It is my life. Go to the place you are called to visit."

I followed the path till I could see that it led up to an opening in the sky, when I heard a voice, and standing still, saw the figures of a man standing near the path, whose head was surrounded with a brilliant halo, and his breast was covered with squares. He said to me, "Look at me; my name is O-Shau-wau-e-geeghick, or the Bright Blue Sky. I am the veil that covers the opening in the sky. Stand and listen to me. Do not be afraid. I am going to endow you with gifts of life, and put you in array that you may withstand and endure." Immediately I saw myself encircled with bright points, which rested against me like needles, but gave me no pain, and they fell at my feet. This was repeated several times, and at each time they fell to the ground. He said, "Wait, do not fear, till I have said and done all I am about to do."

I then felt different instruments, first like awls, then like nails, stuck into my flesh, but neither did they give me pain, but, like the needles, fell at my feet as often as they appeared. He then said, "That is good," meaning my trial by these points; "you will see length of days. Advance a little farther," said he. I did so, and stood at the commencement of the opening. "You have arrived," said he, "at the limit you cannot pass. I give you my name; you can give it to another. Now, return! Look around you. There is a conveyance for you. Do not be afraid to get on its back, and when you get to your lodge, you must take that which sustains the human body." I turned, and saw a kind of fish swimming in the air, and getting upon it as directed, was carried back with celerity; my hair floating behind me in the air. And as soon as I got back, my vision ceased.

I attempted to cut wood as usual, but in this effort I fell back on the snow from exhaustion, and lay some time; at last I made an effort and rose, and went to my lodge and lay down. I again saw the vision, and each person who had before spoken to me, and heard the promises of different kinds made to me, and the songs. I went the same path which I had pursued before, and met with the same reception. I also had another vision, or celestial visit, which I shall presently relate. My mother came again on the seventh day, and brought me some pounded corn boiled in snow water, for, she said, I must not drink water from lake or river. After taking it I related my vision to her. She said it was good, and spoke to me to continue my fast three days longer. I did so: at the end of which she took me home, and made a feast in honor of my success, and invited a great many guests.[29]

It seems almost incredible that a young girl could withstand the physical tests that a ten-day vision demanded. While Indians trained their children very early to endure great physical hardships as against the day when they might find themselves alone and without the possibility of rescue or assistance, nevertheless, this ordeal seems to be on the fringes of what is possible for a human being to endure. Of utmost importance in this story is the repetition of the experience as she was resting in her lodge and finishing the ten-day stretch. Nowhere in the literature can I find a scenario in which the entire vision is repeated. People might be reminded of the elements of a previous experience, but certainly did not find the vision duplicated for them.

PRETTY SHIELD'S VISION

I had slept little, sometimes lying down alone in the hills at night, and always on hard places. I ate only enough to keep me alive, hoping for a medicine-dream, a vision, that would help me to live and to help others. One morning I saw a woman ahead of me. She was walking fast but suddenly she stopped and stood still, looking at the ground. I thought I knew her, thought she was a woman who had died four years before. I felt afraid. I stopped, my heart beating fast. "Come here, daughter." Her words seemed to draw me toward her against my will.

Walking a few steps, I saw that she was not a real woman, but that she was a [apparition] Person, and that she was standing beside an anthill. "Come here, daughter." Again I walked toward her when I did not wish to move. Stopping by her side, I did not try to look into her face. My heart was nearly choking me. "Rake up the side of this anthill and ask for the things you wish, daughter," the Person said, and then she was gone.

Now in this medicine-dream, I entered a beautiful white lodge, with a war eagle at the head. He did not speak to me, and yet I have often seen him since that day. And even more the ants help me. I listen to them always. They are my medicine, these busy, powerful little people, the ants.[30]

35

A Pawnee Woman's Dream

At a recent meeting of the medicine society, when the ceremony had ended, a woman named Yellow Corn Woman arose and said, "I had a vision. I saw Bear-Chief wearing the bear robe over his shoulders and the bear claw neckpiece around his neck. He was painted with yellow earthen clay and had black streaks from each eye down the face. He said, 'My sister, Father (Bear) and Mother (Cedar Tree) have not had any smoke for many years. We (dead people) are watching for our people to have the ceremony. The people think the ceremony is lost. It is not, for one of the Bear men who knows the secret ceremony is still with you. I ask that you tell the people so they can have the ceremony, for it is time.' I woke up and the last few days I have been trying to think that I should be the one to tell you. I have a cow which you can have so you can have the ceremony." Then she began to cry.[31]

Another Pawnee Woman's Visions

One night the woman dreamed of a man with a bundle on his back. He placed the bundle on the ground and walked around it; he sat down on the east side of it and made a small fireplace. Then he sat behind the bundle, which he opened, and took a cat skin from it. The skin had hoofs of ponies and buffalo painted on it. He spread the skin in front of himself. From a dry buffalo bladder in the bundle he took a small pipe. He spread the bladder on the skin and placed the small pipe on it. Then he took out a bag of deer hide, from which he took something clear like glass, which he placed on the hide and covered with the deer hide. Next he took a rope from his bundle. As soon as the woman saw the rope, she recognized both it and the skin, but the pipe and the clear glass-like object she had not seen before. From his tobacco pouch he took a pinch of native tobacco, which he placed in the bowl of the pipe. He held the transparent object over the bowl of the pipe and smoked it. Then he placed the clear thing upon the skin and covered it. He gave four whiffs of smoke to the sun and emptied the ashes in front of the altar. Then he addressed the woman as follows: "Woman, I am the one who gave you the idea of going on the warpath with the men. I made them successful. I gave you the skin and the rope. You found the rope on a mare. You will get the glass and the pipe. You will make the pipe yourself. You must do as I have done. If the clear thing lights the pipe, it will be a sign of success; if not, it will mean ill luck. These things were given you by the sun, so it will be the only one to receive smoke. I am going."

The woman awoke. Ever after this dream she cared for the skin and the rope. She always kept them out of sight so that the men would not see them. She dreamed of the man again. He told her that she was his sister and had the things he wanted her to have, that she was to make the small pipe for her bundle but that the stem of the pipe was to have no perforation. He told her to go on the warpath once more and on her return to make the pipe. After the war party, he told her she would be married, but he warned her that only one male child that she would have would live and that the others would be taken from her by the sun. He told her to give the bundle to her son when he grew up.[32]

Mary Sdipp-shin-mah's Vision

When I was a little girl, five or six years old, my mother said to me one day in huckleberry-picking time, "Tomorrow morning we will go up on the high mountain and pick huckleberries." Next morning she got a horse and we rode double up the mountain. On the way, I told my mother that I saw a spot with many nice, big huckleberries. But she said, "No, we will go farther up the mountain."

Late in the afternoon we were on a high ridge. There we got off the horse and started picking huckleberries. After a while my mother said to me, "You stay here and pick, and you may eat as many berries as you wish. I am going farther up the mountain. I will not be gone long. Nothing will harm you." I picked some berries, and then I sat down and ate them. The sun set, but Mother did not come back. I called and called for her. Then it got dark, and I was frightened, I cried and cried and cried. Then I walked farther up the ridge, crying and crying. After a little rest, I went a little farther. I slept for a while and then I climbed a little higher, still crying.

When the sun came up, I was very tired and sat down on a ridge, facing a gulch thick with forest. I thought I heard something down there, so I stopped crying and listened. I thought I heard the voice of a human being. I listened and listened. Then I saw something coming toward me, coming where the trees were not so thick. A woman and two children were coming. I felt pretty good, now that I knew people were near me. The three turned into the brush, out of sight, but I could still hear them. The boy and girl were playing and having fun. Soon the three of them came right to me and the mother said, "Well, little girl, what are you doing here? You must be lost. We heard you crying, and so we came up here to give you help."

The mother was a middle-aged woman, well dressed in buckskin. Around her shoulders the buckskin was painted red, and she wore trinkets. The little boy and the little girl were pretty little fellows, clean and also well dressed in buckskin "Don't cry anymore, little girl," the mother said. "You come with us." I jumped up and went with them. The children tried to get me to play with them, but I stayed near the mother. She told them, "Leave your little sister alone. She is too tired to play."

When we got to the bottom of the gulch, where the bank was not steep, we stopped to get a drink. I stooped over and drank for a long time, for I was very thirsty. When I finished and sat up, I was alone again. The mother and the children were gone. I cried again until I heard the mother's voice say, "Don't cry, little girl. Come up here."

They were sitting on a bank, and I climbed up to them. Then the mother said, "Now we are going to take you back to your people. When you grow up, you will be a good medicine woman. I give you power over all kinds of sickness. I give you power to heal people. I give you special power to help women give birth to children. But you must never try to do more than I tell you to do. If you do, you will be responsible for suffering and even for death."

"That is all I can tell you now. I have given you your power. These two are your little brother and little sister. I am your mother."

I glanced away and when I looked back, the mother and children were gone. Instead, a grizzly bear sat there beside me, with two little cubs. The mother bear stood up and said, "Now get on my back."

I did. How fast we went, I couldn't say. After a while she stopped and said, "Your people are near here. Walk on a short distance, and you will see them." And I did.

Now you know why I never accept payment for healing the sick or for helping women in childbirth. My power was not given me for reward of any kind. And I cannot tell anyone how I heal the sick.[33]

VISIONS IN TRANSITION

We know today that very few people have visions, and that those who do have encounters that pale in significance and power compared to the visions presented above. What can account for this absence of meaningful relationships with the spirits? It seems that in the process of abandoning the old life and being forced to live in a more structured society, we have lost our connection with the higher powers. Strangely, I have been able to find two transitional visions that bare careful examination. The narratives of these visions suggest that as Christianity began to make inroads into the traditional life, people experienced, or thought they experienced, the entrance of Christ into what would have been wholly traditional vision experiences. Both visions feature a difficult choice for the individuals in that they appear to ask for decisions to be made that would put the people definitely on one side or the other of the two religious traditions.

Since this collection of religious experiences attempts to present the data without taking sides between religions, I have included both accounts as if they were no different from the visions we have discussed above. John Slocum chose the Christian religion; Minnie Enemy Heart chose the old ways. Scholars may dismiss these stories as self-delusion triggered by the intense pressure on the people in the reservation setting. Indeed, they may well be the product of overactive imaginations. On the other hand, they may be as valid as the other stories. Since the scholars in whose works they were found reported them sincerely, and since we were not present during any of these visions to render judgment, we should treat the accounts as real experiences of these people. They raise the question of whether in the spiritual realm there is not an interchange of possibilities offered us by compatible spirits working in different traditions.

JOHN SLOCUM'S VISION

The Shaker church among the Indians of the Columbia Plateau and Pacific Northwest came from a vision reported by Slocum. Note that when suffering from a serious illness, he first went to five Indian doctors who could not cure him, and in a near death experience, which he attributed to Christ, became a convert to Christianity.

> The witnesses have spoken the truth. I was sick about two weeks, and had five Indian doctors. I grew very weak and poor. Dr. Jim was there. He could not cure me. They wanted to save me, but my soul would die two or three hours at a time. At night my breath was out, and I died. All at once I saw

a shining light—great light—trying my soul. I looked and saw my body had no soul—looked at my own body—it was dead.

I came through the first time and told my friends. "When I die, don't cry" and then I died again. Before this I shook hands and told my friends I was going to die. Angels told me to look back and see my body. I did, and saw it lying down. When I saw it, it was pretty poor. My soul left my body and went up to judgment place of God. I do not know about my body after 4 o'clock.

I have seen a great light in my soul from that good land; I have understood all Christ wants us to do. Before I came alive I saw I was a sinner. Angel in heaven said to me "You must go back and turn alive again on earth." I learned that I must be good Christian man on earth, or will be punished. My soul was told that I must come back and live four days on earth. When I came back, I told my friends: "There is a God—there is a Christian people. Good friends be Christian."[34]

MINNIE ENEMY HEART'S VISION

While incorporating the new religion into the old religious structure seemed natural to many people, it was solidly rejected by others. Sometimes, during a vision quest, people are asked to choose what form of spiritual practice and leadership they would like and would feel most comfortable practicing. This vision suggests that clear boundary lines must still be drawn between the different forms of spiritual expression. Goodbird, a Sisseton Sioux, reported this vision in his autobiography, so it must have had credence on the reservation.

On this reservation lives a medicine woman, named Minnie Enemy Heart. When a girl, she went to the mission school and learned something about Jesus Christ. Afterward, as her fathers had done, she went into the hills to seek her god. She says that she fasted and prayed, and Jesus came to her in a vision. One side of his body was dark, like an Indian; the other was white, like a white man. In his white hand he carried a lamb; in the other, a little dog.

Jesus explained the vision. "My body," he said, "half dark and half white, means that I am as much an Indian as I am a white man. This dog means that the Indian ways are for Indians, as white ways are for white men; for Indians sacrifice dogs, as white men once sacrificed lambs. If the missionaries tell you this is not true, ask them who crucified men, were they Indians or white men?"[35]

These transitional visions should be read with some degree of skepticism because the self-serving interpretation that deals with practical choices of people seems a little unlikely. Gathering dreams and visions of modern people will have this same ambiguity because people live in entirely different environments and danger comes from the thoughtlessness of other people rather than war parties and animals.

CHAPTER TWO

POWERS CONFERRED ON THE MEDICINE MEN

* * * * * * * * * * * * *

HEALINGS

One of the primary gifts to people in dreams or visions is the power to heal illnesses. It appears that sometimes the medicine man calls on the bird or animal spirit, and they respond by using their medicine knowledge working through the medicine man. That is to say, the medicine man takes on the appearance of a bear, or wolf, or even duck. They briefly seem to demonstrate the physical form of their patron creature or make sounds the animal usually makes. Luther Standing Bear cited his experience with this phenomenon. "I was once in a tipi where a medicine-man was giving a patient treatment. The medicine-man happened to be a Duck Dreamer, so, of course, the duck was helping him to find a cure for the sick man. The medicine-man asked me to bring him some water, so I brought him a vessel holding two quarts or more. He drank every drop and then quacked in perfect imitation of a duck. In a moment or so he called for more water and that he drank, too."[1]

This format seems most prevalent when there is a very serious illness. At other times, the medicine man appears to diagnose the problem and takes the appropriate action to resolve it. At times, the medicine man will look at the patient and announce that he cannot heal that kind of illness. Sometimes, he will recommend another medicine man; other times, he will simply walk away. Below are some typical stories of healing practices that illustrate the breadth of powers exercised.

THUNDER CLOUD RECEIVES HEALING POWERS

Most healing powers are given during a dream or vision and are the result of a gift presented to a human by a bird or animal. If wind, water, or thunders bestow the healing powers, they are usually represented by a spirit in human form that later transforms itself into a helpful animal. Paul Radin recorded in a story how Thunder Cloud, a Winnebago medicine man, received his healing powers. In his case, which appears to be unusual, the spirits in the sky instructed Thunder Cloud first on the procedure of healing and then tested him by making him perform certain other tasks to give him confidence that their gift has substantial power.

> Brother-in-law, this is how I learned to cure human beings. I was carried up to the spirit village of those who live in the sky, a doctor's village, and there I was instructed as follows. A dead and rotten log, almost completely covered with weeds, was placed in the middle of the lodge. This log I was to treat as though it were a sick human being. I breathed upon this log and the spirits in the lodge breathed on me. Twice, three times, four times, we did the same. Finally the log that had seemed dead was transformed into a young man, who arose and walked away. "Human being," said the spirits, "you are indeed a holy person!"
>
> Brother-in-law, from the middle of the ocean, the spirits came after me, from a shaman's village situated there. They, too, bestowed their powers upon me and they too, made me try my powers. They asked me to blow upon waves they had created, all of them as large as the ocean, and I blew upon them and they became quiet as water in a small saucer. Three times I did this and three times I succeeded. Then the spirits created a choppy ocean, where the waves piled one upon the other furiously and I was told to blow upon it. I did so and that

ocean of waves, mighty as it was, subsided and became quiet.

"Human being," they said, "thus will you always act. There will be nothing that you cannot accomplish. No matter what illness one of your fellow-men may happen to have, you will be able to cure it."[2]

NAVAJO DIAGNOSTICIANS

Today, in several tribes, medicine men work closely with Western-trained doctors. The most publicized cooperative effort between Western doctors and medicine men seems to be happening on the Navajo Reservation in Arizona. Perhaps it is fitting that this joint effort should occur there, because Navajo healing powers are immensely complicated. They use a two-step process of diagnosis and healing that is as sophisticated as Western practices, but often more thorough. According to Leland Wyman: "The function of the diagnostician is to discover not only the cause of illness but also to recommend the treatment to be used (sometimes he recommends actual therapeutic measures, although usually he simply tells what kind of chant should be sung over the patient), and to recommend a particular practitioner who can apply that treatment. This sometimes results in a change of Medicine men during an illness."[3]

There are three kinds of diagnosticians used by the Navajo: 1.) the Hand Trembler; 2.) the Star Gazer; and 3.) the Listener. Franc Newcomb explained the differences in this way: "When it is a case of diagnosing some stubborn ailment, or when it is a desire to learn if a past event has cast a malicious influence over a certain person or family, the Shaking Hand ceremony is generally employed." On the other hand, "if an important decision is to be made that will affect the whole family, such as whether to move from one section of the reservation to another or whether part of the family should undertake a long journey, the Star-gazing or the Sun-gazing rite is often used to influence the decision and also to determine the proper time to start."[4] And, Newcomb reported, "Once in a while grown people go to distant places to obtain employment and months pass during which their family has no word from them. In such cases, the Listening Rite is considered most effective in locating the lost animals or children and in obtaining information concerning distant relatives. This ceremony is also used if a Navajo has been having very bad luck and thinks that someone is casting an evil spell over him."[5] As Wyman described the three modes of diagnosis, we can see a distinguishable difference in the ritual:

> During prayer and thereafter the diagnostician sits with eyes closed and face averted, and as soon as the singing begins his extended hand usually begins to shake. Although it was said that the motion of the hand usually begins any time, even during prayer (in which case the prayer is discontinued and a song begun), it more often than not begins at the start of the song. ... While the hand is moving the diagnostician thinks of various diseases or causes of diseases. When something happens which tells him that he is thinking of the correct one, he then thinks of various chants which might cure the disease; then, of what medicine man might be the best one to give the chant; then perhaps of plant medicines or other therapeutic measure which might be used. After all the desired information has been divined the shaking stops and the diagnostician opens his eyes and tells those assembled what he had discovered.[6]

The Star Gazer uses a crystal and needs an assistant to perform his ritual. Actually, the two procedures have little in common, and it is unusual to have two such different practices in the same tribal religious tradition. So the Star Gazer takes one person with him and leaves the house. Outside he prays the star-prayer to the star spirit, asking the star to show him the cause of the sickness. Then he begins to sing star-songs and while singing gazes fixedly at a star or at the light of a star reflected in a "glass rock," or quartz crystal, which he holds in his hand. Soon, it was said, the star begins to "throw out a string of light and at the end of this the Star Gazer sees the cause of the sickness of the patient, like a motion picture."[7]

If these strings of light are white or yellow the patient will recover; if red, the illness is serious or dangerous. If the white light falls on the house and makes it light as day around it, the patient will get well.[7]

Finally, the Listener uses techniques similar in some respects to the Star Gazer, yet there is a considerable difference in the method, since the Listener hears audible responses, whereas verbal communication is missing from the other two methods:

> The dried and powdered ear-drum of a badger is used in place of the lenses of bird's eyes; the Listener dips a finger in the powder and then places it in each ear. Then he takes one man with him, goes out of the house, and prays to "listening," saying "I want to hear, etc" and then begins to sing (star songs may be used) and to listen. The cause of the sickness is determined from the characteristics of something heard, such as the rattling of a rattlesnake, the roar of a bear, or thunder. If someone is heard crying, the patient will die.[8]

While Wyman developed strict classifications of the result that could be expected using each of these methods, we can see that medical diagnosis is the primary function of each of the ceremonies. I would suggest that, considering the two-step procedure, perhaps this Navajo specialization testifies to the longevity of healing arts among the Navajos as opposed to the other tribes who combine the two functions.

FINDING THE CURE

We wonder sometimes how the spirits know the proper medicine to use. Where an animal spirit has its own medicine and gives it willingly to a medicine man, the transfer of healing powers is relatively simple. However, the case becomes immensely complicated when the disease to be cured has been previously unknown to the people. European diseases virtually depopulated the continent in a series of epidemics beginning shortly after contact was made. Russell Thornton pointed out the terrible fatality rates suffered by some tribes in his book *American Indian Holocaust and Survival*. What would be the response of a medicine man—and his spirit—in seeking to find the proper medicine to be used? Morris Opler recorded a ceremony in which the medicine man and the spirit worked cooperatively to find the proper cure. Whether this procedure was used by the medicine man of other tribes, we do not know. But this Chiricahua Apache story makes a great deal of sense and described a process vaguely akin to the scientific method.

> Now he sang songs about different medicines. He sang about one herb and then another. There was no sign that any of these would help. Then he started on the trees. He got to juniper. Then he stopped. His power had showed him that juniper was good. "What kind of juniper," he asked. His power told him to name the junipers. "Alligator bark juniper?" he asked. "No." "Rock juniper?" It was not right either. "One-seeded juniper?" "You've got it," said his power. He started another song. Right at the beginning he stopped. He nodded. "There are four," he said, "slim medicine (*Perezia wrightii*), sumac, pinon, and one-seeded juniper. The roots of the first two can be used and the needles of the last two."[9]

It is singularly difficult to obtain eyewitness accounts of the powers of the medicine men of the eastern tribes. These selections come from the distant past in New England. They do not vary much from thousands of stories old and contemporary, white and Indian, regarding individuals with unusual healing powers. Since these stories are almost the only accounts we have of the northeastern tribes, I have felt obliged to include them. I suspect that, along with the procedure for healing, some songs were sung to obtain the assistance of healing spirits. Gladys Tantaquidgeon, a respected elder, reported some healings performed by Dr. Perry, a Massachusetts Indian doctor, that are close enough to other healing accounts to be given credence.

DR. PERRY OF MASSACHUSETTS

The daughter of a white family was suffering from tuberculosis and several doctors and specialists had been called in to treat her but she was steadily becoming worse. Her father in desperation decided to ask Dr. Perry to look at his daughter and offer treatment. Dr. Perry visited the girl and lamented the fact that she had been allowed to endure so much suffering. He told her parents that he could help her and that before long she would be out riding her fine horse. This seemed improbable but Dr. Perry administered some herb medicine and in a short time the girl was feeling stronger. After a while he ordered her to sit up and then in a few days she was out of doors. She made rapid progress under his care.[10]

The other story is quite similar and suggests that Dr. Perry was used when all other forms of healing had failed. Critics, of course, will pass these healings off as psychosomatic events, and they may well be. It does seem strange, however, that white doctors who know the culture and religion of the patient and are presumably capable of using the latest medical techniques should fail to use procedures and methods that could deal adequately with psychosomatic illnesses. Obviously, the mental state of the patients would play an important role in recovery from illness. Yet Dr. Perry, with a few herbs, could start the patient on the road to recovery in a very short time, suggesting that there was no psychosomatic problem at all.

On one occasion a boy had become ill and was losing his mind. Several doctors had been called in on the case but they were unable to cure the boy. Dr. Perry appeared after the boy's mother had expressed a desire to have him see her child. She knew that Dr. Perry was far away and it would be impossible to reach him. He said that he knew of the trouble and right away started back to Herring Pond.

The sick boy sat up in bed constantly casting out an

imaginary line and catching fish. When Dr. Perry looked at him, he remarked, "You won't catch many more fish, my boy." Dr. Perry went out in the back yard and returned shortly with some roots which he had dug up. He prepared the roots and made a strong tea which he administered to the boy who fell into a deep sleep. After several hours, the boy awakened and called for his mother. He said, "Where have I been?" His mental and physical conditions were normal and he had no more trouble.[11]

Warriors often had special medicine to use in warfare. Crazy Horse painted hailstones on his face, wore no feathers, and had a stone that kept him immune from wounds. Roman Nose's warbonnet fulfilled the same function. In various stories in this collection, we can find individuals protected by a variety of sacred objects. But what happens if the individual has no power to make himself immune and must take his chances? Many men had special rituals or protectors to enable them to survive wounds that otherwise would prove fatal. Sitting Bull's powers included the power to heal himself.

SITTING BULL'S SELF-REMEDY

A Sioux named Sitting Bull, who had long lived with the Northern Cheyennes and was called by them Short Sioux, while retreating in a running fight with the Crows, was shot in the back. The ball had gone through his body; blood was flowing from the wound in the back and in the breast, and from the man's mouth. After the Crows had left them, Sitting Bull said to those near him: "I must find an ant-hill. Look for one." When an ant-hill was found, Sitting Bull dismounted, collected a handful of ants, and put them in his mouth and swallowed them. "Now," he said, "I shall be well." He mounted and rode all through the night, and at last recovered.[12]

From various accounts, it appears that some medicine men could diagnose illnesses and heal patients in a purely intuitive fashion, singing no songs, barely touching the patient, and effect a cure. What exactly happened on these occasions? Was the illness one over which the medicine man had absolute control, or was it a psychosomatic reaction to events that dissolved quickly when the medicine man appeared on the scene? We can speculate forever and not solve the problem. Nevertheless, taking reports as a true rendering of the situation, below are two stories for analysis and reflection.

WHITE CROW'S HEALING

> One day when my father was away, my stepmother became ill and lay on her bed in great pain, unable to rise. I sent for White Crow who brought with him no medicinebag, rattle, not the usual drum; neither did he sing or talk to mother, but merely sat and looked at her as she rolled in pain. After a while he took a small piece of root which he had with him and cut it into two smaller pieces, telling mother to chew one of the pieces and swallow it and also to chew the second piece and rub it on her chest where the pain was. This mother did as quickly as possible, for she was seriously ill. Her recovery was almost immediate, for it seemed no more than five minutes before she was up and preparing food for White Crow. I was so delighted and curious, that I offered White Crow my best horses if he would give me the name of the plant. He refused and I then offered him fifty dollars for it, but I found that it was not purchasable at any price.[13]

Standing Bear's report emphasized the power of the medicine, but also suggested that White Crow could look inside the woman and see some kind of organic or chemical deficiency and the medicine she needed to overcome her illness. But this ability should not overshadow the fact that White Crow's knowledge of plants must have been spectacular, since he was able to find the right root to give her.

The next story was printed in a newspaper—thus raising a question of accuracy in the telling—but it is presented in such a straightforward manner that there should not be excessive doubts raised. Apparently, it was the custom of vessels in the higher latitudes to allow large numbers of natives to board their ships and entertain and bargain with the crew. Considering the hazardous weather in the Alaska-Aleutian region, the practice also helped to keep sailors from jumping ship. At any rate, the story is impressive.

INSTANT NAUTICAL HEALING

An American ship captain, M. J. Healy, reported a healing done by a medicine man. A young woman fell deathly ill when the natives were visiting his ship, *The Bear*, somewhere in the Alaskan islands. In recounting this incident, the captain expressed his surprise at the ease with which the medicine man restored the girl to health:

> The strangest thing I saw happen on board my ship one day. There were about 100 of these natives aboard. One of the natives, a girl, fell down with a hemorrhage and vomited blood all around. The blood came from her lungs in streams. She was lying there on the deck as pale as death, and I thought she would die there, so I rushed a man off to get Dr. Yeamans, the Bear's surgeon.
>
> Before the doctor could get there the chief medicine man rushed out, and, going to the girl, he blew first into one ear and then into the other, and then tapped her on the chin, and she got up and was all right again, and she began dancing around on the ship as healthy and active as though there had never been the least thing the matter with her. And mark you, this wasn't two minutes from the time she had hemorrhages. I never saw anything so marvelous in my life. There was all the blood before me on the ship too.[14]

REVIVING THE DEAD

The eminent anthropologist Ake Hultkranz did prodigious work on shamanic healing and the concept of the soul found in North American

Indian people. Being quite orthodox, however, his views reflect the prevailing notion that American Indians are somehow linked to the people of Siberia via the mythical Bering Strait, which now, it seems, needs to be open and available for travel for uncounted millenia. But the Siberian link meant that Hultkranz concentrated his efforts on those stories and accounts that would help bolster a faltering fiction.

In like manner, one of my purposes in collecting these stories and presenting the material in the fashion I have is to give as much support to the notion that American Indian medicine traditions are a wholly North American phenomenon. That is to say, I think both American Indians and Siberians are relating to the basic energy of reality, but I believe that except for a few similarities, they originate in entirely different experiences in the natural world. The land we live on is a major force in Indian traditions, and while there are instances of "soul loss" to be found in our tradition, this phenomenon does not occur with great frequency.

Soul loss is much better discussed in relation to the Indian concept of souls, and while Hultkranz has written on this subject also, I believe it is far more complex in a philosophical sense and reveals much more variety in actual empirical events. The basic premise of soul loss is that the vital parts of the soul depart from the unity they once enjoyed, and the person who suffers from this malady actually, physically dies. Below are three accounts cited by Hultkranz that give us an idea of how the illness is seen in Indian experience and how it is treated.

Northen Barred Owl's Remedy

A Saulteaux shaman (Lake Winnipeg area) by the name of Northen Barred Owl was sent for to cure a girl who was very ill. She died shortly after the shaman's arrival. Nevertheless, he did not give up. He lay down beside her, tying a piece of red yarn around the girl's wrist. Then he went into a trance so deep that he did not move at all. His soul now followed the girl on her way to the realm of the dead. There he found her, with the help of the red yarn, in the crowd of the dead, and he then brought her back to the land of the living. The spectators saw him move a little. As he moved, so did the girl. He moved more, and the girl did the same. She was restored to life. (We might say that this was a case of apparent death.)[15]

Hultkranz reviewed the case of an Indian policeman's son who had lost consciousness, and that condition perhaps placed the healing in the category of soul loss. This incident occurred in 1910 but was well known and accurately reported in the community. When he fell sick and lost consciousness, his parents sent for the medicine man.

He declared that the soul (free-soul) had gone, and only breath (symbol of life soul) remained. This was a serious situation. All that was left for the medicine man to do was to "die" (go in a trance) and catch the lost soul in the realm of the dead. Said he, "When I have died my soul will go to the world of the departed to hunt the boy's soul. But in order to bring me back to life you bystanders must give me three kicks in the back."

So he died, and lay dead on the ground. After half an hour he received three kicks in the back. The people standing around could hear him give a deep breath; his soul had returned. After the medicine man regained consciousness, he told of his experiences in the land of the dead. He said that he had found the boy's soul on the other side of the (western) mountains, playing with dead boys over there. The medicine man had great difficulty in persuading the boy to come back with him to his home again. At last the boy consented and went with the medicine man. The medicine man assured the policeman that the boy had come back and that he would be quite well again. The boy recovered and grew up to be a man.

A Crow Indian mother had lost her little girl, who was three or four years of age. Morgan Moon's sister said: "The child is dead; there is nothing to do." But her brother retorted,

"No, the soul has just temporarily left the body. I shall bring it back." He touched the top of the child's head, stroking it round the crown. The child opened her eyes and looked at him. He soul was close to the body and entered it through the top of the head. Next day the girl was playing again. She was quite well.[16]

These incidents may well be examples of near death experience viewed from the perspective of an observer. We might argue that, given the lack of knowledge of medicine by the Indians, the patients were actually lapsing into a coma and required but a little attention to be brought back to consciousness. That argument, however, overlooks the fact that Indians viewed illnesses from a spiritual point of view, some medicine men simply touching the person or observing them and prescribing the proper root medicine to cure them. That the medicine man said he had been to the realm of the dead and returned with the soul suggests a spiritual power of great strength. Indian near death experiences describe the other world in familiar terms, a world not much different from our own. I would tend to give these stories credence until we fully investigate the dimensions of the other world.

HEALING SEVERE GUNSHOT WOUNDS

It is well known that European diseases quickly ravaged the Indian nations and nearly exterminated them. The Chinooks on the Columbia River, for example, lost about 90 percent of their people in just four years (1829–1833) to a flu epidemic. One would have thought that the weapons of the Europeans would wreak a proportionate loss, and, at first, they certainly killed many people while frightening the others into a state of submission. It has been argued that the diseases came too quickly for the medicine men to adjust and find a cure. The medicine men seemed to adjust quickly to guns, and the following stories show just how complete a change they made.

BLACK ELK'S EXPERIENCE

Black Elk remembered a healing done by a bear medicine man that seems highly unusual, if not spectacular. It occurred during the summer of 1876, when the Sioux were fighting with the soldiers almost every week. The healing impressed itself on Black Elk, and he paid strict attention to it because he thought that, someday, he would have to perform similar healings.

> The wounded man, Raffling Hawk, was shot through the hips and was wounded in the Rosebud fight. It seemed to be an impossibility to heal him. They gave him a holy stick painted red. There were two women with the man [the bear medicine man] on either side. One of them had a cup of water and I looked into the cup expecting to see something in it like a blue man. It was impossible for the wounded [man] to get up and the chief bear told the girls to give the water and herb to the man and then it came to my mind that someday I will have to perform this myself. [Because of the cup of water in his vision] Then when they gave the wounded the stick, he stood up. The two girls led [him] out of the tipi and faced the south. Then all six bears began to groan like bears and you could see flames coming out—all kinds of colors—and feathers coming out. They did this toward the wounded man. Then after this the man began to walk with this sacred red cane.[17]

EAGLE SHIELD'S TRIUMPH

A similar healing involving a dreadful gunshot injury took place after the people went on the Standing Rock Reservation. Unfortunately, we do not know what medicine animal, if any, Eagle Shield used to affect this cure. From the description of the injury, we can speculate that bear medicine was used, because it usually had very strong powers to deal with illnesses. However, gunshots were not the unusual kind of sickness. Of more importance, perhaps, is the fact that this healing occurred *after* white doctors had given up on the patient,

suggesting that traditional healing powers can be used both as a pre-
ventive and as a last resort.

> Eagle Shield said that he had treated men shot through the
> body and they had recovered. One man thus treated was per-
> sonally known to the writer. The man had attempted suicide
> by shooting himself in the left side, the bullet passing through
> the body and breaking the edge of the shoulder blade. As a
> result of the wound his arm was paralyzed, and two doctors of
> the white race said that it must be amputated. Eagle Shield
> undertook the treatment of the case and did his work so
> effectually that the man appears to have as free use of one arm
> as of the other.[18]

OMAHA BUFFALO MEDICINE MEN

Francis La Flesche reported a healing performed by the Omaha Buffalo medicine men that seems incredible; yet there is good evidence
that his account is accurate. He and some other boys were playing
gambling games in the woods when they heard a series of shots indicating older boys were firing pistols. Then they heard someone cry
out in despair that he had committed murder. The account is quite
long, and I have excerpted the critical descriptions of the healing. La
Flesche wrote:

> I made my way through the crowd, to see who it was that was
> killed. Peering over the shoulders of another boy, I saw on the
> ground a dirty-looking little form, and recognized it as one of
> my playmates. Blood was oozing from a wound in the back of his
> head, and from one just under his right eye, near the nose ...
>   Soon there was an opening in the crowd, and I saw a tall
> man come up the hill, wrapped in a buffalo robe, and pass
> through the opening to where the boy lay; he stopped over
> the child, felt his wrists, then of his breast. "He is alive," the
> man said, "set up a tent, and take him in there." The little body

was lifted in a robe, and carried by two men into a large tent which was hastily erected. A young man was sent in haste to call the buffalo medicine-men of another village. All the buffalo medicine men came and lifted the bottom of the tent so people could see what they were doing …

All the medicine men sat around the boy, their eyes gleaming out of their wrinkled faces. The man who was first to try his charms and medicines on the patient began by telling in a loud voice how he became possessed of them, how in a vision he had seen the buffalo which had revealed to him the mysterious secrets of the medicine, and of the charm song he was taught to sing when using the medicine. At the end of every narrative the boy's father thanked the doctor in terms of relationship. When he had recited his story from beginning to end, and had compounded the roots he had taken from his skin pouch, he started his song at the top of his voice, which the other doctors, twenty or thirty in number, picked up and sang in unison, with such volume that one would imagine it could have been heard many miles. In the midst of the chorus of voices rose the shrill sound of the bone whistle accompaniment, imitating the call of an eagle.

After the doctor had started the song, he put bits of root into his mouth, grinding them with his teeth, and, taking a mouthful of water, he slowly approached the boy bellowing and pawing the earth, after the manner of an angry buffalo at bay. All eyes were upon him with an admiring gaze. When within a few feet of the boy's head, he paused for a moment, drew a long breath, and with a whizzing noise forced the water from his mouth into the wound. The boy spread out his hands and winced as though he was again hit by a ball. The man uttered a series of short exclamations, "He! he! He!" to give an additional charm to the medicine. It was a successful operation, and the father, and the man who had wounded the boy, lifted their spread hands towards the doctor to signify their thanks. During this performance all the medicine-men sang with energy the song which had been started by the operator.

The next day the Indian agent at the Omaha Agency arrived and demanded that the boy be sent to the agency since he was a qualified doctor. The Omaha chief and the boy's father rejected his order and the agent went into the tent to look at the boy and when he touched him the buffalo medicine men immediately told him to stop. So the agent left, declaring that the boy had a short time to live with the wounds he had.

The boy's head was swollen to nearly twice its natural size, and looked like a great blue ball, the hollows of his eyes were covered up, so that he could not see, and it made me shudder to look at him. Four days the boy was treated in this strange manner. On the evening of the third day the doctors said that he was out of danger, and that in the morning he would be made to rise and meet the rising sun and to greet the return of life ... In the morning there was a mist in the air, as the medicine-men had foretold there would be; but as the dawn grew brighter and brighter, the fog slowly disappeared, as if to unveil the great red sun that was just visible over the horizon. Slowly it grew larger and larger, while the boy was gently lifted by two strong men, and when up on his feet, he was told to take four steps toward the east. The medicine-men sang with a good will the mystery song appropriate to the occasion, as the boy attempted this feeble walk. The two men by his side began to count, as the lad moved eastward, "Win (one), numba (two), thab'thin (three)." Slower grew the steps; it did not seem as if he would be able to take the fourth; slowly the boy dragged his foot, and made the last step; as he set his foot down, the men cried, "duba" (four), and it was done. Then was sung the song of triumph, and thus ended the first medicine incantation I witnessed among the Omahas ... in about thirty days he was up again, shooting sticks, and ready to go and witness another pistol practice.[19]

BEYOND HOPE

The Omaha healing has other important aspects because it is one of many instances where, after the white doctors had given up hope, the Indian doctor easily cured the illness. I'm certain that there are stories equally as important where the white doctors were able to effect a cure when the medicine men could not heal. The combination of the two would be a powerfully effective health measure. Hultkranz cited an instance where the Indian medicine worked, reported by Dr. Garro at the medical department at Winnipeg, Canada.

HEALING WITCHCRAFT

An Ojibway man awoke one morning to find that he was lame in his legs and hands. He was transported to a hospital, but the doctors there were unable to explain his disability. They gave him a pair of crutches and some arthritic pills, and then they sent him away. He was home for a week, without experiencing any improvement. A medicine man was called in. He could state that the man's illness was due to witchcraft, brought about by a jealous individual. This individual had injected foreign substances into the patient's members and thus incapacitated him. The medicine man sucked these objects out through a tube that he put on the afflicted places. The man soon recovered and has since then not suffered from similar pains.[20]

In another case cited by Hultkranz, "There is a report of a woman who could not be cured by white doctors. A Native doctor then came to her assistance. He told her husband that her guardian spirit had left her and was now stuck in the mud of the river. The shaman's guardian spirit then listened for the song of the woman's guardian spirit. He caught it up and started to sing. Then the woman rose and sang it together with him. Her guardian spirit returned, and she was cured. Only a shaman is able to sing a foreign spirit's song."[21]

We learn a great deal in this story. It appears that the guardian spirits are responsible, at least in part, for the physical energy of the living person. It also seems that they can be detached from the physical body to such a degree as to cause disability in the person they are bound to protect. The medicine man seems able to tap into the conditions of the spiritual world and act with some degree of efficiency in resolving them so that they do not continue to hinder the individual. On the other hand, if we are as vulnerable to spiritual dislocation as the story implies, we live in a world much more hazardous than we presently believe.

SOUTHWESTERN HEALING PRACTICES

Charles Lummis summarized the standard practice in many tribes of the medicine man using a sucking device, such as a hollow bone, a feather, or a wand. Often, the medicine man himself would suck the bad spirits out of the patient's body. This practice was rather widespread among many tribes and exemplified the Indian belief that illnesses were caused by tiny entities invading the invalid's body. Hence, no one was surprised when it appeared that strange objects—shells, parts of plants, stones, and other objects—were produced by the medicine man to demonstrate that he had ejected the entity that had made the person ill. Most critics have vigorously rejected the notion that entirely foreign objects can be lodged in a person's body and cause illnesses.

Close observation of the medicine man raises some serious questions about what has really happened during the healing. For a medicine man to spit out all kinds of objects from his mouth would mean he had hidden them there prior to undertaking his work so that he could show them at the appropriate time. Since many medicine men wore only breechclouts when performing a healing, and the relatives would have been very close to the patient, it is dubious whether even a sleight-of-hand trick would be successful. There have been lots of instances where actual fraud was discovered, so the topic bears scrutiny. But the accusation that the medicine man invoked mass hypnosis cannot stand on the evidence that we have in these stories.

A shaman dances up to a sick person in the audience, puts the top of the feather against the patient, and with the quill in his mouth sucks diligently for a moment. The feather seems to swell to a great size, as though some large object were passing through it. Then it resumes its natural size, the shaman begins to cough and choke, and directly with his hand draws from his mouth a large rag, or a big stone, or a foot-long branch of the myriad-bristling buckhorn-cactus—while the patient feels vastly relieved at having such an unpleasant lodger removed from his cheek or neck or eye![22]

Pawnee Injury and Treatment Incidents

The Pawnees had a special time of the year, probably November, when the medicine men demonstrated their powers in what they called the Doctor's Lodge. Each medicine man would perform some exploit that was seemingly impossible. Some of the stories of performances related by George Bird Grinnell are so far from the norm of behavior that we can hardly not have questions whether or not their performances were mass hypnosis. But since the people they wounded were seen within a short time walking about the camp circle in a normal fashion, these stories seem to have an echo of truth, although they are, in our ordinary world, quite impossible. Again, it was the bear doctors who seemed to have the most powerful medicine.

A man representing a bear came into the ring and was pursued by a number of Indians, who shot arrows at him for some time, without appearing to injure him. At length, however, an arrow pierced him through the bowels, and the wound was plainly seen on each side. The man fell, and appeared to be dying. He was removed to the lodge, and in a short time was entirely recovered.[23]

And Grinnell quoted a similar feat observed by Major Frank North, who saw one of these bear performances in which the pretending bear, having attacked one of his pursuers, was slashed across the abdomen with a large knife, inflicting a cut from which the bowels hung down so they dragged on the ground. The bear was carried off and in a short time was healed and went about as usual.[24]

What do we make of these kinds of events? Surely, there is an argument that the performance was rehearsed and fixed before the bear medicine man began, since the purpose of these demonstrations was to display the relative powers of each man attending the sessions. If the medicine men were advertising their powers, they would cause injuries for the primary purpose of healing them in record time so that people would be both impressed and warned that extraordinary things were possible through the use of these medicine powers.

SUN'S ROAD'S DISCOVERY AND RECOVERY

Grinnell discussed an unusual case of self-diagnosis, and it demonstrated the belief that much illness is a result of spiritual conflict rather than germs and viruses. This incident occurred in 1890, when Sun's Road built himself a fine log cabin in a valley and then fell victim to sickness and bad fortune. Then he discovered an awful truth, but was able to overcome his difficulties. This is the story of …

> Sun's Road, who, about the year 1890, built a cabin on Muddy Creek, and soon after moving into it, became sick, and for a long time was in bad health. Nothing seemed to help him, though the tribal doctors and the agency physician did what they could. At length, however, he discovered the cause of his illness. In the hills on the north side of the Muddy, standing out a little from the higher bluffs, is a peculiar conical peak odd in shape and color, and on the south side of the stream is another odd-looking peak. Sun's Road's house was in the line between these two peaks, and thus was on the trail traveled by the spirits dwelling in them, when they went from one peak to the other to visit. Since the doors at the front and back of the house faced up and down the stream, it appeared evident that when the spirits passed to and fro they could not pass through the house, but were obliged to climb over it.

This obstruction in their trail annoyed them, and to punish Sun's Road for troubling them, they made him ill. When Sun's Road awoke to the situation, he at once moved his house out of the line between the hills, and also turned it half round so that if they wished, the spirits might pass through the house, instead of climbing over it, if it still stood in their way. He became better at once, and in a short time recovered his health. Sun's Road often expressed astonishment that he could have been so careless as to build his house in such a situation, and so to subject himself to danger.[25]

PLENTY CROWS'S, A FAMOUS MEDICINE MAN OF THE CHEYENNE, HEALING

According to John Stands in Timber, Plenty Crows had received bear medicine from a bear while on a long trip as part of a war party. His son, Fighting Bear, had a severe hemorrhage, and the white reservation doctor could do nothing to stop the bleeding. Plenty Crows had been off the reservation, but was found and hastily returned to doctor his son. As Stands in Timber told it:

> Another time I saw Indian doctoring was when his son Fighting Bear got a nosebleed and they could not do anything about it. The doctor said something was broken in his nose, and a bandage could not stop it. He nearly bled to death. At last they brought the old man. He was not on the reservation at the time, but they found him. I did not see it, but my uncle and others told me what happened. They told Fighting Bear his father was coming, and he said, "Good, now I may be saved." When the old man got there he sang a song, and then he stood on his knees in front of his son and started making bear noises. They could see his teeth grow and stick out like tusks on the side of his mouth. He shook his head like he was after something, and came to his soft nose and started blowing, and they heard little bears begin squealing and growling. And

they said, "Those bears will lick blood from his nose."

When he got through, his nose bleed did stop. I went over to see Fighting Bear, as he was my relative, and he was sitting up; he wanted to eat right away. He had eaten nothing before. And he got well and lived to an old age. I heard Plenty Crows doctored others the same way too, showing his teeth, and they could hear the little bears in his mouth or somewhere.[26]

THE HORSE DOCTOR

To conclude our examination of the healing powers of medicine men, we have a story recorded by Robert H. Lowie in his study of the Assiniboines that seems so unlikely as to be pure fiction, yet Lowie felt it was important enough to relate at length.

Once a shaman who had received supernatural revelations from a horse was treating a sick man. A lodge was erected, the entrance facing south. At some distance a lodge-pole having some flannel attached to it was planted in the ground. A horse, which had flannel tied around his neck and calico and feathers around his mane, was tied to the pole.

Paint was put on, beginning from his mane and passing down the entire back, and the top of his nose was reddened. Some singers entered the lodge and sang according to the shaman's directions. After several songs, the performer walked to the horse, untied him, and brought the rope to the lodge, the horse still remaining in the same position. The shaman unpinned the front of the lodge, so that the horse could enter. At the next intonation of the song, the horse walked into the lodge, and began smelling the sick man, who was not even able to turn from one side to the other. Whenever the horse drew a breath, smoke of various colors—blue, red, black— issued from his mouth. He placed his mouth over the sick man, and several round objects fell on the patient's breast. The shaman ordered the man to swallow them, which he did.

The horse walked out to the pole and stood facing the lodge-entrance. The patient suddenly felt like rising. First he sat up, then he rose unaided, stepped out of the lodge, walked around the camp, returned, and sat down. He said that he no longer felt weak, but was inclined to walk about. Previously he had not been able to eat, now he was hungry. The shaman said, "it is going to rain presently. When it rains, strip naked, go outside, and get washed by the rain. Before this, you must not touch your wife. If you disobey, you will only live a very short time; it will be like thrusting a knife into your throat." A cloud appeared, and grew in size.

The doctor and his singers left. The rain-drops began to fall. The convalescent's wife approached. Her husband bade her enter. She refused, saying, "No, you are not allowed to touch me until you are well." The man said he was quite well. Though the woman had not heard the doctor's directions, she knew it was not good for her husband to embrace her. However, he insisted until she reluctantly approached. Then he seized her. She bade him release her, again warning him, but nevertheless he embraced her. She went home. After a while, the shaman returned. As he entered, the horse began to neigh. The doctor said, "You have transgressed my orders, I shall not treat you any more." He turned the horse loose, and went away. The patient was taken sick again, with pains in every part of his body. He died the next noon.[27]

Trying to determine the sequence in which the healing power manifested itself is a major task. While the medicine man was able to diagnose the illness and seemed to be in control of the horse, it was the initiative of the horse to place its mouth next to the man's face and provide him with the objects to swallow. And the horse neighed as the shaman approached to give his patient further treatment. But how did the medicine man know that the horse could cure the man of his illness? All we can do is place the story in the category of unknown and unresolved.

LOCATING LOST OBJECTS

One of the primary powers given to medicine men is that of locating lost objects, be they animate (people, horses) or inanimate (rifles, utensils, religious power objects). These powers are usually found in the small sacred stones used by the Plains people and the power boards, or cedar shakes, used by the Indian nations of the Pacific Northwest. Sometimes, medicine men simply have an extended vision that enables them to see such a long distance that they locate the missing thing.

One characteristic of the sacred stones is that they remain within our chronological time while looking for lost objects. That is to say, they disappear and the people wait, sometimes for an hour or more, until the stones return. It must be a spectacular experience to suddenly discover that the stones, which are laid out on a soft buckskin or on top of the bag in which they are carried, suddenly disappear. You would find them gone, and the only indication that they have been there a slight popping, if they choose to go through the sides of the tipi instead of using the door. The power boards also take some time to find things. We will discuss stones later in a different context. Suffice it to say that they are amongst the most valuable religious objects that medicine men can have, since they perform menial tasks for them.

We will begin our investigation of the power of stones with two stories collected by Frances Densmore at Standing Rock. We must note that the stones, in addition to retrieving things, provide information on where the missing objects were found and what the circumstances were. Often, in early reservation days, there was theft of tools, weapons, and horses, so finding the object also meant warning the owner how it had become lost.

GOOSE FINDS A RIFLE

Goose found a rifle which had fallen into the water. This occurred near the present site of Pierre, S. Dak. Some horses were being taken across the river on a ferry and others were compelled to swim. In the confusion a white man dropped his rifle into the river. The man regretted his loss, but made no effort to recover the rifle. After the man had gone, Goose decided to try to find it by the aid of the sacred stones. Accordingly he took the stones with him, and rowed on the river until the stones told him to dive. Doing so, he found the rifle on the bed of the river, a strange circumstance being that when he was in the water it appeared clear instead of cloudy as usual. Goose afterwards had an opportunity to restore the rifle to its owner, who rewarded him liberally.[28]

WHITE SHIELD'S TASKS

A remarkable demonstration of the sacred stones by White Shield was related by Siya'ka. Siya'ka said that on one occasion he had lost two horses and asked White Shield to locate them. Before being bound with sinews, White Shield asked, "What sign shall the stone bring to show whether your horses are by a creek or on the prairie?" Siya'ka replied: "If they are by a creek, let the stone bring a little turtle and a piece of clamshell, and if they are on the prairie let the stone bring a meadow lark."

White Shield then sent the stone on its quest. While the stone was absent the people prepared a square of finely pulverized earth as already described. It was evening when the stone returned. The tepee was dark, as the fire had been smothered, but there was dry grass ready to put on it when White Shield ordered light. At last the stone appeared on the place prepared for it, and beside it was a little turtle with a small piece of clamshell in one of its claws.[29]

Such events were not unusual in the old days.

Does this feat tell us anything about turtles, other than that they were summoned by the stone and made their appearance accordingly? Standing Bear remembered a strange characteristic of turtles when he was recounting the Sioux knowledge of the natural world. He remarked that the people never saw turtles moving from one watering place to another. They just suddenly appeared in different places and seemed to have abandoned other locations. Surely, there must have been at least once when someone saw turtles migrating from one pond or creek to another. On the other hand, the Plains Indians were constantly observing the behavior of birds and animals and keeping a sharp eye on the weather, so very little ever escaped their attention.

> After the appearance of the stone and verification of its pow-ers, White Shield, without any apparent oral communication with the stone, told Siyaka: "Your horses are 15 miles west of the Porcupine Hills at a fork of the Porcupine Creek. If you do not want to go for them there is a traveler coming that way who will get them and bring them in for you." This proved true. A neighbor of Siyaka's had been out looking for wild fruit and on his way home he saw the horses at the fork of the Porcupine Creek; recognizing them as Siyaka's, he brought them back.[30]

White Shield was very talented in locating lost objects, and from all indications, he had such power that he need only fix his attention on a task and he was guaranteed success. Densmore cited another of his exploits with his stone. The following account of a performance by White Shield differs from preceding narratives in that it took place in a house, and the stone was held in White Shield's hand instead of being laid on the ground. The narrative was given by Bull Head, who witnessed the performance. He said it occurred when the govern-ment first issued

> harness and wagons to the Indians. At that time the old peo-ple 'kept close track' of everything which was issued to them by the government and prized it very highly. One old man lost part of a harness. Knowing that White Shield often recovered

lost articles by the aid of the sacred stones, he appealed to him, asking him to find the missing part of his harness and also a handsome tobacco bag and pipe.

White Shield came, and in giving the performance held the stone in the palm of his hand, saying, "This will disappear." Bull Head said that though he watched it very closely, it suddenly vanished from before his eyes. The length of time that a stone is absent depends on the distance it must travel in finding the lost object. In this instance the stone was gone a long time. At last a rattle was heard at the door. White Shield stopped the singing, and said, "The stone has returned; be ready to receive it." He then opened the door, and the stone was found on the doorstep.

White Shield brought it in and heard the message. The stone said that the missing articles had been taken by a certain man who, for fear of detection, had thrown them into the river. The stone said further that the articles would be brought back that night and left where they had been last seen. The next morning all the missing articles were found in the place where they had been last seen. Their appearance indicated that they had been under the water for several days.[31]

BEAR NECKLACE'S STONES

Sometimes, the stones participated in other ceremonies. In the following story, we see phenomena that belong to both the spirit lodge and the yuwipi, or binding, ceremony, testifying that the spiritual world is a seamless unity. Presumably, the five stones that appear to give assistance all belong to Bear Necklace. He could have sent the stones on their errand without the other phenomena; however, it was the custom of medicine men to demonstrate the scope of their powers to impress their audiences. On the other hand, the information required at that sitting might have required a demonstration of faith by the medicine man, and therefore, he had to perform these preliminary feats before the stones would work for him.

Charging Thunder said that his father [Bear Necklace], while on a buffalo hunt, was thrown from his horse, falling on a pile of stones and injuring his head. He lay unconscious almost all day and was found in the evening. His wound was dressed, and when he regained consciousness he said that all the rocks and stones "were people turned to stone."

After this he found some stones. He could talk to them and depended on them for help. Once a war party had been gone two months; no news of them had been received, and it was feared that all were killed. In their anxiety the people appealed to Bear Necklace, asking him to ascertain by means of the sacred stones, what had become of the war party.

Bear Necklace requested them to tie his arms behind him, then to tie his fingers and toes, interlacing them with twisted sinew. He was then wrapped in a buffalo robe and tied with ropes. His medicine drum, medicine bag, and a bell were hung high on the tent poles, and he was laid on the ground beneath them. The tent was darkened, he sang the following song and told his dreams. Then the tent began to tremble, the articles hanging from the pole dropped to the ground, his cords loosened, and he stood entirely free. As soon as the medicine articles fell to the ground there appeared a row of four or five small round stones ready to tell him what he wanted to know.

Sitting Bull was present and made an offering of a buffalo robe to the sacred stones and asked that he might become famous. Bear Necklace wrapped one of the stones in buckskin and gave it to him. Sitting Bull wore it in a bag around his neck to the time of his death, and it was buried with him. Bear Necklace then gave correct information concerning the absent war party. At that time he proved his power to give information by the help of the sacred stones, and afterwards the stones always told him the names of those who were killed in war, the names of the survivors, and the day on which they would return. This information was always correct.[32]

Young Bird's Psychic Powers

He told us to come to his camp in the early morning and wait for him and when he came out of his tepee and walked away from it to follow him and he would tell us where the horse was. So he went and I noticed he pointed down the river to Ashland and up the other way before he spoke. Then he said: "That horse was stolen from the time it disappeared. A man rode it between Ashland and Burney and then turned it across the river and it drifted back up the other side and is now at the head of Deer Creek across from the dam." And sure enough, a white man named Shortly Caddell found the horse right there a few days later. He said he had seen the notice we had posted at the OW ranch near there, so he went back to where he remembered seeing the horse and got him, and we gave him the twenty-five dollars reward.[33]

John Fornsby's Guardian Power Boards

In the Pacific Northwest, the Indians use what are called power boards. These helpers are cedar boards about fifteen inches by a foot—recognizably rectangular—that have the same function as the sacred stones on the Western prairies. Two men hold the boards while their owner sings power songs. As the songs proceed, the boards begin to move in the hands of the two assistants and act out in some hardly discernible pantomime the answers to questions asked by their owner. The motion seems to be easily interpreted by the singer. At first, they exhibit a rotary motion about chest high on the holders. They move in the direction where a missing person or thing is. If the missing person is alive, they rise straight up. If he or she is dead, the boards go down and make a motion outlining a grave and covering it with soil. In this lengthy account, we can see how the boards behaved in solving a problem of some missing money.

A widow asked Fornsby to locate a can that held $1,000 in gold coins hidden by her late husband.

Fornsby volunteered to find it. I said, "If somebody will help me, I will try and find it." I got four men and made a guardian power board. Those men from the Nooksack tribe didn't know how, but I had two Skagit with me. I made two guardian power boards, just tied with a rag. I had the first one and the four of us caught hold. We went out. The rest just followed us.

There was a little log right at the end of the garden. I asked, "What were you folks doing here?" when the power boards touched the log. Those guarding powers knew. They took me right into that bush. I asked that lady. "We buried this money right here in that bush. He buried it right in that place." They dug about three feet deep, about the length of my cane. They dug deep. Guarding powers searched around there. The old man had kept moving the money. He dug a big hole to keep potatoes in near the house. He kept the money there.

The lady talked to me, "You had better go to that dead man who owned the money." We went to the little dead man in the house. My guarding powers searched the man, searched his hands and head. Guarding powers searched the man. He used to keep the money at the head of his bed. He kept that money three or four days in that place. The house was like a barn, with no floor. We made a fire in the middle and warmed up the guarding powers. We had a hot fire to warm them up. Guarding powers looked all around, looked in the corners, looked all around. They took us into a hole. They took a board and threw it away. I asked the woman what was in the hole. "Your man had money there?" She said, "Yes, he had money there long ago." The man kept money in the hole two or three days so no one could get it.

Then the guarding powers went out in the garden. They went straight into the hole where the fellows had been digging in the morning. It was three or four feet deep, three feet wide. The power stopped right in the middle where they had been digging. The guarding power knew the money was buried there. They stopped quick. I told the people that I wouldn't give up. I looked. The Nooksack didn't tell me how much money it was. "Give me something to dig with. You have some kind of shovel?" I wouldn't give up. I gave my guarding power board to my partner. I dug with my hands. The ground was soft. I found out that the ground was soft. I dug around, dug as far down as I could. I felt something down there. It was two feet below where the people were digging. I asked that lady what the money was in. She said, "can." I felt around, it was kind of loose. I got it loose and pulled it up. "Here are you."

My aunt said, "Now you save me. I was going to hang myself, I had nothing to wrap my man in. I was going to die with my husband." I took that can, sat down, and opened the can. There were twenty dollar gold pieces in the can, a thousand dollars. I covered it up. The old lady wrapped the can and took it away.

That guarding power is a powerful thing. He knew where the old man was working, digging two or three places. He hid the money outside. Guarding power knew that the old lady was standing up, watching for people when the old man buried that money. "You were sitting down on the log," I said to her.[34]

While the power seems to reside in the boards, Fornsby made the boards for this occasion, indicating that his power actually came from the songs and the relationship with cedar. The boards appear to have followed some kind of psychic vibration left by the deceased husband, since they followed his trail in deciding where to hide the money. Generally, the boards can also work healings and make predictions and were used by a wide variety of people not necessarily otherwise regarded as medicine men in the traditional meaning of the term.

Densmore reported on another medicine man, Dr. Jim in British Columbia, who was able to locate missing objects through the technique known as trembling—extending one's arms, singing, and allowing the vibration of the lost person or object to attract the medicine man's attention. We have already encountered trembling when we discussed the Navajo diagnosticians. Since this power is widespread through many tribes and is not regarded as unusual, not very many instances of the practices are available for examination. Densmore regarded the ritual as primarily one of singing rather than trembling.

Dr. Jim's Song

A certain medicine man living at Carmanah is able to locate lost persons and articles. It is his custom to dance with his arms held out and shaking, his fingers extended and trembling, this manner probably being in accordance with his dream. It was said that a man once went out hunting and became lost. This doctor danced for about 3 hours before he was able to locate the man, then he told the people where they would find the hunter. The people went to the place indicated by the doctor and there they found the man.[35]

Unusual Predictions

One of the major motivations of people in every society in seeking the advice of the spirits is the desire to know the future. Knowing something about the person seeking advice often gives the psychic an advantage in predicting the immediate future for the client. Since it is possible for a skillful individual to guess or hypothesize with some degree of accuracy, and since phrasing a response in general terms usually supports the idea that the psychic is correct, only those stories that provide predictions that could not possibly be the result of guesswork should be cited in any discussion of predictions. These stories that follow I feel would qualify themselves as real exercises of special powers. The first story concerns the experience of the French soldiers during a war with the Spanish for control of the Louisiana region.

PREDICTING FOR THE FRENCH SOLDIERS

When we [the French soldiers] were surrounded by the Spaniards in Dauphin Island, and were expecting help from France from day to day, we wished to know whether it was on the point of arriving, which could only be known by means of the savages whom we had with us. They were then made to conjure, and having done this they reported that five vessels would come the next day, three of which were large and two smaller, that they were loaded with soldiers, that one of the little ones would not arrive as soon as the others, because it was separated and was still a long way off, but that all would have arrived the day after that toward evening. This actually took place, for the next day at eight in the morning the first vessel was discovered, and about three or four in the after-noon, four were anchored at Dauphin Island, but the fifth did not come in until the day following.[36]

The next story is rather long, but its richness of detail makes it believable. A person would have to have almost photographic long-distance vision to make the predictions found in this account. Witnesses of this incident were frontiersmen accustomed to the medicine men's powers and hence could not be easily fooled. So many witnesses were available to support the veracity of this story that it became one of the favorite stories of early Minnesota.

THE TOBACCO PREDICTION

About twenty years ago, a large party of Indians, collected near Lake Traverse, were quite destitute of tobacco; not know-ing how to procure any, they applied to Tatankanaje (Standing Buffalo), a prophet of some distinction, and the uncle of the present chief of the Kahras. This man usually carried about him a little stone idol, carved into a human shape; this he called his little man, and to it he always applied when consulted in the way of his profession.

Tatankanaje being requested to advise the best means of obtaining tobacco, made answer to them, that if they would go to a certain place, which he pointed out to them, they would find his idol, and, by examining it, they would observe in its hand a piece of tobacco. They did as he bade them, and found in the little fellow's hand a piece about four inches long; and this was brought to the camp, and was thought to redound much to the credit of both the prophet and the idol; but Tatankanaje then observed, that he would consult the little man, and ascertain where he had found the tobacco, and how he came by it. This he did by putting interrogatories to him, to which he pretended that audible answers were returned, though of the many present not one heard them beside himself.

The purport of these answers, however, as he subsequently informed them, was, that at a spot on the St. Peter, near to redwood river, there was a boat, loaded with goods; that the commander, a French trader, having been murdered by the Sioux, the crew had been alarmed, and had run away, leaving the boat unguarded, together with her cargo, consisting principally of tobacco; that the little man had seen her and finding a piece of tobacco on a keg, had brought it up. The prophet having invited them to seek for it, they repaired to the spot, found the boat, and took the tobacco, and returned the rest of the goods to the first French traders that passed up the river.

This event happened, as we were informed, in the presence of Renville and Freiners, two French traders of reputation, both considered as intelligent and enlightened men; they were the fathers of the two half-breed traders with whom we were acquainted. The story is given with all the particulars that might be wished for: the name of the owner of the boat was Benjamin la Goterie, a name well known in that country. The story has been current ever since. The traders, who appear to credit it, state that it was impossible for the prophet to have visited the spot and returned without his absence being known; from whom he received his intelligence they never knew.[37]

Predicting the Traders' Arrival

Jonathon Carver, a late-eighteenth-century traveler in the Great Lakes area, reported a ceremony undertaken to ascertain when an expected boat of fur traders would arrive at an Indian village. The Indians seemed eager to impress Carver with their special powers, and his report sounds credible, although most of the things he claimed to have experienced in his book have come under severe criticism from scholars for a long time. His account rings true, however, and since it has similarities with the predictions about the French soldiers, belongs here with the other stories.

> When everything had been properly prepared, the king came to me and led me to a capacious tent, the covering of which was drawn up, so as to render what was transacting within visible to those who stood without. We found the tent surrounded by a great number of the Indians, but we readily gained admission, and seated ourselves on skins laid on the ground for that purpose.
>
> In the center I observed that there was a place of an oblong shape, which was composed of stakes stuck in the ground, with intervals between, so as to form a kind of chest or coffin, large enough to contain the body of a man. These were of a middle size, and placed at such a distance from each other, that whatever lay within them was readily to be discerned. The tent was perfectly illuminated by a great number of torches made of splinters cut from the pine or birch tree, which the Indians held in their hands.
>
> In a few minutes the priest entered; when an amazing large elk's skin being spread on the ground, just at my feet, he laid himself down upon it, after having stripped himself of every garment except that which he wore close about his

middle. Being now prostrate on his back, he first laid hold of one side of the skin, and folded it over him, and then the other; leaving only his head uncovered. This was no sooner done, than two of the young men who stood by took about forty yards of strong cord, made also of an elk's hide, and rolled it tight round his body, so that he was completely swathed within the skin. Being thus bound up like an Egyptian Mummy, one took him by the heels, and the other by the head, and lifted him over the pales into the inclosure, I could also now discern him as plain as I had hitherto done, and I took care not to turn my eyes a moment from the object before me, that I might the more readily detect the artifice; for such I doubted not but it would turn out to be.

The priest had not lain in this situation more than a few seconds, when he began to mutter. This he continued to do for some time, and then by degrees grew louder and louder, till at length he spoke articulately; however what he uttered was in such a mixed jargon of the Chipeway, Ottwaw, and Killisinoe languages, that I could understand but very little of it. Having continued in this tone for a considerable while, he at last exerted his voice to its utmost pitch, sometimes raving and sometimes praying, till he had worked himself into such an agitation, that he foamed at his mouth.

After having remained near three quarters of an hour in the place, and continued his vociferation with unabated vigor, he seemed to be quite exhausted, and remained speechless. But in an instant he sprung upon his feet, not withstanding at the time he was put in, it appeared impossible for him to move either his legs or arms, and shaking off his coverage, as quick as if the bands were burned asunder, he began to address those who stood around in a firm and audible voice. "My Brothers," said he, "the Great Spirit has deigned to hold a Talk with his servant at my earnest request. He has not, indeed, told me when the persons we expect will be here, but to-morrow, soon after the sun has reached his highest point in the heavens, a canoe will arrive, and the people in that will inform us when the traders will come." Having said this, he stepped out of the inclosure, and after he had put on his robes, dismissed the assembly.

The next day the sun shone bright, and before noon all the Indians were gathered together on the eminence that overlooked the lake. The old king came to me and asked me whether I had so much confidence in what the priest had foretold, as to join his people off the hill, and wait for the completion of it? I told him I was at a loss what opinion to form of the prediction but that I would readily attend him. On this we walked together to the place where the others were assembled. Every eye was again fixed by turns on me and on the lake; when just as, the sun had reached his zenith, agreeable to what the priest had foretold, a canoe, came round a point of land about a league distant. The Indians no sooner beheld it than they sent up a universal shout, and by their looks seemed to triumph in the interest their priest thus evidently had with the Great Spirit.

In less than an hour the canoe reached the shore, when I attended the king and chiefs to receive those who were on board. As soon as the men were landed, we walked all together to the king's tent, when according to their invariable custom we began to smoke; and this we did, notwithstanding our impatience to know the tidings they brought, without asking any questions; for the Indians are the most deliberate people in the world. However, after some trivial conversation, the king inquired of them whether they had seen anything of the traders? The men replied, that they had parted from them a few days before, and they proposed bring here the second day from the present. They accordingly arrived at that time greatly to our satisfaction, but more particularly so to that of the Indians, who found by this event the importance both of their priest and of their nation, greatly augmented in the sight of a stranger.[38]

THE BLACKFEET PROPHET

John Mason Brown wrote an article on Indian medicine men in which he began with a devastating critique, accusing them of atrocities instead of healings. After thoroughly chastising them, he relented a bit and cited some things they had done that defied rational explanation. And, he recounted a marvelous feat of prediction for which he had no explanation. Note that the details contained in his prophecy were made before there was any hint that the party that he described was lost.

> The medicine-man whom I knew best was Ma-que-a-pos (the Wolf's Word), an ignorant and unintellectual person. I knew him perfectly well. His nature was simple, innocent, and harmless, devoid of cunning, and wanting in those fierce traits that make up the Indian character. His predictions were sometimes absolutely astounding. He has, beyond question, accurately described the persons, horses, arms, and destination of a party three hundred miles distant, not one of whom he, not any one in his camp, was before apprised.
>
> The Wolf's Word knew this party was lost and had sent four young men to find them and said they would look for four days and finally locate the missing party. On the afternoon of the last day, four young Indians were seen, [by the lost party] who, after a cautious approach, made the sign of peace, laid down their arms, and came forward, announcing themselves to be Blackfeet of the Blood Band. They were sent out, they said, by Ma-que-a-pos, to find three whites mounted on horses of a peculiar color, dressed in garments accurately described to them, and armed with weapons which they, without seeing them, minutely described. The whole history of the expedition had been detailed to them by Ma-que-a-pos. The purpose of the journey, the personnel of the party, the exact locality at which to find the three who persevered, had been detailed by him with as much fidelity as could have been done by one of the whites themselves.[39]

CHAPTER THREE

CONTINUING COMMUNICATIONS

★ ★ ★ ★ ★ ★ ★ ★ ★ ★ ★ ★ ★

The medicine vision or dream is permanently imprinted in the minds of medicine men and forms the context within which they live their lives. It is always a frame of reference within which they exercise their powers with the assistance of the spirits. There are ceremonies that become important in the continuing communications between these people and the spirits. Two ceremonies in particular stand out, if only because they are found in such widespread places. In the Plains, there is the yuwipi, or the binding with ropes, in which a medicine man is tied up firmly with strong ropes with thongs around each finger and toe so that he is almost completely immobile. The Algonquin peoples have the spirit lodge, in which a temporary shelter is made from poles and skins and the spirits come and converse with him.

In nontribal religions, we have the concept of revelation, in which a sacred message is given that is supposed to cover all future contingencies, and those traditions then develop an interpretive literature to explain the basic revelation over the succeeding centuries in terms of the events of their generation. Indians did not regard the vision as having less applicability to the external world, but more to their own psychological makeup and sense of vocation. Thus, these two ceremonies, among others, serve to provide them with a continuing source of information that is relevant to the immediate situation

in which they find themselves. They are also able to continue healing powers of great potency, as we have seen above.

In order to understand the efficiency of this kind of relationship,
we will examine the practices of these two major ceremonies. In
each ceremony, there seems to be the opportunity to receive messages from the spirits on current problems, to receive predictions about
the future, and to heal illnesses. The information given is precise and
does not have the mystical and garbled symbolism of predictions in
the nontribal religions. That is to say, there are no mystical riddles for
the medicine practitioner to solve. Note how specific these spirit
messages are.

THE YUWIPI CEREMONY

In the yuwipi, the practitioner is firmly bound up with ropes: each
finger is tied with knots, the hands are firmly tied, and often the feet
are tied in a similar manner. Then blankets—or in the old days, buffalo robes—are wrapped around him very tightly and bound with
ropes. The man is placed on the floor, or, preferably, the ground, and
the tipi or lodge is sealed so that total darkness prevails. Around the
room are distributed a large number (usually 405) of very small
pouches of tobacco wrapped in red cloth—gifts to the spirits who will
come and participate in the ritual, healing and answering questions.
The practitioner begins to sing his yuwipi power songs, and soon the
blue sparks of the spirits are seen coming into the room or tent.
Often, they come into the place at the highest corners. People attending the ceremony feel the brush of bird wings; sometimes, they hear
the patter of animal feet; sometimes, they feel a great wind that strangely
does not disturb anything; and, frequently, they hear animal noises or
strange languages used by the spirits attending the practitioner.

In this state, the practitioner can heal people, find lost objects,
and predict the future. The minds of everyone attending are clearly
read by the practitioner, and messages are passed back and forth
between himself and the spirits. Sometimes, there is a long silence as the
practitioner goes to other times and places and gathers information
needed by someone in the group. During this time, it is necessary for

the people to pray for the return of the medicine man, since his soul has left his body and has gone to search for answers.

Finally, the medicine man brings the ritual to an end, either when all the answers have been given or when the spirits inform him they are departing. Lights are lit and there is the practitioner, often with only a breechclout, wholly free of the robes, which are now neatly folded and piled in a stack, and the ropes that had bound him are now perfectly coiled and stacked. People remember that there was no noise of what should have been an intense struggle of the practitioner to free himself of the wrappings and ties. Sometimes, the spirits dance in a circle and give off enough light so that the wrapped body of the medicine man is barely visible to those individuals close to where he lies. People then realize that there was not sufficient time to free him from his bondage and neatly arrange the pile of blankets or ropes. Even if a helper were to unwrap the confined medicine man, there is never any evidence that he has done so, since there is no indication that the helper has done anything except sit and sing the songs he has been taught to sing during the ceremony. The tobacco pouches are missing or empty, and since there are 405 little pouches of tobacco, it would have taken the entire duration of the ritual for them to have been collected. No rational explanation can be given for what people have experienced.

THE YUWIPI SPIRITS

William K. Powers, in his book *Sacred Language*, identified the spirits that participate in the yuwipi ceremony. "Not only are all aspects of the Lakota universe represented in the meeting in terms of ritual paraphernalia and altar decorations, but also all generations are represented. The generational aspects of yuwipi are made more consistent by the fact that all yuwipi spirits, human and animal, are actually spirits of those who once lived on the earth, hence the Oglala feel the sense of continuity between the living and nonliving, and their belief that the spirit world is simply an extension of the earthly world is reinforced."[1]

We should, perhaps, amend that explanation in that there is

always a continuity of spirit in the world. The real division occurs when we make distinctions based on whether the spirit is incarnate or not and assume a break in continuity. The apprehension of Wakan tanka, as the spiritual energy creating and supporting the world, means there could be no discontinuity except in the manner in which we experience life. Here the presence of spirits and their participation in the ritual negates any division that the passage of time might have created in our minds.

Powers goes on to explain the songs used in the ritual and their essential role in helping to maintain the feeling of continuity. "It is as if some of these songs, although learned through the personal experience of the vision quest, continue to be taught to fledgling medicine men by the same spirits. It is believed that they reoccur because they are taught to initiates by medicine men who are now living somewhere between earth and the clouds in the West, and who join in those very meetings that they once conducted. Once they cured their patients through the mediation of the spirit helpers. Now they appear to those seeking visions as one of the spirit helpers themselves."[2]

There are many books and articles describing the sequence of experiences in a yuwipi. Lame Deer has much valuable information on this ritual. Powers has devoted a book to the yuwipi, and Thomas Lewis described the ceremony in his book *The Medicine Men*. In a collection stressing short pieces, it is impossible to reproduce the entire ritual. G. H. Pond, a missionary to the Sioux and Chippewa in Minnesota, described the ceremony while expressing his doubts and theological misgivings. Since it is such an early rendering of the ritual and fits nicely into this collection, I have reproduced it here.

RED BIRD'S YUWIPI

A man had been sick a considerable time, and many of the wakan-men had attempted, to the extent of their ability, to exorcise him, without any favorable results. Red-Bird had in his service many of the gods called Taku-skan-skan. It was decided in council that the case should be referred to them.

Accordingly, in the evening, a feast was prepared for the gods to which they were called by chants, on the part of the medicine-men. A tent of parchment was prepared for them. The doctor was bound, carefully weaving strings and tying them firmly in all his fingers and toes. Then his arms were bound behind his back and he rolled up in a buffalo robe, and carefully bound it by cords around it outside. He had a little boulder in his bosom, a symbol of the gods. He charged those who bound him to do it thoroughly, assuring them that the boys—his gods—would come and release him. He was so bound that he could not stir and then was rolled into the tent, and the sick man was placed by his side. Over him was hung a drum and a deer hoof rattle; a large number of spectators were in atten-dances—men, women, and children.

Red Bird ordered that certain men present should chant to the gods, which they did. The doctor, in the mean time, was very demonstrative with his wakan jargon. A young man, who had been appointed for that purpose, then gave a wild yell, and all lights were suddenly extinguished. At the instant, a strong wind struck the tent, and the doctor cried out, as if he were in great fear, "Boys come carefully, your father is very weak, be careful!" But the gods did not seem to regard the admonition and beat the drum, shook the rattle and heaved the tent furiously. The tent seemed to be full of them and they were very talkative and rude, but their voices were so fine, so soft, that we could not comprehend their meaning. They per-formed the ceremony of exorcising the sick man. The sounds they made were so different from what we had been accus-tomed to hear and so ludicrous that we could scarcely refrain from laughter, though we had been forewarned that if any one should laugh he should be knocked down.

The gods called for a pipe, and smoked many pipes-full, indicating a large number of them, but it was dark and they could not be seen. Suddenly the gods were all gone, and the doctor ordered the torches to be lighted. All expected to see him still bound, as he was thrust into the tent; but, to their surprise, he was out of the robe, and all of his fingers and toes slipped out of their fastenings, though not a single knot had been untied. The sick man began from that time to recover, though all sick persons who are treated in this manner do not recover.[3]

How powerful is this ceremony? Stephen Feraca records an event that boggles the mind and demonstrates immense spiritual powers. "Some years ago, by order of the agency superintendent, who was in charge of the Pine Ridge Reservation, Horn Chips's meeting was held in a lighted room. Indian police were present, and the police chief himself carefully tied and wrapped the yuwipi man. Lights flashed on the ceiling. Horn Chips was untied when the flashing ceased."[4] Horn Chips is regarded as the most powerful medicine man in the tribe's memory, and this demonstration is nothing short of spectacular because it was performed in daylight, when there could not be the slightest hint of trickery.

THE SPIRIT LODGE RITUAL

One of the most profound ceremonies among the Algonquin peoples is that of the spirit lodge, often called the "shaking tent" by anthropologists. In this ritual, a medicine man and his helpers build the framework for an extensive skin lodge. The lodge is sometimes as high as ten feet and composed of heavy timber poles, so that it usually takes several men to construct and put in place. Once the framework of poles is complete, the helpers then cover it tightly with animal skins, leaving a little entrance at the bottom of the structure. The medicine man goes inside, and after blessing the enterprise by smoking a pipe, he begins singing sacred songs, summoning the spirits to the ceremony. Sometimes, people are allowed into the tent; most of the time, it is the medicine man alone who enters.

After a while, sometimes as long as half an hour, the edifice begins to shake, primarily at the top of the lodge, increasing in violence until the spirit enters it. Then strange voices are heard, usually easily distinguishable from the voice and language of the medicine man. The timbers used for the framework start to bend and vibrate back and forth, showing an amazing flexibility that did not exist when the poles were firmly planted in the ground. On occasion, the tent rocks back and forth so violently that it appears it will tip over on its side. Then the spirit begins to communicate through the medicine man, using a language only he knows, but loud enough so that people outside can hear clearly.

People attending a sweat lodge often remark that they can hear the spirits coming to the ceremony as they hit and penetrate the skin or blanket covering. The spirit lodge seems to surpass the sweat lodge in intensity, and the noises often reach a crescendo and sometimes appear to be several different voices. At this point in the ritual, the medicine man asks the questions that people have posed and receives answers from the spirits. The answers are often complex and involve knowledge of the immediate social and physical environment that could not otherwise be obtained. After all the questions have been answered, the tent becomes stable again, and the medicine man emerges, totally exhausted. Some tribes tie the medicine man's fingers and toes together with leather strings or wrap him first in robes, as is done in the yuwipi ceremony. Other tribes have the medicine man enter completely naked and carrying a pipe.

This ceremony appears to be found almost exclusively among the Algonquin peoples, and they are scattered over an extensive area, from the Blackfeet in Montana to the tribes in Quebec and northern Canada. There are variations among the tribal practices, but, on the whole, the examples reproduced here are representative. Many non-Indians have observed this ritual over several centuries, beginning with Samuel Champaign and continuing until the present day, where it is still being performed in Canada. On the whole, non-Indian observers have reported the ceremony accurately but have rejected what they experienced as some kind of trickery.

No one can offer any good explanation of how this ritual functions. Most often, the excuse is given that the medicine man himself shakes the tent. However, on occasion, the tent shakes for several hours, certainly sufficiently long enough to sap the strength of anyone trying to move the structure in the powerful way that the shaking occurs. Critics also fail to reflect on the fact that stout poles and timbers, immovable otherwise, demonstrate great flexibility during the ceremony and are stiff and inflexible before and after the ceremony takes place.

Critics also claim that the medicine man engages in double-talk to make it appear that he is conversing with different spirits. Yet people have to admit that the voices are different and that they engage in conversation with some voices appearing to be speaking from the top of the tent, while others are definitely heard at ground level. No one seems to give a definitive and sensible explanation of the phenomenon. The best answer, of course, is that people witness a demonstration of the power of the spirits attending the ceremony.

The first selection illustrating this ceremony comes from *The Jesuit Relations*, and the Jesuit observer is not inclined to credit the medicine man with the positive spiritual powers he displays. The quick answer for the Jesuit, of course, was that the ceremony was the work of the devil and his demons. However, considering all the physical phenomena that take place during the ritual and the accuracy of the information obtained from the spirits, this practice certainly stands on its own feet and remains incapable of explanation by Western logical standards. Since the ceremony is designed to assist people in illness, in finding lost objects, and in finding game—all efforts to assist people—I am puzzled that the ritual would be seen as the devil's work.

THE JESUIT REPORT

> Towards nightfall, when I was resting, some young men erected a tent in the middle of our cabin. They planted six poles deep in the ground in the form of a circle. To the top of these poles they fastened a large ring which encircled them. This done, they enclosed the edifice with blankets, leaving the top of the tent open. It was all a tall man could do to reach to the top of this round tower, capable of holding five or six men standing upright.

The tent completed, all fires in the cabin were put out in order that the flames should not frighten away the khichi-gouai (spirits). A young juggler crawled in under the blanket covering and closing the opening behind him, for there must be no means of entrance or exit save the opening at the top. He began to moan plaintively and the tent began to quiver, at first gently but with growing vehemence until I feared he would break everything to pieces. He commenced to whistle in a hollow tone, and as if it came from afar, then to talk as if in a bottle; to cry like the owls of these countries, then to howl and sing constantly varying the tones. I was astonished at a man having so much strength; for after he had once begun to shake it, he did not stop until the consultation was over, which lasted about three hours.[5]

It hardly seems likely that one man could conceivably perform this feat over the period of one hour when it took several men a considerable time to create the lodge. Jesuit descriptions of Indian ceremonies are usually accurate, but characterized by tortured efforts to explain away the phenomena they had just experienced.

ANDREW J. BLACKBIRD'S ACCOUNT

Andrew J. Blackbird, a Chippewa historian, undertook to write what he knew of his people's history, culture, and beliefs in the 1880s—one of the first Indians to recognize that the more information whites had, the better were the chances of creating an understanding between the races. His description of the spirit lodge ceremony is objective in that he sought only to discuss the general procedures of the ceremony and did not seek to encourage belief in the reader. The information we get from his narrative holds for the majority of practitioners.

The forms of these lodges was like a tower in circular form built with long poles set deep in the ground ten or twelve feet high, then covered tight all around with canvas of skins of animals, except the top is left open. Now the magician or performer comes with the little flat magician's rattle like a tamboone. They always build a fire close to the lodge so that the attendants and spectators could light their pipes, as they generally smoke much during the performance. The magician sits by the fire also, and begins to talk to the people, telling them that he could call up various spirits, even the spirit of those who are yet living in the world, and that they should hear them and ask any questions they wish. After which he begins to sing a peculiar song which scarcely anyone could understand.

Then he either goes into the lodge by crawling under or sits outside with the rest of the audience, and simply throws something of his wear in the lodge—his blanket or his robe or coat. And immediately the lodge begins to tremble, appearing to be full of wind. Then voices of various kinds are heard from top to bottom, some speaking in unknown tongues, and when the spectators ask any questions they would receive replies sometimes with unknown tongues, but among the spirits there is always a special interpreter to make known what other spirits say.[6]

HENRY R. SCHOOLCRAFT'S REPORT

Henry R. Schoolcraft gave a negative summary of the spirit lodge, and, from the description, it seems likely that he was repeating what he had been told, since there is no mention of the tent shaking violently or the change of voice reported by other knowledgeable people. Nevertheless, his account is worth considering because it provided some additional understanding, as, for example, the fact that the poles composing the framework of the tent must be of different kinds of wood—a very difficult task if the medicine man is to do this ceremony with any degree of frequency or at some location chosen by the people who want to have the ritual performed.

To prepare the operator in these mysteries for answering questions, a lodge is erected by driving stout poles, or saplings, in a circle, and swathing them round tightly from the ground to the top with skins, drawling the poles closer at each turn or wind, so that the structure represents a rather acute pyramid. The number of poles is prescribed by the jossakeed [medicine man], and the kind of wood. There are, sometimes, perhaps generally, ten poles, each of a different kind of wood. When this structure has been finished, the operator crawls in, by forcing his way under the skin at the ground, taking with him his drum, and scarcely anything beside. He begins his supplications by kneeling and bending his body very low, so as almost to touch the ground. When his incantations and songs have been continued the requisite time, and he professes to have called around him the spirits, or gods, upon whom he relies, and he announces his readiness to the assembled multitude without, to give responses.[7]

Paul Kane's Experience

Paul Kane was an artist who took two extended tours of the West, including a return trip through Canada, in 1848, to paint Indians and landscapes. He was particularly interested in the customs and costumes of the people and produced more than thirty paintings. This experience occurred on the return trip of his second journey, and his account has an added dimension in that he was not supposed to attend the session, and when he crept to the edge of the circle of Indians to listen to the proceedings, the ceremony stopped and he was exposed.

> In the evening our Indians constructed a jonglerie, or medicine lodge, the main object of which was to procure a fair wind for next day. For this purpose they first drive ten or twelve poles, nine or ten feet long, into the ground, enclosing a circular area of about three feet in diameter, with a boat sail open at the top. The medicine-man, one of whom is generally found in every brigade, gets inside and commences shaking

the poles violently, rattling his medicinal rattle, and singing hoarse incantations to the Great Spirit for a fair wind. Being unable to sleep on account of the discordant noises, I wrapped a blanket round me and went out into the woods, where they were holding their midnight orgies and lay down amongst those on the outside of the medicine lodge, to witness the proceedings. I had no sooner done so than the incantation at once ceased, and the performer exclaimed that a white man was present. How he ascertained this fact I am at a loss to surmise, as it was pitch dark at the time, and he was enclosed in the narrow tent, without any apparent opening through which he could espy me, even had it been light enough to distinguish one person from another.[8]

Exactly how medicine men are able to identify the source of disharmony during a ceremony and remove its cause remains a puzzle. Certainly, Kane thought his presence was unknown and, in fact, undetectable. People report this phenomenon in sweat lodges also when a disbeliever or otherwise unworthy person is in the room. Regina Flannery reported an incident among the Gros Ventres that has a touch of humor, but is so typical that it cannot be challenged without good cause.

Just before the spirit made this last speech, two little boys in the lodge had been playing during that ceremony and the spirit told them: "Be quiet because I am going to tell you what happened." And before they knew what happened to them these two little boys landed outside the lodge. The spirit must have pushed them out! And everybody was certainly quiet after that.[9]

Sometimes, the conjuror doesn't even have to be in the spirit lodge. A. Irving Hallowell, in his study of the Saulteaux, recorded a story he received from an old man who lived on Lake Winnipeg at the settlement of Jack Head. In this story, the conjuror's brother warned the medicine man that skeptics were present, thereby motivating him to answer their disbelief with actions so convincing that they could not be refuted.

SAULTEAUX CONJURING

On one occasion when he was conjuring some white people were present. They were overheard to say that it was the conjurer who was doing the singing, not the spirits. So my informant uncle, who knew a little English, called out to his brother, the conjuror; and told him what the white people said. An agreement was made to repeat the performance the next night and the four white men told the conjuror that they would give him five dollars apiece if he convinced them that he did not do the singing.

So the conjuror ordered a lodge of forty poles built the next day and to each corner had ropes attached. These were tied to stakes in the ground like a tent so that the structure could not be shaken. When everything was ready the conjurer first walked around the lodge and shook it a little from the outside. It was very firm. Then he told the skabewiss to raise the canvas covering. Taking off the new black broadcloth coat he was wearing he folded it up and shoved it into the lodge which began shaking at once. Then he sat down outside a little distance from the lodge. It not only continued to shake, but Pawaganak came to it and sang just the same. So the white men paid him the money they promised.[10]

Schoolcraft also included a rare and important narrative regarding the spirit lodge. We have already discussed the puberty vision quest of Catherine Wabose, and it is our good fortune that she also told the story of how she, as a medicine woman, performed this ceremony. It was rare that a woman was able to conduct this ceremony. Since we have no record by a man telling how the ceremony unfolded from his perspective, the narrative of someone, especially a woman, describing what she felt, gives us additional understanding of this ritual.

CATHERINE WABOSE'S EXPERIENCE

One evening the chief of the party came into my mother's lodge. I had lain down, and was supposed to be asleep, and he requested of my mother that she would allow me to try my skill to relieve them. My mother spoke to me, and after some conversation, she gave me her consent. I told them to build the Jee-suk-aun, or prophet's lodge, strong, and gave particular directions for it. I directed that it should consist of ten posts or saplings, each of a different kind of wood, which I named. When it was finished, and tightly wound with skins, the entire population of the encampment assembled around it, and I went in, taking only a small drum. I immediately knelt down, and holding my head near the ground in a position, as near as may be, prostrate, began beating my drum, and reciting my songs or incantations. The lodge commenced shaking violently by supernatural means. I knew this by the compressed current of air above, and the noise of motion. This being regarded by me and by all without as proof of the present of the spirits I consulted, I ceased beating and singing, and lay still, waiting for questions, in the position I had at first assumed.

The first question put to me was in relation to the game, and where it was to be found. The response was given by the orbicular spirit, who had appeared to me. He said, "How shortsighted you are! If you will go in a west direction, you will find game in abundance." Next day the camp was broken up, and they all moved westward, the hunters, as usual, going far ahead. They had not proceeded far beyond the bounds of their former hunting circle when they came upon tracks of a moose, and that day they killed a female, and two young mooses nearly full grown. They pitched their encampment anew, and had abundance of animal food in this new position.[11]

Sometimes, the person conducting the ceremony is thrown violently around the tent, but in this case, Wabose simply lay down in a position that was most comfortable for her and enabled her to receive the spirit into her body. Today, we would say she was channeling the spirit and obtaining her information that way.

Half a century later, we have another description of this ritual. James W. Schultz, a white man who lived a good part of his life with the Blackfeet of Montana and married into the tribe, wrote a considerable number of books on his experiences. This selection from *My Life as an Indian*, generally regarded as his most reliable volume, reported on a spirit lodge ritual performed almost as entertainment by the medicine man Old Sun.

James W. Schultz's Report

Sometimes of a dark night, he would invite a few of us to his lodge, when all was calm and still. After all were seated his wives would bank the fire with ashes so that it was dark, and he would begin to pray. First to the Sun, chief ruler, then to Ai-sopwon-stan, the wind-maker, then to Sistsekom, the thunder, and Puh-pom, the lightning. As he prayed, entreating them to come and do his will, first the lodge ears would begin to quiver with the first breath of a coming breeze, which gradually grew stronger until the lodge bent to the blasts, and the poles strained and creaked. Then thunder began to boom, faint and far away, and lightning to simply blaze, and they came nearer and nearer until they seemed to be just overhead; the crashes deafened us, the flashes blinded us. Then this wonderful man would pray them to go, and the wind would die down and the thunder and lightning go on rambling and flashing into the far distance until we heard and saw them no more.[12]

Sir Cecil Denny's Experience

Sir Cecil Denny, a Canadian Northwest Mounted Police official, reported his experience with the spirit lodge ceremony. Police officials being astute observers of everything, his version of the experience suggested that the ceremony cannot be explained according to the standard way we judge phenomena. In fact, Denny did not offer a defensive explanation of the experience, nor did he seek to explain or belittle his experience.

> I happened to be camped on the Red Deer River in 1879 close to a large Blackfoot encampment. One moonlight night I walked over to the camp with my interpreter, Billy Gladstone. We intended visiting the lodge of the medicine man which was pitched a little distance from the main camp. We entered his lodge which had only a small fire in the center. The medicine man was seated wrapped in his buffalo robe at the side of the teepee smoking one of their long medicine pipes. He paid no attention to us. We sat down near him, and also proceeded to smoke quietly. He still gave no sign of recognition of our presence.
>
> Everything was still, while outside from the main camp sounded beating drums where dances were being held. We sat this way for quite a time when I was startled by the ringing of a bell above the top of the lodge. I could see nothing, and the medicine man made no move. Presently the teepee began to rock, even lifting off the ground about a foot. When it is remembered that such a tent as this consists of a dozen long poles crossed at the top, wide apart at the bottom and covered with heavy buffalo robes making it impossible to lift one side, as I now witnessed, for these teepees are built so that no ordinary wind could blow them over. And remember the Indian did not touch the tent.
>
> After some time the rocking motion ceased. I hurried outside to see if anyone had been playing tricks. Not a human being was in sight near us; the moon was clear and you could see a long distance. I returned, resumed my seat. The tent

began to rock again, this time so violently that it sometimes lifted several feet on one side so that both myself and the interpreter could plainly see outside. My interpreter was thoroughly frightened by this time, and I was not much better; yet the Indian never stirred. We had seen enough and left, returning to the camp thoroughly mystified.[13]

Stephan Schwartz reported on a variant version of the shaking tent ritual that indicated that the practice continued until very modern times. I have verified that the practice continues as it always has been with a Canadian Cree man who told of even more startling exploits of medicine men who live far away from civilization. Since the Schwartz version cannot be improved upon, I cite it at length.

THE MONTAGNAIS PRACTICES

In the late 1950s, a researcher named Stiles, of the Museum of the American Indian, made one of his periodic visits to a tribe of Algonquin people, known as the Montagnais, who lived in eastern Canada. He brought back from that trip an observation that, being an anthropologist with a healthy sense of professional survival, he did not choose to publish but did present his paper to Professor C. W. Weiant, who, a few years later, entered it into the literature. What Stiles described was a situation in which "certain members of the Montagnais habitually repair to the woods, set up a log shelter about the size of a telephone booth, get inside and, when the power is sufficiently strong, make contact with a friend or relative who may be hundreds of miles away. A two-way conversation is carried on seemingly by clairaudience. If no contact is made, it is assumed that the person with whom contact is sought has died."[14]

Some skeptics never resolved their doubts, and we have two stories in which, years after the experience, when they felt the Indian medicine man should have confessed to trickery, skeptics were told the exact same story of the experiences of the spirit lodge by the aged and dying practitioner. In the interim, the medicine men were never shaken into changing what they had experienced.

J. G. KOHL'S STORY

Thirty years ago, said this white man, I was present at the incantation and performance of a "jossakid" (local name for a medicine man) in one of these lodges. I saw the man creep into the hut, which was about ten feet high, after swallowing a mysterious potion made from a root, he immediately began singing and beating the drum in his basket-work "chimney." The entire cage began gradually trembling and shaking, and oscillating slowly amid great noise. The more the necromancer sang and drummed, the more violent the oscillations of the long case became. It bent backwards and forwards, up and down, like the mast of a vessel caught in a storm and tossed on the waves. I could not understand how these movements could be produced by a man inside, as we could not have caused them from the exterior.

The drum ceased, and the jossakid yelled that the spirits were coming after him. We then heard through the noise and crackling and oscillations of the hut two voices speaking inside, one above, the other below. The lower one asked questions, which the upper one answered. Both voices seemed entirely different, and I believed I could explain them by very clever ventriloquism. Some spiritualist among us, however, explained it through modern spiritualism, and asserted that the Indian jossakids had speaking media, in addition to those known to us, which tapped, wrote, and drew.

There was a sequel to this story. Thirty years later (i.e. shortly before he met Kohl), the narrator came across a very old Indian, lying on his death-bed, whom he recognized to be the very jossakid who had given the strange performance described above. Since that date, this Indian had become a Christian, and, of course, had renounced his former pagan practices. Kohl's narrator sat down beside the dying Indian, and began to talk to him.

Uncle, he said to him, Dost thou remember prophesying

to us in thy lodge thirty years ago, and astonishing us, not only by thy discourse, but also by the movements of thy prophet-lodge? I was curious to know it how it was done, and thou saidst thou hadst performed it by supernatural power, "through the spirits." Now thou art old, and hast become a Christian; thou art sick and canst not live much longer. Now is the time to confess all truthfully. Tell me, then, how and through what means thou didst deceive us?

"I know it, my uncle," the sick Indian replied. "I have become a Christian, I am old, I am sick, I cannot live much longer, and I can do no other than speak the truth. Believe me, I did not deceive you at the time. I did not move the lodge. It was shaken by the power of the spirits. I only repeated to you what the spirits said to me. I heard their voices. The top of the lodge was full of them, and before me the sky and wide lands lay expanded. I could see a great distance about me, and believed I could recognize the most distant objects.[15]

A. IRVING HALLOWELL'S CONFESSIONS

Hallowell, in his report *The Role of Conjuring in Saulteaux Society*, returned two conflicting confessions about the spirit lodge and whether or not the medicine man made the tent move. He cited Wau-chus-co, a medicine man who died near Mackinac in 1840 who made a similar deathbed statement.

I possessed a power which I cannot explain or describe to you. I never attempted to move the lodge. I held communications with supernatural beings, or thinking minds, or spirits which acted upon my mind, or soul, and revealed to me such knowledge as I have described.[16]

His informant "M" had a slightly different interpretation of the experience in the tent.

> As soon as I got inside and put my hand on one of the posts it seemed as if the lodge were very easy to move. It is something like beating a drum; it was almost as if it shook itself. I knew just what to do, what songs to sing and everything else. There are more then thirty different songs. The inside of the lodge was not dark; it was light as day. I saw wisakedjak plainly before me there. He told me what was the matter with the woman. So I said to her father: "You have done something wrong. You have used medicine you got in the midewiwin for bad purposes. You made a man suffer illness for three winters." I told him to give up the medicine at once or else his daughter would die.[17]

This confession that the lodge might have been flimsy does not square with all other accounts. I suspect that "M" meant that once the lodge was constructed, it took on a holy aspect all its own, and that when the spirits came, it was not difficult for them to move it— it was already in a different kind of physical state.

MUSKOGEE PRACTICES

John R. Swanton reported a recognizable practice among the Creeks. Instead of building a separate tent, they apparently simply enclosed the medicine man's cabin for the ritual, and it shook as if it were a temporary tent erected for the occasion.

> The savages have much confidence in their medicine men; the cabin of the jugglers (jongleur) is covered with skins which serve him as a covering or clothing. He enters it entirely naked and begins to pronounce some words which none understands: it is, says he, to invoke the spirit; after which he rises, cries, is agitated, appears beside himself, and water pours from all parts of his body.

The cabin shakes, and those present think that it is the presence of the Spirit; the language which he speaks in these invocations has nothing in common with the language of the savages.[18]

CHEYENNE SPIRIT LODGE RITUAL

The Cheyennes have their own unique spirit lodge that has often been classified by scholars as a "shaking tent" ritual, although the people themselves feel it should not be described in a generic sense with other lodges used by more eastern and northern Algonquins. The Cheyenne ritual could only be offered by a holy person who had the power to do so. The previous selections we have examined make no distinction as to the status within the tribe of the men who performed this ritual. In the nineteenth century, Stone Forehead, Keeper of the Sacred Arrows, and Box Elder, Keeper of one of the Sacred Wheel Lances, had this power, suggesting that is was used sparingly by the people. Stone Forehead offered the spirit lodge in an effort to locate Medicine Snake and his warriors. He was told they were all dead, killed by the Pawnees in one of the great disasters for the Cheyennes.[19]

> The man unwrapped his sacred things; the singers chanted their spiritual songs, and the fire was permitted to die down, until the lodge was dark. Before the fire was out, the man who was calling the spirit was tied with four bowstrings. Each finger of each hand was tied separately to the next finger, in a hard knot and the ends of the bowstrings on each hand were tied together, behind his back, so that he hands were tightly bound there. His feet were tied together in the same way, each toe being tied to the next one in a hard knot, and the feet bound together by the bowstrings. Thus tied, he sat at the back of the lodge, and sometimes was tied to one of the lodgepoles. At times a little shelter, shaped like a sweat-lodge, was built in the middle of the lodge, and the man was put in that.

After the fire had gone out, in some interval of the singing, the lodge was shaken as if by a strong wind, the poles creaked, and suddenly in the lodge a strange voice was heard, talking to the man. The secret helper was perhaps called to ask where there were buffalo, or where there were enemies; where missing people were; or even where lost horses might be found. Some times the secret helper told what was happening at a distance; or perhaps warned the camp of enemies near at hand. After the spirit had gone, and a light had again been made, the man was found to be untied, and the bow-strings were lying in the door, tied in innumerable knots. It was believed that the spirits untied him.[20]

Sister Bernard Coleman recorded a story about the use of the spirit lodge ritual after an Indian village in Minnesota had been plagued by scabies, a skin disorder, and doctors and even lumberjacks with their folk cures had failed to stop the epidemic. The story follows the expected traditional format quite closely, suggesting that this ritual has continued to be practiced even in an industrial social setting.

THE SPIRIT LODGE CURE

When I was a young boy, my family lived near Mora, Minnesota, in an Indian village of about 400 people. At one time all of the children were afflicted with scabbies. The parents tried every remedy they knew of to cure the children. They even tried remedies suggested by the lumberjacks in the camp across the river—sulphur and molasses, and wagon grease. But all of these failed, and the scabbies continued to spread. Finally the Indians resorted to the djasakid. I remember watching the men place eight ironwood saplings firmly into the ground in the shape of a circle. They laced small branches between the saplings and covered the entire frame with a blanket. This small lodge or cage was about four feet wide and eight feet high.

The djasakid entered the lodge after the men had bound

him with ropes. I remember hearing voices within the lodge and seeing the lodge shake from side to side. This meant that the spirits were approaching. An old man near the lodge spoke for the Indians. He said, "Our children are sick with scabbies. We have tried all the medicines of the India and the white man, but we cannot save our children. Now the old people are getting sick and they will die."

Then the tent came to a stop, and the djasakid answered, "Don't be afraid. Elect two men to be your scouts. Have them make a strawman and set it up in the village. They must wear moccasins, paint their faces, and wear feathers on their heads. Let them shoot until the strawman burns to ashes."

The next morning as I was running down to the dam to get fish for breakfast, I saw the scouts carrying the strawman over the hill. They brought it to the center of the village. Then I saw the scouts running back and forth, shouting and shooting. Soon the strawman was only ashes, and not long after, the scabbies were gone.[21]

A KIOWA SPIRIT LODGE

A very unusual practice was used by the Kiowa in which the spirits of the departed participated. They appear to have some of the power of the woodlands ceremonies, and it is uncertain whether this ceremony is designed specifically to communicate with and receive the blessing of departed souls or whether it has as its goals the healings and predictions found in other accounts. It is interesting and features not simply a spirit lodge for the living, but a small lodge for the spirits.

The rite was held at night in a darkened tipi. On the west side opposite the door was placed a miniature tipi one to three feet high. The spectators sat in the other part of the large tipi. At some performances it was necessary for them to lie face downward with heads covered. To peek was dangerous, for it would anger the spirit, who might kill the offender, or at least throw dirt in his eyes. At other performances this precaution was not necessary.

The shaman began by smoking and praying, sometimes assisted by the singing of some old men. Presently a roaring noise was heard, the large tipi was shaken and filled with wind, and then the small tipi vibrated. At this time drumming and low singing were sometimes heard coming from the small tipi. The spirit of a dead person, often a reknowned warrior or shaman, came in the form of an owl. The flapping of wings was heard outside the smokehole; then the owl entered and fluttered against the small tipi. From within the small tipi was heard the voice of the spirit asking why he had been summoned. At performances in which deer hooves and a whistle had been placed beside the firepit in advance, the spirit blew the whistle and rattled the hooves before speaking. The shaman asked who had come, and the spirit replied with the name of some dead person. The shaman then smoked a pipe, offered the stem to the spirit to smoke, and put the question to him. The spirit might answer at once, or fly out of the tipi to return in half an hour or so with the answer. The spirit spoke in a high muffled, nasal voice, and repeated everything twice.

At one seance, after the question has been answered, a woman spectator asked to speak to her dead brother. The owl, apparently acting as intermediary, consented and rushed from the tipi. Presently there was a surge of wind in the tipi and the spirit of the woman's brother spoke. They carried on a brief conversation during which he mentioned that his world was a land of plenty and contentment. Then the spirit departed with the usual rush of wind.[22]

CHAPTER FOUR

INTERSPECIES RELATIONS

* * * * * * * * * * * * *

INTERSPECIES COMMUNICATION—BIRDS

Some people have described the role of other creatures as that of intercessor on behalf of the human in both dreams and visions. Some birds and animals may indeed play that role. One thing seems certain: dreams, daytime encounters, and visions all consist of communications from higher powers who already know much about us and who have a specific purpose in revealing themselves to us and, at least for American Indians, appear in the form of birds and animals. Higher spirits may appear as a specific bird or animal with a specific purpose for bestowing powers. Quite frequently, within dream and vision experiences, we observe a change of bodily form so that birds become animals, animals become birds, and human persons take on other shapes. The Spider, *Iktomi* in the Sioux tradition, is noted for moving back and forth in various shapes during the course of these events. Sometimes, this phenomenon occurs to teach the human that in spite of different shapes and talents, the universe is a unified tapestry and not a collection of isolated, unrelated entities.

For much of the recorded material that we have, however, it seems as if the other creatures are waiting for humans to make an overture to the higher spirits, and once the quest for a relationship is set in motion, they join in, bringing their knowledge to add to our understanding and enabling us to receive special roles in life and

107

powers to fulfill the roles. Often, it appears that certain birds or animals have been watching particular individuals, and, detecting an
attitude of respect, they then initiated communications with them,
either by dreams or during a vision experience. When plants and animals come to us in dreams, they take the first step in establishing a
relationship with us.

The memory of talking with other creatures goes back far into
the mists of early planetary time. Karl L. Schlesier, writing about the
Cheyennes' understanding of interspecies communication, said: "in
Tsistsistas [Cheyenne] memories, animals talked with humans, took
pity on them, protected and taught them, gave to them special power
and knowledge, healed them from wounds and sicknesses, kept them
alive with self-sacrifice, and, finally, became human themselves to
help them in great need."[1] For many tribes, this phenomenon of
interspecies communication has always been present, and hearing a
voice generally involves hearing a specific voice from a particular
bird or animal.

When we begin to gather the stories of talking with other creatures, we find that three kinds of communication are involved. The
first instance is when another creature appears in an encounter with
the sacred and plays a vital role in the unfolding scenario. We can call
this phenomenon a vehicle for the sacred to manifest itself through
the medium of other creatures. The second kind are those instances
where the bird or animal appears in circumstances in which the
human is extremely vulnerable and the bird or animal assists with
information or powers that will resolve a particular situation, such as
providing direction for people who are lost, identifying where the
game is, or warning of possible disaster from as yet unknown forces.
The third kind is more secular and consists of the objective knowledge possessed by humans of birds and animals speaking the tribal
language and often simply acting as a commentator on human activities, sometimes even teasing and provoking people by flaunting their
knowledge of us.

LUTHER STANDING BEAR

Luther Standing Bear identified several birds that spoke to people, echoing, in part, the Cheyennes' memories of early days. "The prairie chicken, the meadowlark, and the crow are birds that make sounds that can be interpreted into Sioux words. We Sioux knew, of course, that birds and animals had a way of talking to one another just as we did. We knew, too, that the animals and birds came and talked with our medicine men. Our legends tell of the time when bird and animal life communicated with man."[2] Melvin R. Gilmore, an early scholar on the Plains Indians, reported:

> They say that the meadow lark imitates the speech of human beings. They say that meadow larks come close to the dwellings of human beings at night and listen to what the people say, and that next morning the larks mock the people, singing out what they have heard the night before. The Dakotas say that if you pay attention when the meadow lark sings, you can plainly distinguish words and sentences. But they say that it is not only the meadow lark which thus sings words and sentences of human speech, but some other kinds of birds also do this. Two other kinds of birds which thus talk are the brown thrasher and the red-winged blackbird. They talk while they fly, and sometimes as they sit in the trees.[3]

Communication with birds in particular seems to have become secularized over the centuries, as many people report talking with birds as a regular part of daily life. Charles Eastman said that his grandmother told him, "When I had grown old enough to take notice, I was apparently capable of holding extended conversations in an unknown dialect with birds and red squirrels."[4] Indeed, Luther Standing Bear humorously reflected: "The larks in our state [South Dakota], at that time, talked the Sioux language—at least we inferred that they did; but in California, where I now live, it is impossible to understand them. Perhaps they are getting too civilized."[5]

As previously noted, people hear things because they are supposed to hear things. Lame Deer said, "Butterflies talk to women. A spirit will get into a beautiful butterfly, fly over to a young squaw, and sit on her shoulder. The spirit will talk through the butterfly to the young squaw and tell her to become a medicine woman."[6] Why is it essential that a particular young woman become a medicine person? We can suggest that some spiritual entity, aware of and planning for the future of the tribe, has chosen a young woman to play a vital role for her people and has begun the process of awareness that will blossom as she grows older. While these anecdotal beliefs provide a context in which we can understand the popular understanding of interspecies communication, they certainly do not provide a basis for affirming it. The most generous interpretation might be that people became so intimately acquainted with the sounds of birds and animals that they were often able to apprehend the emotional posture of the other creatures much as we are able to discern the moods of our cats and dogs. Modem psychologists may object to this interpretation of interspecies communication, but in these cases, no useful information is transferred. We simply have a demonstration of the creature's ability to talk with humans about mundane things.

Jungians, on the other hand, might insist that the appearance and apparent communication by the other creature is merely a projection from our collective unconscious of something we already knew, either through some form of psychic heredity or because that information had been discovered earlier and was filed away in the collective unconscious. This argument would imply that we have a power of retrieval to locate and extract from the collective unconscious a bit of otherwise irrelevant information that happens to coincide with precisely what we need at that moment. It would be a form of synchronicity, although trivial to be sure. But birds mocking us, other than the mockingbird itself, seems rather unusual.

A great many tribes did not welcome communications from the owl. This bird was a messenger of death, or at least ill fortune, for many people. Frequently, the owl is linked to the appearance of ghosts, as in the case of the Chiricahua Apaches. Morris Opler quoted an Apache elder on this subject: "If you hear an owl, you know a ghost is near by, for the owl is connected with the ghost. Owls talk the Chiricahua language. They say different things to different people. To me it seems like they are saying: 'All you people are going to get killed.'"[7] Whether this belief originates in past experience or is a superstition is certainly open to inquiry. We should note that the frequency of the appearance of owls has declined significantly since the Apaches went to live on a reservation.

INTERSPECIES COMMUNICATIONS—ANIMALS

BLACK ELK'S EXPERIENCE

Let us move beyond gossiping meadowlarks and analyze a more concrete example. Black Elk, the famous Oglala Sioux holy man, was out hunting when a blizzard came up. As the storm increased in fury, he made a shelter near the bank of a hill, where he could escape the wind, and settled down in his buffalo robe to wait out the storm. Then, he related: "The wind went down that night and it was still and very cold. While I was lying there in a bison robe, a coyote began to howl not far off, and suddenly I knew it was saying something. It was not making words, but it said something plainer than words, and this was it: 'Two- legged one, on the big ridge west of you there are bison; but first you shall see two more two-legged over there.'"[8] The next day, Black Elk found an old man and a boy huddled together to wait out the storm as he had been. They had also been hunting, had survived the storm, and were terribly hungry. After encountering them, Black Elk went over the hill to the west where he discovered seven buffalo stranded in the snowdrifts and easy to kill. They killed several animals and took meat back to their camp.

Critics may reply that this incident merely illustrates the capability of human beings to extract themselves from nasty situations. Indeed, Carl Gustav Jung, trying to understand the appearance of the other creature in dreams during human crises, would have described the phenomenon as "the motif of the helpful animal intervening when everything is impossible and people expect a catastrophe—help out of a tight corner. What do these animals mean? They are merely representatives of lower instinctual forces in man and helpful in the same way."⁹ We should beware when a thinker describes something as "merely." There is no crisis here for Black Elk. He comfortably survived the snowstorm and, in continuing the hunt, discovered the two other people who also survived the blizzard, thus verifying part of the message. Finding the buffalo confirmed that the entire message of the coyote was accurate.

Could anyone extract from the collective unconscious the specific data that is transmitted to Black Elk in this experience? Here we have elements of time: "tomorrow, this will happen." We have spatial directions: "over the ridge to the west." We have the two-leggeds Black Elk met prior to discovering the buffalo. This message cannot have been a hallucination, because it had considerable empirical content. Because the coyote did not speak in human language, we may have doubts, but this objection judges a complete event by a criticism based on different criteria. Transmitting accurate information, we learn, is not dependant on language at a more profound level of relationships. It can pass from one entity to another quite easily if the receiving party is alert. There need not even be a face-to-face encounter—Black Elk did not even see the coyote.

Here we can draw a comparison with the discoveries of quantum physics. Ian Wilson, seeking to reconcile near death experiences with quantum, said, "According to quantum theory there are certain conditions under which, in the case of two very distant sub-atomic particles, if the behavior of one is altered the other can be expected to change instantaneously in exactly the same way, despite no apparent force or signal linking them. It is as if each particle 'knows' what the other is doing."¹⁰ Certainly, the coyote knew the situation of Black Elk, and, as he howled, Black Elk received a message meaningful only to his situation. But the two—the coyote and Black Elk—were not physically connected at all. The unity of life on the spiritual level enabled man and animal to exchange ideas. There remains the mystery of why the coyote felt obligated to inform the man of events that were to occur the next morning. Did he, perhaps, need Black Elk to kill the buffalo so he could feast on the remains? The helpful animal occurrence needs considerably more serious thought for an adequate explanation.

WHITE BULL'S EXPERIENCE

White Bull, a Minneconjou Sioux and relative of Sitting Bull, reported a similar experience when he became lost in a blizzard while trying to get home after an ill-fated hunting trip. As Stanley Vestal reported it:

> He was riding up a dry creek-bed, his horse could hardly go against the wind and the cold, and he himself held his head down, wailing and crying. Suddenly his horse stopped, snorting, with rigid ears, staring at something ahead. White Bull looked up and saw a big buffalo bull facing him. The bull was singing: "My mother and father said so." White Bull stared at the buffalo in amazement. The great bull said: "Friend look at me. I am going to a good people. My father and mother are taking my trail. They want something." After the bull said this he rolled in the snow, and when he got up, one side of his body seemed covered with white paint. The other side was red. Tied to his horn on the white side was a white shell, and tied to his horn on the red side was a streamer of red flannel.
>
> The buffalo said to White Bull, "My friend, I want you to be my friend, and I will show you what to do. Look me over well." Then the buffalo turned and turned, so that White Bull could see first one side of him, then the other. Sometimes the bull would paw and lick.
>
> The bull said: "Now I have shown you what I want and what I wish you would show the people. And this is all I wish to show you. Go now on your way and you will be saved."
>
> White Bull kicked the ribs of his pony and pushed on through the whirling snow. Soon after, it stopped snowing, the skies cleared, and White Bull's pony carried him on in a daze and stopped at Sitting Bull's tipi.[11]

It is difficult to classify this experience, because it has strong elements of a daytime vision since the buffalo appeared in physical form. However, it appears that in times of human emergency, some animals do manifest their concern and communicate with humans to help them resolve their problem.

There are many stories of animals and birds warning the people when they are in danger. This phenomenon occurs more often than we would suspect and testifies to the idea that meaning can be conveyed by an unusual sound made by the nonhuman that translates immediately into a coherent—and badly needed—warning or solution to the human's problem.

WILLIAM ROWLAND'S STORY

A good example is from the Cheyennes, who seem to have had an amazingly close relationship with the higher powers. In 1854 or 1855, William Rowland was in the Cheyenne camp in late autumn. About nine or ten o'clock at night, a coyote near at hand set up a great howling. Soon after, an old man went around through the camp and announced that a war party of Pawnees was near and was about to attack the camp, that all must be prepared. The next morning, the camp was attacked by Pawnees, who were driven off.[12]

JIM BRIDGER'S EXPERIENCE

This phenomenon was apparently not restricted to Indians. Some white men came to know the Indian ways so closely that they could interpret the sounds of animals like the Indians and reported similar experiences. Jim Bridger, scouting for General Connor's expedition in Wyoming in 1865, one night heard a strange coyote howl and knew, from his familiarity with the Indian beliefs, that danger was near:

> All the way from Laramie thousands of big gray buffalo wolves had surrounded the camp, making the night hideous with their infernal howling. Jim Bridger found their racket reassuring; where wolves were plenty, Injuns were generally scarce. He slept soundly through their wild concert, for the wolves had sung him to sleep for nearly forty years.
>
> But that night Jim heard a howl which brought him wide awake and sitting up in his blankets with prickles running up

and down his spine.

It was the howl of a wolf that he heard, but it was no ordinary howl. The sound was weird and eerie—exactly like the death wail of an Injun woman. Jim and his fellow scouts stared at each other across the dying campfire with wide and troubled eyes. They all recognized that sound—it was the howling of a "medicine wolf."

Bridger warned General Connors of the meaning of the howl. Connors rejected Jim's explanation and said he would not be turned back because the scouts and Indians were superstitious. "That's no Injun," he argued, "you can tell an Injun's howl from a real wolf easy enough. A real wolf don't have no echo."[13]

When Connor and his soldiers refused to listen and poked fun at Bridger, he packed his goods, left along with two other experienced mountain men, and camped some distance away from the soldiers. The Connor expedition was a complete disaster from then on, the general eventually losing close to 600 horses and his mission collapsing. He fell into disgrace.

How could a white man appropriate some of the powers of the Indian medicine men? A common phenomenon among people living on the frontier was their propensity to adopt Indian ways. Doctors, missionaries, trappers, and traders—none were immune from the change that overtook them when they had to adjust to the conditions of life under which Indians lived. John Mason Brown, writing an article on "Indian Medicine" in the *Atlantic Monthly* in 1886, observed: "It cannot be denied that the whites, who consort much with the ruder tribes of Indians imbibe, to a considerable degree, their veneration of medicine. The old trappers and voyageurs are, almost without exception, observers of omens and dreamers of dreams. They claim that medicine is a faculty which can in some degree be cultivated, and aspire to its possession as eagerly as do the Indians."[14]

Animals, it appears, like to share in the exploits of humans. While we appreciate the intervention of animals to help us, there is an opposite effect also, as the next story shows. Here a coyote led a Cheyenne war party to locate a camp of Utes, whom they subsequently attacked and took prisoners. The Utes, no doubt, did not appreciate the coyote taking sides.

THE COYOTE HELPS THE WAR PARTY

In 1858, Dives Backward, a Cheyenne who could understand what the coyotes said when they howled, was with a war party to the south, which had just reached the Rio Grande del Norte, when a coyote was heard to howl close to the camp. "Hold on," said Dives Backward. "Across that big river are some lodges of people whom we ought to attack." They crossed the river and went on. Before they reached the place, they joined a war party of Arapahoes, and a little later a coyote howled again, telling them that the enemy were close by. They found the camp—six lodges of Utes—attacked it, and captured Yellow Nose, then four years of age, and his mother, who afterward escaped.[15]

ANIMAL POWERS

Earlier, we discussed the experience of Goose, who could not shoot the antelope even though he fired sixteen shots at it. The failure to hit the animal was attributed to the fact that Goose was being brought into a confrontation with the sacred, and his failure to hit the animal alerted him that something unusual was taking place. This phenomenon of being unable to kill game was again a common experience of the Indians. Different tribes might interpret it in different ways, but the fact of being unable to hit the game was seen by the Indians generally as the ability of the animal to protect itself and refuse to give its body as food to the Indians.

LUTHER STANDING BEAR'S EXPERIENCE

Luther Standing Bear reported an instance in which he was baffled by a white-tailed deer:

Among our tribe there is a superstition concerning the black-tailed deer. It is said that if this deer becomes aware of the hunter who is about to aim at it, the animal can deflect the bullets of the hunter and save itself. Many times I heard this story, then one day I had an amazing experience with this animal that puzzled me as it had other hunters. A friend and myself were hunting on horseback. The wind being right, we came close upon a black-tailed deer before it saw us. I quickly dismounted to shoot while my companion held the reins of my horse. The deer did not run, but stood looking at me as I aimed, wagging its tail steadily back and forth. With every assurance of getting my game I fired. To my astonishment the deer stood still and looked intently at me. I was a good marksman, the animal was only a short distance from me, and fully exposed, yet my shot had gone astray.

Seven times I shot at the animal, missing every time, the deer never moving. The seventh bullet was my last and I could shoot no more. My ammunition was gone, and there the deer and I stood looking at each other. So close were we that I could see its lips twitching. It pawed the earth once or twice with its front hoof, then dashed away. My friend accused me of being nervous, but I am not a nervous person. When I reached home, I got some more ammunition and tried out my gun. It was in perfect working order. According to my tribespeople, the prairie dog and the prairie chicken both have the power to keep a hunter from hitting them.[16]

The Sioux tradition reported that certain animals had the power to render themselves invulnerable to hunters if they so chose. This belief came down over the centuries, but was always verified by the behavior of the animals, so the people rarely questioned it. The list of animals with this kind of power may be much longer, and all the animals may possess this power for all we know. By the same token, it appears that birds and animals knew when they were going to die. Exactly how the creatures exercised this power is unknown, but since some of them gave the same power of invulnerability to humans, we can rely on this belief.

YELLOW FISH'S TRAGEDY

The Blackfeet, who lived farther west from the Sioux in Montana, had a different interpretation of the animal power that prevented the successful hunting of them. James W. Schultz related an incident that happened when he, Yellow Fish, a Blackfeet guide for himself, and George Bird Grinnell, the famous scholar and writer, were hunting bighorn sheep. Finding himself unable to bring down his animal from close range, Yellow Fish became despondent, and Schultz inquired about the sudden change in temperament and received this unusual response.

> "That every shot I fired failed to kill was a warning to me, a sure warning that some relative, someone dear to me is dead," dejectedly he answered. And, though hard we tried we could not turn him from that belief. Such warnings were well known, he said, and he named several hunters who had had that experience: missed, time and time again, game at close range that they had shot at, and returning home, found that someone dear had died.
>
> Said Grinnell: "Well, friend Yellow Fish, though you had bad luck, your hunt was not all for nothing. That little stream you followed up to where it heads, we name for you. From now on, it is Yellow Fish Creek, and next north of it is Yellow Fish Mountain. Later, when we arrived at the agency, we learned that, early on the morning of the day of Yellow Fish's unsuccessful hunt, his mother had died And he said to me: "Apiknui [Schultz' Blackfeet name], now you know that my warning was true. It is that we Lone People (Indians) receive messages from our gods that the whites are never given by their different kinds of gods."[17]

A more enigmatic story that really begs credibility was nevertheless reported in a Roman Catholic scholarly journal, written in good faith by the scholar, and was presented almost as a gratuitous comment, as if it were a routine experience of the people. I reproduce it here as an interesting experience that seemed ordinary to the Gros Ventres and may seem to refer to the origins of life. It would certainly explain how vacant lands become populated.

BUFFALO OF THE SUN

> The Gros Ventres were traveling and they got to a place where there is a mountain on both sides. They were going to look for buffalo. The men went out and then heard a man hollering for all the others. They all looked and saw a herd of buffalo coming from the sky. Iron Bucket (Singer's husband) was one of that party. The herd dropped close by. When the people see anything like that they say it is a holy thing. The men chased these buffalo and killed one. It was bigger and fatter than the real kind and that is how they knew. They talked about this a whole lot. They had not prayed for this. It just happened. The man who first saw these bufffalo gave a war whoop and then yelled: "Come See!" The others all looked and here the buffalo were. When the buffalo landed, the earth shook and the dust iust came up.[18]

The empirical aspects of this story are important. Other than the usual preparations for hunting, which might have included special prayers, this event occurred without any effort by the medicine men intervening in order to receive special hunting dispensation from the sun. It was one of those strange, unexplainable incidents where the sacred intrudes upon secular activities. The sun buffalo hit the earth and raised clouds of dust as they achieved their balance, reacting in the way we would expect animals coming from some height would behave. This adjustment to the ground would indicate that they were not simply another group of buffalo feeding as usual, but not seen by the scouts. The buffalo were "bigger and fatter" than the ordinary animals they hunted. And the scene of animals coming out of the sun did not stun them so that they were afraid to hunt the animals. The memory was short and succinct and apparently not regarded by them as unusual. The casual nature and simplicity of the report testifies to its accuracy.

Unexplained in modern science is the manner in which life reconstitutes itself after a geological era has ended in catastrophe. We have estimates that as high as 80 percent of the species might have been extinguished after death-dealing asteroid/meteor impacts on the planet. With such a high death toll, it is unlikely that the right predator/prey and symbiotic species would survive to continue life as they had formerly functioned. Yet when we find fossils of organisms, there is nearly unanimous opinion that they are complete organisms and change very little thereafter. The Indian solution to this problem may be contained in this little account. Perhaps, somehow, when people say they are children of the sun, they are speaking in a very literal sense. Pending the discovery of many missing links that would affirm present beliefs, I believe we should file this item away in our minds for future consideration.

There are hundreds of stories in which animals play a crucial role in visions and dreams, and since they are familiar to many people of different tribes, it is repetitive to reproduce them here. The examples cited above, however, are accounts illustrating the independent action of the animals in assisting humans. Birds and animals are not always subservient to the higher powers, but have their own secular relationship with us. Modern people lack the years of sustained contact with the natural world that would enable them to understand the different kinds of sound made by other creatures and to gain information from them. The early mountain men eventually gained sufficient experience to understand the animal sounds and used tribal medicine men whenever they could to assist them in their endeavors.

ANIMALS ADMONISHING HUMANS

Lest we begin to believe that animals are always helpful, we must think in terms of mutual exchange of ideas with the animals. Sometimes, the dream projects a possible adversarial relationship between human and animal. Animals can demand corrective action on the part of humans to preserve the arrangement they enjoy. Many Tail Feathers, a Blackfeet, related the story of his father's dream, a critical exchange of information that required the Blackfeet to refrain from hunting the buffalo in the destructive manner of running them off cliffs in the buffalo jump.

MANY TAIL FEATHERS'S FATHER'S DREAM

> My friend, my vision was powerful. As I slept I, my shadow, went forth upon discovery of whatever I might see. It was that, as I was walking in a valley strange to me, a buffalo bull came out from a grove, came toward me, stopped and raised high a right forefoot, making as it were, the sign for peace. So, peace I also signed, and he came on. Soon we met and he said to me: "I have been looking for you. It is that I must give you warning about something you and your kind are doing that is very wrong. It is that with your piskans you are rapidly killing off us buffalo. If you keep on doing it you will soon put an end to the very last ones of us. So this I say, stop using your piskans if you would prevent something dreadful happening to all of your kind."[19]

Although couched in polite terms, clearly, here the buffalo warned humans about their destructive practices that were injuring the animals. Thereafter, the Blackfeet abandoned their practice of driving the animals off cliffs into corrals and hunted on horseback or by sneaking up to the herd, a reform that should calm the attacks of environmentalists regarding the style of hunting used by the Indians. This dream resulted in a change of behavior of the human and a better relationship between the two.

The Bears Warn the Hunter

A tale told by Schultz about a Blackfeet hunter illustrated eloquently the idea that, at times, humans go beyond the bounds of decent behavior. In this story, bears overheard a man who apparently had no respect for them and warned him not to hunt them. As it turned out, he ignored the warning and thereafter fell into a series of misfortunes that eventually crippled him so that he was virtually helpless. As the hunter remembered:

> The night before we started, I had a powerful vision: I saw myself standing upon a big log in a heavy forest, standing there looking for game. Away to my right, some thick brush shook and swayed and, watching, I saw two big real-bears come out of it and straight toward me. As I was about to raise my rifle to aim at one of them, he called out to me: "Stand as you are, for we have come to talk to you." I was very much surprised to be so addressed, by a real-bear, in perfect Pikuni language.
>
> They came on and on toward me, and, when quite close, sat up on their haunches, and the one said to me: "We heard you talking about going to Two Medicine Lake to hunt, you and two others. Well, go, kill all the grass-eaters that you want, but don't shoot at any of our relatives. I warn you now that you must not attempt to harm them. If you do, you will be sorry for it so long as you live!" I tried to think quickly what I should say to them, and, before I could make up my mind, they suddenly disappeared, my shadow came back into my body. I awoke with a loud cry, and found myself sitting up in bed, my body wet with perspiration.[20]

The hunter did not respect this warning and in a series of accidents, was reduced to almost a helpless cripple.

Rising Wolf's Protective Warbonnet

Rising Wolf's son told Schultz how his father got his protective warbonnet. The story is unusual because although the human was instructed on how to make the bonnet and what should be in it, the helpful wolf was not satisfied with his effort and took the materials and fashioned them the way he wanted. In almost every other account of visions and dreams, the human seemed capable of performing the task of creating a medicine bundle or special protective device. That the helping animal took over the task of making the bonnet is therefore highly unlikely.

> A wolf came to him and said, "I am chief of these great plains, and I have taken a liking to you; therefore I am going to tell you how to make something that will preserve you in times of danger. Go and get the tail feathers of an owl, skins of weasels and minks, and make a war bonnet."
>
> "As you say," my father, or, rather his shadow answered. He collected the feathers and skins and made the bonnet, but it did not please the wolf; he took it apart, rearranged the materials, singing all the time as he put them together. And when he was satisfied with his work, he put the bonnet on my father and walked around and around him, looking at it, still singing, and at last said. "There, it is as I wanted it. This will preserve you from the enemy, you, and any friend or relative to whom you may lend it. And do not forget this, my song that goes with it, and which you are to sing when you put the bonnet on and face danger. However, your possession of the bonnet, just your having it near you, in your lodge, on your person or your horse when traveling, will itself protect you from the enemy."[11]

CHAPTER FIVE

THE LAND AND THE COSMOS

✶ ✶ ✶ ✶ ✶ ✶ ✶ ✶ ✶ ✶ ✶ ✶ ✶

Among the powers granted to medicine people were relationships with the land, the plants, and the elements. Over the generations, different tribes learned to coordinate their activities with the forces and entities of the natural world, and they produced an amazing knowledge of how the larger world functioned. Thus the Osage and Pawnee planted their corn and then moved the whole village westward in search of game. When a certain flower turned colors, they packed up their camp and the meat they had dried during the hunt and went back to their villages. When they arrived, their corn was ready for harvest. One could say that they had an intimate knowledge of the flora over a 500- to 600-mile radius, since they ensured that their activities were nicely dovetailed with what the plant people were doing in their growth and death cycle.

Stories abound in which certain plants talk to people or appear in dreams to inform humans of their uses. If this were not so, we would have to imagine that through tedious trial and error, knowledge of plants was formed. That may have worked for plants easily located, but what about plants that had no visible presence? How did the people know that they were there or that they were useful? John C. Cremony reported on the plant knowledge of Sons-in-Jah, an Apache who demonstrated that his tribe's knowledge quite easily encompassed all the plants of the immediate environment.

SONS-IN-JAH AND DESERT POTATOES

> There appeared to be no herbage whatever on the spot. The earth was completely bare, and my inexperienced eyes could detect nothing. Stopping down he dug with his knife, about six inches deep, and soon unearthed a small root about the size of a large gooseberry. "Taste that," said he; I did and found it excellent, somewhat resembling in flavor a raw sweet potato, but more palatable. He then pointed out to me a small dry stalk, not larger than an ordinary match, and about half as long. "Wherever you find these," he added, "you will find potatoes." This was in October, and a few days afterward the field was covered with Indians digging these roots, of which they obtained large quantities.[1]

There was another kind of knowledge, the province of the medicine people over and above the sophisticated plant knowledge shared by all members of the tribe, and if we cannot credit superior knowledge with an initial revelation to a medicine person, we can see in the stories presented below a special kind of knowledge about plants that manifested itself in spectacular fashion. This power enabled the medicine people to grow a kernal or seed to its full maturity in a matter of hours. This knowledge was apparently widespread, because we find stories about it in many tribal traditions.

MAKING PLANTS GROW

The first two selections come from the tradition of the Pawnee medicine lodge and were witnessed by many non-Indians who were allowed into the ceremony. Major Frank North, who organized the famous Pawnee scouts for the frontier army, personally testified to the truth of these accounts to George Bird Grinnell. The medicine lodge of the earth village people on the Missouri was extremely potent, and it served as a forum in which the Indian "doctors" could demonstrate their powers. Often, these displays involved competition between the doctors and were designed to enhance their reputations.

Thus, spectators were encouraged to come, and the contest was not a matter of belief or sleight of hand, but performing before a critical audience. If anyone claimed powers and could not appear and demonstrate them before the village, they would be disgraced beyond redemption. Thus, according to Grinnell's description:

THE PAWNEE CORN GROWERS

Major North told me that he saw with his own eyes the doctors make the corn grow. This was in the medicine lodge. In the middle of the lodge, the doctor dug up a piece of the hard trodden floor of the lodge, about as large as a dinner plate, and broke up between his fingers the hard pieces of soil, until the dirt was soft and friable. The ground having thus been prepared, and having been moistened with water, a few kernels of corn were buried in the loose earth. Then the doctor retired a little from the spot and sang, and as the place where the corn was buried was watched, the soil was seen to move, and a tiny green blade came slowly into view. This continued to increase in height and size, until in the course of twenty minutes or half an hour from the time of planting, the stalk or corn was a foot or fifteen inches in height. At this point Major North was obliged to leave the lodge, to take out a white woman who was fainting from the heat, and so did not see the maturing of the corn. All the Indians and white men who remained assured him that the stalks continued to grow until they were of full height, and that they then tasseled out and put forth one or more ears of corn, which grew to full size, and that then the doctor approached the plant, plucked an ear, and passed it to the spectators.[2]

The second account reported a fast growth of a wild plant, not a domesticated food plant, indicating that humans were able to move into the life cycle of any plant and change the tempo of its development. We often hear traditional people say that they must bring a gift when they harvest wild plants, that they must ask permission when they cut trees, take birch bark, and reach agreement with any plant to be harvested for a ceremony. Thus, Grinnell reported:

GROWING THE CEDAR BERRY

Similar to this [growing the corn] was a feat performed with a cedar berry. The berry was passed around among the spectators for examination, and was then planted as the corn had been. Then after a few moments the doctor approached the spot, put his thumb and forefinger down into the soft dirt and seemed to lay hold of something. Very slowly he raised his hand and was seen to hold on the tips of his fingers the end of a cedar twig. Slowly his hand was moved from the ground, the twig growing longer and longer. When nine or ten inches high it began to have side branches. The doctor still holding the topmost twig of what was by this time a cedar bush, continued to lift his hand very slowly, until it was about three feet from the ground, and then let go of the bush. Then presently he took hold of the stem close to the ground and, seeming to exert a good deal of force, pulled up the bush by the roots and all the people saw the bush and its bunch of fresh and growing roots.[3]

THE PAWNEE BLIND MAN

The Pawnees, at the time Grinnell visited them, had a blind man who could only see at night. This condition was not seen as a handicap, since he could detect anything, friendly or not, that might approach the camp and surprise people. At one of the sessions during which the Pawnee doctors demonstrated their powers, this blind man showed that he had special powers not to be regarded lightly.

One of the wonderful things done by this man was at a medicine dance. Everybody was there. He stood up with his bearskin over him, and was led out before the people. A cedar branch was given him, and he sharpened the end where it had been cut off, and stuck it in the ground. Everybody was now asked to pull up this branch, and many tried to do so, but the strongest men in the tribe could not move it. He could pull it up, as if it were stuck in the mud. He thrust the pointed end in the ground again, and asked the doctors to pull up the cedar branch. They tried to do so, but could not stir it. The chiefs were also asked to try to do this. They tried, but could not move it. Something seemed to hold it in the ground.

After everybody present had tried to pull it up, and failed, this blind man went to it, and taking hold of it, pulled with all his strength, and pulled up with it about six feet of roots. There lay the tree with all its roots fresh and growing.[4]

PLENTY FINGERS FEEDS HIS CHILDREN

The power of one of the most remarkable Crow medicine men is recorded in Robert H. Lowie's *The Religion of the Crow Indians*. Where we have no additional information on the breadth of the powers to make plants grow possessed by the spiritual people, our data on Plenty Fingers seems complete, and the man could apparently feed not only his family, but much of the camp as well. Here, because of the variety of fruits and foods, we have a potential commissary. The discussion starts with Plenty Fingers's concern to satisfy his children.

One winter one of these children wanted some berries. Plenty-fingers told them to get him the limb of a cherry tree. When they had brought it, he stuck it into the ground in front of himself, covered himself up and made medicine. When he had removed the blanket the tree was full of cherries, which the children ate. One of the boys wanted plums and in similar fashion he produced plums. Some of the girls would long for wild turnips in the winter time. He would dig in the ground with his fingers, take some out, and give them to his children. He could also produce sarvis-berries and other berries in the winter. When people had no meat, they would go to Plenty-fingers and ask him for some. He would order them to get the bark of a tree, cover himself and the bark with a blanket, and when he was done the bark was turned into dry meat, which was given to everyone to satisfy their hunger. He would similarly transform driftwood into animal intestines.[5]

Charles Lummis, a well-known personality of the Southwest in the 1890s, reported on two different Navajo demonstrations of their power with the corn. One described the familiar pattern of making the corn kernel grow to full maturity quickly. The other feat involved distributing the seeds of many plants in a ritual in which the corn revealed itself as the basic plant with other plants, through their seeds, derived from corn. Unfortunately, Lummis used very derogatory terms in characterizing the medicine men, calling them magicians and jugglers and doubting that they had these powers. He nevertheless admitted that he could not explain how they were able to accomplish these feats.

NAVAJO CORN GROWERS

At sunrise the shaman plants the enchanted kernel before him, in full view of his audience, and sits solemnly in his place, singing a weird song. Presently the earth cracks, and the tender green shoot pushes forth. As the magician sings on the young plant grows visibly, reaching upward several inches an hour, waxing thick and putting out its dropping blades. If the juggler stops his song the growth of the corn stops, and is resumed only when he recommences his chant. By noon the corn is tall and vigorous and already tasseled out, and by sunset it is a mature and perfect plant, with its tall stalk sedgy leaves, and silk-topped ears of corn! How the trick is performed I have never been able to form so much as a satisfactory guess;

but done it is, as plainly as eyes ever saw anything done, and apparently with as little chance for deception.[6]

NAVAJO SEED GIVING

Early in the spring, the Navajos would perform a special ceremony to determine how their crops would do in the year ahead. They would send three medicine men to the Rio Grande at a time when no plants had yet emerged from their winter hibernation. In a ritual conducted on the banks of the river, they would be given green corn and wheat stalks to bring back to the assembled audience in the medicine hogan used for ceremonies. A senior medicine man would examine the stalks and predict the anticipated harvest in the fall. Then, according to what Lummis was able to understand, they performed this ceremony of the seeds.

> The last service of the medicine-dance before the benediction-song is the "seed-giving," which is itself a sleight-of-hand trick. The chief fetich of the shamans is "the Mother"—an ear of spotless white corn with a plume of downy white feathers bound to the head. It represents the mother of all mankind, and during the whole medicine-dance one of these queer objects has been sitting in front of each medicine-man. Now, as all in the audience rise, the chief shaman and his assistants shake their "Mothers" above the heads of the throng in token of blessing; and out pours a perfect shower of kernels of corn, wheat, and seeds of all kinds, in a vastly greater quantity than I would undertake to hide in ten times as many of those little tufts.[7]

This power was apparently obtained from the Pueblos after the Navajos came into the southwestern area near them. William E. Curtis, also an astute observer of Indian rituals, writing a report to the *Boise Daily Statesman* newspaper, gave the important explanation of the ceremony that Lummis apparently did not know. There often are people who accurately report a ceremony or feat without knowing the basic reason the Indians are performing these specific rituals. Curtis noted that this ceremony was called "seed grass," and its primary function was to predict the approximate size of the harvests once the seeds were planted in the spring.

PUEBLO SEED GRASS CEREMONY

It is celebrated at the planting season, and the result is interpretive as a prediction of the success or failure of the harvest. If the trick fails, as it sometimes does, the whole community goes into mourning and takes measures to intercede that the tribe may not starve. When the worshippers are gathered in the estufa one of the priests shells an ear of white corn into a blanket. It must be a perfect ear. The more perfect the better the results. Then, after two or three hours of chanting, dancing and incantations, at a signal to the chief priest all present arise and direct their gaze upon the blanket, which all this time has been lying folded in the center of the group.

No hand has touched it. It has not been interfered with in any way, but when it is opened it is found to contain a bushel or more of different kinds of seeds—corn, wheat, beans, peas, watermelon and other seeds used by the Indians in their gardens. The quantity indicates the comparative volume of the harvest. There may be an abundance of corn and very few beans, or wheat may be plenty and corn scarce. Sometimes the blanket will contain two or three bushels of seeds which by some mysterious process have been evolved from the handful of white corn that was originally concealed in the folds of the blanket.[8]

Now, say what we will, many different seeds, all essential to the Navajo agricultural practices, cannot come from an ear of white corn as a rule. Nor can medicine men hide the great variety of seeds that this ritual produces. Whenever we try to visualize these feats of the medicine men, we must remember that these people are within feet of their audience and usually wear very few clothes so as not to be accused of a sleight-of-hand trick. It would take but one season of nonproductive crops to discredit this ritual and the men who performed it. Casting aside Lummis's skepticism as seen in his characterization of the medicine men, we can say that he has preserved the essence of an agricultural ritual for our edification.

The New York Times reported a more recent instance in which the spiritual elders were able to change the rate of the passage of time for another entity. This talent has been reported in other parts of the world, and it has always been inexplicable to secular observers. I am told that medicine men in other tribes, particularly the southwestern tribes, have this gift today, that it always takes several men working together because the occasion is so special. I am unable, however, to find a more modern description or observation of this ritual. We can only hope *The New York Times* was more accurate in its reporting in 1922 than it is today.

ZUNI CORN GROWERS

Preparation is made for this extraordinary Zuni performance by spreading a large square of clean yellowish sand on the ground before the southern aperture of the medicine lodge. This sand is carefully smoothed and packed so as to present a firm level surface. Around the edges of the sand square are then drawn, by means of a ceremonial arrow, figures representing the Great Spirit, the earth, the sun, the sky, and the rain. There are also the symbols for corn and for a bountiful harvest. The indentations made by the arrow are then filled in with pigments, the clouds and sky with blue, the earth with black, and the harvest with chrome yellow. The centre of the square is left vacant. When completed, this sand paining is a fine specimen of barbaric art, and is far from displeasing to a civilized eye.

When the hour arrives, the officiating medicine man takes his seat in the opening of the lodge facing the sand square. On his right and left, extending out around the square, the chiefs and warriors range themselves according to rank. When all are in position, the medicine man fills the ceremonial pipe with tobacco, lights it, and blows one puff of smoke to the east, one to the west, one to the north, one to the south, and two to the heavens. He then addresses those assembled, recounting the religious history of the tribe, its wanderings and famine, and the benevolence of the Great Spirit in the past. He closes with a prayer for the continuance of fatherly care.

Then he takes a grain of corn from the medicine bag at his waist, thrusts the sacred arrow into the centre of the sand square, withdraws it, drops the grain into the opening, and carefully smoothes down the sand. Resuming his seat, all the assembled chiefs light their pipes and smoke in silence. If the Great Spirit condescends to answer the prayer of the medicine man, as generally happens, the grain of corn will sprout and send forth a shoot. After an interval of fifteen or twenty minutes the sand seems undisturbed at the spot where the corn was buried.

Soon slender light green blades of sprouting corn appear above the surface. The plant rises naturally and rapidly during the day. By the next sunrise the silk and tassel appear. By noon the ear and stalk have reached full maturity. Then the ripening begins. Finally the blades and husks turn yellow and rattle when they are shaken by the wind. All this, mind you, has been done in thirty-six hours. On the morning of the second day the corn growing is complete. The medicine man now addresses the "watchers," who in company have "watched" the plant grow, for it is never left alone. With appropriate ceremonies he symbolizes the harvest by stripping the ear of its husks. The corn he places in the medicine bag for future ceremonies, while the stalk is pulled up by the roots and hung over the door of the lodge. The long vigil of the watchers is now ended and they seek much needed rest and food in order to be ready for the rain dances on the following day.

Every white man witnessing one of these ceremonies is deeply mystified. Above all, he is filled with admiration for the old medicine man. So natural and mysterious has been the process that the spectator feels at times disposed to believe in the presence of some supernatural power. Yet every sane person knows that this performance has nothing unnatural about it. No white man, however, has discovered the secret. The absence of stage paraphernalia and the crude mechanical knowledge of the Zunis add to the mystery of the whole thing. Various theories have been advanced in explanation. One is that some shrewd old medicine man discovered by accident some peculiar natural chemical that has the power of forcing the growth of a grain of corn and that this secret has been handed down from one generation of priests to another.

Another favorite explanation is that by great skill the medicine man is able to hypnotize the entire circle of spectators and produce the result without apparatus of any kind save a yellow stalk of corn from the last harvest.[9]

It is rather humorous to read the commentary and explanations given by the non-Indian reporter. He told us one would almost think something sacred had occurred. He was unable to explain what he had seen. Carrying over a stalk of corn from the previous year's ceremony and finding a way to sneak it into the hogan seems to be quite a stretch, because that stalk would be dried and brittle after a year out of the ground. Crediting the medicine men with the ability to hypnotize the crowd of onlookers seems even more unlikely. If a crowd of people can be that easily hypnotized, the real feat here would be mesmerizing the crowd to see whatever you wanted them to see, and that is a power not lightly bestowed.

CHANGES IN THE WEATHER

One of the most frequently reported feats of medicine men is their ability to change the weather. Newspaper reporters delight in covering stories where, after dancing, the Indians made it rain, and the Hopi snake dance has been written up many times by scholars who have observed this phenomenon. But skeptics accusing medicine men of fraud are also plentiful. Critics argue that the rain and the dance are mere coincidence. Some critics suggest that the medicine man has a profound knowledge of clouds and times his dance so that a rain, coming anyway, appears to have some relationship with the dance. Sometimes, indeed, the rain doesn't come. There seem to be no good parameters to judge this phenomenon. The concentration on the one aspect of producing rain, the most spectacular feat, hides the scope of the wide variety of powers exercised by medicine men in regard to thunder, clouds, and rain.

A closer examination of the different stories of rainmaking suggests that there is much more involved in the medicine man's ability to produce rain and control weather. I believe this topic can be subdivided into three distinct parts: 1.) when a medicine man is asked directly to produce rain during a drought or dry spell; 2.) when people know that rain, often torrents of rain, will fall without any ceremonial initiative on the part of the human, and they ask the medicine man to change the course of a storm to avoid injury to the camp; and 3.) where medicine men engage in a contest to demonstrate their power or cause changes in the weather to escape conflict or assist them in their ventures.

In the first case, the power to bring rain resides in the special songs and dances given the spiritual elder in a vision or dream and upon which he can call to demonstrate his power. In the second case, the spirits, most often the spirits of a particular location, seem to control the rainmaking, and humans know the consequences of their actions. In the last instance, weather becomes an arena through which spiritual powers give relief to people who would not ordinarily be granted others. Generally, these events give testimony to the presence of a larger universe that supersedes our physical world yet imposes certain limits on us as we pursue our daily lives. Most often, if someone violates a particular prohibition, rain and bad weather will most certainly follow. At other times, the rain appears as a positive thing, allowing us to enter into the place without retribution. There must certainly be many other elements involved here since some stories relate how the weather has changed as we have moved from world to world in the course of earth history. Later in this collection, we will examine the unbelievable powers of the Navajo medicine men to create a complete, if small, thunderstorm.

Bringing Rain

Let us examine first a story that seems to fulfill our impression about how medicine men produced rain. We start with a need for rain and the medicine man's response. The practitioner does a ceremony and rain falls—at least within a short time afterward. We are, unfortunately, not told the condition of the sky when this appeal is made, so there is no way to answer the criticism that the medicine man only performs this ritual when it appears that there would be rain anyway. The only argument we have is that if it appeared cloudy and contained the possibility of rain, no one would ask the medicine man to assist them.

Chiricahua Apache Ceremony

In *An Apache Lifeway*, Morris Opler reported on the Chiricahua ceremony for bringing rain that seems typical of the powers found in the people of many tribes.

> There is a ceremony to bring rain when it is very dry. Then we get rain by calling on White Painted Woman and Child of the Water. The world is White Painted Woman. The thunder is the Child of the Water. Sand, a whitish sand from Old Mexico, is used in this ceremony to call the rain. It is blown to the four directions. Also Lightning is called on when the sand is blown, and a blowing noise, "hoo, hoo!" is made. In the prayer there is mention of the number of days it should rain.[10]

The Unfortunate Mexican

Herbert Lehmann, a captive of the Apaches for many years, reported on a less than benign practice for bringing rain with, incidentally, dire consequences for the Apaches.

Once I knew of them [the Apaches] vainly trying, but the drought continued, so the medicine man came into camp and placed the blame on a Mexican who was staying with us. This Mexican was firmly bound, hand and foot, with rawhide, and carried away upon the mountain and bound to a flat rock, and near him was staked a large rattlesnake. The snake was placed just near enough to strike the Mexican whenever he moved. We returned to camp and the incantations were repeated and there came a regular waterspout. Our wigwams were washed away, one white child captive was drowned, several horses went down in the raging torrent which rushed down the arroyo on which our camp was situated, and we had to flee to the mountain for safety."[11]

This story suggested that the petition for rain was once dependent on human sacrifice, since we do not hear of the ultimate fate of the Mexican. It seems to me a rather extreme way of bringing rain.

When I lived near the Lummi Reservation, just west of Bellingham, Washington, I was told that the Lummis had a rain dance. That part of Washington state receives an ungodly amount of rain during the year, and one is tempted to look for webs on the feet of the people. Why on earth they would need a rain dance baffled me until they explained its use. Some years, the cold coming down from Alaska overcomes the warmth brought by the Japanese current, and instead of raining, it snows for a long time—it covers everything to an incredible depth. If the snows are too deep and cover the longhouses, people are trapped inside and die of starvation and sometimes even suffocation. So the Lummi rain dance was performed as the snow was falling and began to accumulate to a hazardous depth. On those occasions, a tribal member possessing the power to make rain performs a ceremony and sings a song that changes the snow into rain and melts the snow on the ground, relieving the Lummis from danger. I was told that this power was passed down within one family over the centuries, and that while it might not be used in a generation, it was necessary always to maintain that power lest the snow overtake them in an unfortunate year. The ability to change weather thus has a useful social purpose.

CHANGING THE NATURE OF A STORM

By far, the most frequent reports suggested that a storm's path, progress, and severity can be changed by a medicine man. Almost every tribe had people who had the thunder power and could alter the effects of a storm. John R. Swanton reported the traditions of the Alabama tribe in Texas in a summary of incidents. These stories were, at the time Swanton gathered them, memories of the olden days and, since no medicine man is named, had become part of the legends of the tribe.

THE TEXAS ALABAMA TRADITION

The Texas Alabama tell of a prophet who stopped rain by fasting and putting medicine on the water of a creek. Another stopped a storm which was brought on when his companion shot a buzzard, mistaking it for a turkey. On another occasion some people were in the middle of a lake and were surrounded on all sides by enemies who had lighted fires all about on the banks so that they could not escape during the night. However, a prophet among the people in the water made it rain, thereby putting out the fires, and enabling them to get through the lines of their enemy. Still another prophet brought on rain in the following manner. He sent a boy out to catch fish, and when they were brought he dived within them to the bottom of a creek and gave them to certain long, horned snakes living there which go under both the water and land.[12]

Swanton also reported on the ability of an Alabama medicine man to change the nature of a storm: "When a storm was coming up an Alabama doctor would blow into his clasped hands, rub them together, and then wave them upward and outward. Then, even if it rained, the wind would not blow. The same person claimed to be able to cause rain or drought."[13] Eliminating the wind would be a most useful power almost anywhere Indians lived.

WOODEN LEG'S STORY

Wooden Leg, a Cheyenne elder, related how the medicine men of his band demonstrated their power over the weather to educate the young men regarding the great mysterious power that made everything possible—including the power of humans to participate in a changing of the weather on certain occasions.

> Three medicine men invited some of us young men into a tepee on one certain occasion when I was about fourteen or fifteen years old. They said: "We will show you how to make the winter go away so that the grass may grow, for the good of the young colts coming to our herds." Just at that time there was a big snowstorm making the people and the horses shiver. But the three medicine men went confidently at their ceremony.
>
> They sent a young woman out to gather some certain kinds of sprigs of vegetation. It was not tobacco, but pretty soon the medicine men had it changed into tobacco. They formed a circle around us, loaded the pipe, and soon it was passing from one to another. To each of us in turn they said: "Draw in only a little of the smoke, but draw it in slowly and deeply. Hold it there a short time then let it flow out from wide open lips not in puffs from firm lips." We did as they directed. While the smoking was being done the three old men made prayers. After a while one of them said: "Look outside." We looked. The storm had quit, the sky had cleared, the ground was wet but bare of snow, green grass was peeking up everywhere.[14]

LAST HORSE'S MIRACLE

Luther Standing Bear, an Oglala Sioux, reported a feat performed by Last Horse at the Rosebud Agency after the people had settled on the reservation there. His story is typical—perhaps archetypical—of similar accounts that can be found in the oral traditions of many other tribes. As Standing Bear told it:

> In 1878 I saw Last Horse perform one of his miracles. Some of my band, the Oglalas, went to visit the Brule band and by way of entertainment preparations were made for a dance and feast. The day was bright and beautiful, and everyone was dressed in feathers and painted buck-skin. But a storm came up suddenly, threatening to disrupt the gathering, so of course there was much unhappiness as the wind began to blow harder and the rain began to fall. Last Horse walked into his tipi and disrobed, coming out wearing only breechclout and moccasins. His hair streamed down his back and in his hand he carried his rattle. Walking slowly to the center of the village he raised his face to the sky and sang his Thunder songs, which commanded the clouds to part. Slowly but surely, under the magic of the song, the clouds parted and the sky was clear once more.[15]

These accounts are typical of many tribal stories wherein medicine men are prevailed upon to intervene and prevent bad weather from disrupting human activities. Again, we can argue that this event is a happy coincidence; however, this explanation leveled against all exercises of spiritual power begins to wear thin when cited for every skeptical thought. We cannot always have these kinds of coincidence when medicine men perform feats and at no other time. We have no way of knowing, apart from the testimony of those present, whether these events are coincidence or not, but certainly the presence of the medicine man changed the manner in which events happened. People do not otherwise change the paths and nature of thunderstorms.

THE BLACKFEET MEDICINE MEN CONTEST

Walter McClintock, in his book *The Old North Trail*, related an experience he had while living with the Blackfeet of Montana. Two medicine men, Mastepene and Spotted Eagle, decided to test their powers one day, as was frequently their custom. McClintock observed the contest, and his dramatic account demonstrated how special powers were often used to remind the people that there was something greater than the forces of nature they saw daily.

A dark cloud, with its eastern side extending far out over the plains, was seen slowly advancing along the main range of the Rockies towards the encampment. The people anxiously watched the medicine men, who were quick to realize that the occasion had great possibilities of success, or failure for their office. Spotted Eagle and Mastepene standing in front of their people, entered into a sort of competition as weathermakers, but with much better success than the competing prophets of Baal. Mastepene, blowing his whistle and facing the black cloud, called in a loud voice:

"Behold! A storm comes from the mountains and you people would get wet, but I am powerful and my medicine is strong. I will now dance to keep the weather clear."

He left the booth, and stepping forth into the circle danced, circling around with agile step, he held an otter skin towards the north, south, east and west which, with a final gesture, as if driving back the clouds, he waved over his head. A sudden change in the wind averted its course and it divided, as Mastepene predicted. Spotted Eagle, jealous of the success of his rival, then left the booth. He wore the powerful medicine handed down to him by Four Bears. On his head was an otter-skin cap to make him strong and active; in his hair an eagle feather to preserve him in battle; while around his waist was a medicine belt to keep his body free from sickness. In one hand he carried a magpie and in the other a mink skin. Standing before the waiting people, he said, "Mastepene, you are wrong, for my supernatural power over the weather comes from the Sun, and is therefore stronger than yours. The storm has indeed separated, but it will again unite and return to west the people." Again the eyes of the Indians eagerly watched the divided clouds, which actually came together and continued to spread until they passed over the encampment with a heavy rain.[16]

It is not difficult to argue that we have two experienced observers of the weather making predictions as valid as our evening news reporters. The event apparently impressed the people in the camp and McClintock, although we cannot vouch for his willingness to be impressed or deceived. However, if the event is taken seriously in an Indian context, what does it tell us? First, that not all the use of medicine powers was devoted to the serious business of securing a better life for the people. Medicine men can occasionally use some powers to demonstrate their status in the tribe and in competition with other medicine men. Second, we can perhaps identify a hierarchy of powers in the spirit world. Mastepene apparently relied on his ordinary powers, and these were sufficient to divide the storm. Spotted Eagle's powers were not derivative, since they came directly from the sun. But did enlisting the additional entities turn the tide? Did the mink, magpie, and eagle feather together give him the edge? These considerations must be examined before any final understanding of the phenomenon is possible.

FULFILLING BIG BEAR'S REQUEST

Ernest Wallace and E. Adamson Hoebel recounted a story of relatively modern times with a twinge of humor in their book on the Comanches. The basic theme of the story is that when we ask for something, we should be very careful to specify exactly what we want. This event occurred during the early reservation days but was still a topic of conversation when they interviewed the Comanches.

The rain-making medicine of Big Bear called for the use of an outside tall feather of a black eagle. With his power it was necessary only to dip the feather into water and sprinkle towards the sun four times. "A cloud will soon appear and shortly it will rain." Big Bear overdid it once when living in a tipi northeast of Cache, Oklahoma. He made medicine for a rain with some wind in it. Came a cloud. It grew bigger. Then came rain and a big wind that blew his tipi down. His wife got after him for not asking for a nice soft rain.[17]

ENLISTING THE WEATHER AS AN AID

It seems only natural that medicine men would use their powers in warfare, since much of their work involved looking into the future to predict the outcome of proposed ventures. We have seen that animals frequently told them of events ahead or warned them of danger. There are a goodly number of stories on how the ability to change the weather led to practical success, and they cover some unusual events that might seem unlikely, but nevertheless occurred. We begin with a clear instance of this power.

THE SIN'-O-PAH WEATHER CONTROL

Grinnell related how a certain band of the Blackfeet possessed the power to change the weather to protect them during warfare. This power would seem to be unique in that the major spirits of the winds, thunders, and directions would not ordinarily take sides whenever a dispute between two tribes occurred. More likely, the power they exercised was simply to help them escape perilous situations, and in that sense, they could call upon higher powers.

> People who belonged to the Sin'-o-pah band of the I-kun-uh'-kah-tsi, if they were at war in summer and wanted a storm to come up, would take some dirt and water and rub it on the kit-fox skin, and this would cause a rain-storm to come up. In winter, snow and dirt would be rubbed on the skin and this would bring up a snow-storm.[18]

We have no idea how often this power was used, but presumably only on rare occasions.

The Gros Ventres had a similar story, in which changing the weather served to protect them from a band of Sioux. In this story, a Ghost Helper had predicted the outcome of a raid made by the Gros Ventres against the Sioux.

> Having tried to steal some ponies from the Sioux, the Gros Ventres found themselves hard pressed to escape once the ire of the Sioux was aroused. So they called on Morning-Star-Appeared to cause such weather that the Sioux could not catch them. He sang his song, using his robe to enclose himself, and said: "We wish rain." At once a cloud appeared and in a short time grew into a great black storm cloud; then came a perfect cloudburst, with thunder and lightning, in which you couldn't see any distance. Under this cover the Gros Ventres escaped from the pursuing Sioux and got back to camp safely with no loss of life, although two of their number had had narrow escapes, just as the Ghost Helper had said.[19]

CHIRICAHUA STORM MEDICINE

A Chiricahua medicine man admitted to Opler that he had powers to change the atmosphere significantly.

> I have a ceremony which, if carried out on the desert would cause a sandstorm. But this would be uncomfortable for the people, and so I dislike to do it. It is a prayer. I used it when men were going to make a raid for horses so that they would get away without being detected. I throw sand into the air, blow against it four times, say the prayer, and it causes sand to blow around so thick that you can't see.[20]

Ruffled Feathers Calms the Waters

There are many stories about medicine men calming otherwise rough waters, sometimes by merely speaking to the wind or water, other times offering tobacco, as we will see in the story below. While this power does not strictly fall into the category of changing the weather, since calming the waters depends in large part on changing the effect of the wind on the waters, it is most appropriate here. Ruffled Feathers, an Ojibwa, performed this feat.

> In his youth he had a dream of smooth, quiet water, and he related an incident when the power given him in that dream enabled him to appeal to the Spirit of the Water. He was traveling with a party of Indians in northern Minnesota. When they reached a certain river they found the water too rough for them to cross. Someone asked: "Does anyone know how to treat with the Spirit of the water?" Niski'gwun volunteered for the task, strewed tobacco on the water, and made his appeal. In half an hour the wind veered, the water became smooth, and the Indians went on their way.[21]

Rain as an Affirmation of a Blessing

The temptation to regard ourselves as the ultimate actor in the physical universe is quickly put to rest when we hear these things, and we always need to approach the larger spiritual world with some degree of humility, a commodity in scarce supply. We must always ask why phenomena happen when medicine men are present, and why, in the ordinary course of events, they do not happen as a regular part of planetary activity.

We can begin our examination of the spontaneous appearance of rain as an affirmation of a blessing with a simple reminder of old Black Elk standing on Harney Peak in the Black Hills of South Dakota, raising his pipe, and praying. He had informed John Neihardt that if his prayer was sincere, there should be some rain as an acknowledgment by the spirits. And, of course, a few drops fell, sufficient to comfort the old man and validate his understanding of his life's mission, meaning, and experiences. We can interpret the rain as an affirmation of Black Elk's vision, or we can view the incident as confirming the sacredness of Harney Peak that served, on occasion, to represent the center of the world.

THE OLD HUNKPAPA SIOUX CHIEF

Stanley Vestal, a popular writer who devoted a good deal of his writing to the people at Standing Rock, particularly Sitting Bull and his relatives, reported an incident in which he was involved that gives evidence of the great powers these old men possessed. Out on the reservation, collecting stories from the local people, Vestal, for some reason, devoted his efforts to getting an old man to tell the story of his vision and its subsequent realization, a sharing that few medicine men would endorse. Finally, the old man, to be polite, succumbed to Vestal's pleadings. As Vestal remembered:

> Though the chief had promised to tell me the full story of his life, he was somewhat reluctant to relate this vision, and requested that I hear it when there was no one else in the cabin. *He explained that, whenever he told this story, a fierce thunderstorm followed,* and therefore he told it very seldom. The old man does not see well and is rather deaf. He told the story at four o'clock in the afternoon. He had been sitting with his back to the north wall of the cabin, inside, and the sky was cloudless. We finished the conference at seven o'clock that evening and had supper. By that time thunder-clouds had piled up in the northwest, and my interpreter pointed out certain features of the clouds which indicated a storm about to break. Immediately after supper, a terrific thunder-storm burst upon us. The cloud was small and swept out of the north directly for my cabin, where the story had been told. No rain fell on the adjacent cabins with a few yards on either side, *but the wind was so strong that I had to move my car to keep it from rolling over the bluff.* The Chief made no comment on this

appalling fulfillment of his prediction. He took the storm for granted.[22] (Emphasis added)

CHAPTER SIX

Sacred Stones and Places

★ ★ ★ ★ ★ ★ ★ ★ ★ ★ ★ ★ ★

Sacred Stones

One of the most prevalent entities in the traditional Indian spiritual universe was the sacred stone. Almost every tribe had its own understanding of the important role stones play in the physical/spiritual universe. The largest stones, of course, are the mountains. They often represent the center of the universe or the center of each nation's hoop, as Black Elk discovered, and in this sense, they provide a cosmic perspective that the people must always keep in mind. Sacred mountains also have certain powers, and some rock formations, such as Spider Woman Rock in Chaco Canyon, the Bear's Lodge (Devils Tower) in Wyoming, or Mount Shasta in California, provide an empirical verification of the ancient stories of origins and previous worlds. Some mountains are revered as places of emergence into this world, while others sustain life, such as the Blue Lake of Taos Pueblo in New Mexico.

The Menominees of Wisconsin have a stone located near their reservation that is supposed to mark their tribal longevity. Tradition has it that the rock was once very prominent at the beginning of the world, and when it has worn down to nothing or fragments apart, there will be no more Menominees. Spirits inhabit many mountains and are sometimes seen by medicine men, and Bear Butte in South Dakota is a place where the Cheyennes received their holy objects. Among other tribes, certain rocks have spirits that can bestow good fortune, and even special powers, when approached with the proper respect.

THE PICTURE ROCKS

There are also stones that give forewarning of events to come. Early in the morning, medicine men come to view the stones, and on them are visible a preview of the events to come, often events of the immediate day and sometimes things that may occur in the next week or so. Generally, these stones are large, immovable granite erratics that are found at many places on the northern Plains. They can be almost buried in the earth but must have some surface area showing on which prophecy pictures appear. Some rocky cliffs have the same powers. John Neihardt, apparently quoting an unnamed Indian, listed the messages of picture rocks as one of the four most important ways that Indians foretold the future. "There is a place in the Black Hills, also on the Little Big Horn, a bank of solid rock where there are inscriptions that only a medicine man can read. It is a mystery. There is one in the Black Hills that only a medicine man can read (pictograph). We don't know who wrote it, but a medicine man can decode it and get the meaning. We would camp and when we would come back there would be more writing."[1]

BLACK ELK

The Deer Rocks in Montana are well known as a location where tableaus of future events have appeared and been read by spiritual elders. In the Neihardt interviews, published in *The Sixth Grandfather*, Black Elk remembered how the bands were scattering after the Battle of the Little Big Horn. They passed by Deer Rocks, and he said:

> Next we stopped at a sacred place where a big rock bluff was. The Indians claim that before the Custer fight the whole thing was pictured on it. No man could possibly get up to where the picture is. Things are foretold here always. When there was a man hanging down headfirst, why something will probably happen that year. And a year before the Custer fight

there was a bunch of soldiers with their heads hanging down pictured on this bluff. The rock is called Rock Writing Bluff. This rock stands right next to the water on the Rosebud. Here we camped and the drawing of the Custer fight was still there and other people also saw it.[2]

There are several of these cliffs in the Black Hills that were used by the people for a long time. By some coincidence, several frequently visited picture rocks were included inside several reservation boundaries when they were established, relieving people of going off the reservation where they would be disturbed. Night spirits are said to create the scenarios found on the rocks, and, presumably, over time, they give a continuing preview of events to come so that medicine men, remembering the previous messages, can properly read them whenever they appear.

INCIDENT AT CANNON BALL

A. McG. Beede, an Episcopal missionary on the Standing Rock Reservation in 1919, reported on an incident with a sacred picture stone that he could not explain and generally supported the Indian interpretation of the event.

A rock of this kind was formerly on Medicine Hill near Cannon Ball Sub-station. Some years ago we were assembled, three hundred tents, for a religious gathering at St. James Church, half a mile from this rock. Old Indians came to me, at about 9 o'clock A.M., and said that the lightning would strike somebody in camp that day, for a picture (wowapi) on this holy rock indicated such an event. The picture had appeared while the dew was on the rock (as such pictures do always appear, if at all), but they did not tell me until 9 o'clock. And the lightning did strike a tent in camp and nearly kill a woman (whose name I now forget), at about 4 o'clock P.M. I poured into her mouth a little consecrated wine, at the request of the Indians, while they silently prayed, and the woman recovered. I have known several similar things, equally foretelling events to come. I can not account for it.[3]

There is a possible explanation of how the inscriptions are made on the rocks; it comes from a Blackfoot source. An old woman told this story many years ago, and Ella E. Clark included it in *Indian Legends from the Northern Rockies*. She said that birds, directed by the spirit of the place, do the actual sketching of the pictures. This explanation means, however, that the spirit of a place has access to the larger cosmic time sequence; hence, if true, it enhances our conception of the power of the spirits of sacred places.

OLD MANDAN'S PICTURE ROCK

My father, Old Man Mandan, told me about the cliff. When he was a boy, he went there and slept at the foot of it, hoping to have his dream vision. For two nights he did not dream anything or see anything.

The third night, a man came to him in his dream and said to him, "My boy, why are you here?"

"I am staying here," the boy answered, "because I hope that some spirit will give me power. I want a spirit to give me power so that I may become a brave warrior some day."

"That is good," the man answered. "I am the spirit of this place. You shall get your wish, if you stay here one more night. In the morning you will see all of my children. They are the ones that make the pictures on the Writing Stone. We know what is going to happen ahead of time, and my children draw the pictures that tell what is going to happen."

So my father slept at the bottom of the cliff another night. When he woke up early in the morning, he looked at the stone. At first he did not see anything. The second time he looked, he saw many little birds of every color fly from above and light on the cliff. Some of them were blue, some red, some yellow. They were pretty birds of all colors.

My father sat there and watched them for a long time, as they were doing something on the rock. After they had finished the whole flock darted up at once and flew away. He did not see the birds again during the day, but when he looked at the cliff, he found new pictures.

Then my father knew that the man who had spoken to him was a bird. The boy stayed there all night and slept there a fourth night.

That night the man came to him again and said, "My boy, I have come to give you my power to become a brave warrior. In the days to come, you will be a great warrior and a chief. You will also have the power to heal the sick, and the power to know ahead of time what is going to happen."

"You have seen my children, the birds. In the days to come, you will have as many horses as there are birds in that flock. Your horses will be many colors. Remember that I like to help people and that you are the kind of person I like to help. Whenever you need anything, call on me. I give you many powers." ... The pictures on the rock tell the future. In the old days, before a war party started on a raid, the men went to the cliff and looked at the pictures. If anyone saw his own picture there, he knew that he would be killed.[4]

SWEAT LODGE STONES

In the old traditional way, stones to be used in a sweat lodge ceremony were gathered in a special way. When a medicine man went in search of stones, he wandered around telling the stones that he was going to hold the ceremony and asking different stones if they wished to participate. George Tinker told of helping a medicine man to gather stones and said that instead of simply taking the available stones nearby, he had to canvass the whole field to find the proper stones, a good distance from the car in which they were to be hauled. Following the ceremony, the stones are always returned to their original location, since it is their home.

Medicine Stones

Let us now turn to the small rocks that spiritual leaders use in exercising their powers. These stones have many thrilling stories of their own and are much more important in the daily lives of people than the sacred mountains and the picture rocks. In the Southwest, the holy men and healers use a variety of stones and crystals to diagnoses illnesses, perform healings, and retrieve lost things. We find mention of two kinds of sacred stones in the northern Plains: small, round stones found on top of buttes and fossil bones that have some kind of residual spiritual powers. These are the stones used in rituals that perform tasks for the medicine men.

These stones are usually about golf-ball size, round, and earth-colored. They are especially created by the thunders, have immense knowledge and special powers, and yet willingly serve medicine men by performing services that do not have time and space limitations. This stone is regarded as the most perfect form of life, since it has a physical integrity in itself and needs no other forms of relationships. Lame Deer explained the belief quite well: "A medicine stone is a perfect work of Wakan Tanka, the Great Spirit. It is made up of one kind of matter only. Its surface has no beginning and no end. Its power lasts forever."[5] Indeed, the principal spirit in the Sioux creation story is Inyan, the stone, who sacrifices his body by causing it to shrink and dispersing energy to create the universe.

The stones are found on the top of buttes, usually immediately after thunderstorms. The requirement in obtaining a stone is that it must be completely free from the soil on which it rests. Its independence from the earth is taken as a sign that it is ready for a human relationship. Any stone that is even partially covered by earth must not be touched, or dire circumstances will follow for the miscreant. This prohibition of picking up a stone has some interesting implications. If people are restricted to taking only the freestanding independent stones, wouldn't the supply of them have been exhausted centuries ago? That one could now find independent stones available for use by the medicine men seems highly unlikely. Nevertheless, contemporary medicine men continue to find them. They are said to be produced by the thunders and have the thunder powers. This belief that the thunders create the stones must have some spiritual substance, or the supply would have been exhausted thousands of years ago.

HORN CHIPS'S STONES

We have already noted that Horn Chips was one of the most powerful medicine men of the last century. He used his sacred stones in everything he did. He had quite a few stones and could lend them to people with the assurance that when the stones wanted, they would go back to him again. Standing Bear was very impressed with Horn Chips; they may even have been relatives. He explained the wide variety of circumstances in which Horn Chips used the stones:

> He would go into the sweat-bath and there locate lost articles or horses and absent people. While taking the purification ceremony the tunkes [sic tunkan], or hot stones, brought great inspiration to Chips, so when he went to the place of vigil they came to him in spirit and offered him service. So Chips always carried stones, some of them painted in colors, in his medicine bag. When he was making medicine they would fly to him and they could be heard striking the tipi and after we moved into houses I have heard them dropping down the chimney and have seen them lying about on the floor where they had fallen.[6]

Painting the stones indicated great knowledge of the powers of each stone so that the appropriate color could be used. Horn Chips also had to learn the particular talents of each stone, since there was no reason to send more than one stone to do any of his errands. Frances Densmore noted that several medicine men at Standing Rock had more than one stone and loaned them out or even sold them, but they always returned to the original owners and did better work for them. Horn Chips, in my estimation, represents the highest level of spiritual development with stones.

BUFFALO STONES THAT CALL THE BLACKFEET

The Blackfeet use sacred stones, but they have a different way of coming into possession of them, a tradition much different from that of the Sioux, Cheyennes, and other neighboring tribes. Their stones are called buffalo stones. George Bird Grinnell explained their understanding of the stones.

> A small stone, which is usually a fossil shell of some kind, is known by the Blackfeet as I-nis'-kim the buffalo stone. This object is strong medicine, and, as indicated in some of these stories, gives its possessor great power with buffalo. The stone is found on the prairie, and the person who succeeds in obtaining one is regarded as very fortunate. Sometimes a man, who is riding along on the prairie, will hear a peculiar faint chirp, such as a little bird might utter. The sound he knows is made by a buffalo rock. He stops and searches the ground for the rock, and if he cannot find it, marks the place and very likely returns the next day, either alone or with others from the camp, to look for it again.[7]

This buffalo stone can be dug from the ground; it is generally a fossil of some kind; and it takes the initiative in contacting humans and offering itself as a helper. It is found on the prairie, not on the tops of buttes. And it is useful primarily in hunting the buffalo; it therefore has a restricted importance perhaps different in capability to the small, round stones of the other tribes.

MEDICINE CROW'S MOTHER'S STONES

The people who have them can find evidence that the stones are alive in keen observations. Not only do the stones talk to their owners, but also, they sometimes change during the course of a year in a discernible manner. This story from the Crow tribe illustrated this phenomenon. The way and time of change is not usually discussed with people except other medicine men.

When Medicine-crow's mother showed her husband the medicine, she had four stones,—one suggesting a bird, another a buffalo, the third a horse, and the fourth a person. They were light in weight early in the spring, but grew heavier by the summer; in the coldest winter there would be frost on them, for they breathed. These rocks told Medicine-crow's stepfather where the Crow should spend the winter so as to avoid a famine; and he would announce such instructions."[8]

From this account, it appears as if the woman was the owner of the stones, but her husband used them for prophecy. Unfortunately, we do not know if the stones that looked like people and animals had special powers regarding these personages.

Two Leggings, the Crow warrior, revealed another startling phenomenon regarding the stones that seems unlikely, as critics could argue that there is too much room for deception. However, we have no basis for assuming an effort to deceive because Two Leggings mentioned this fact in passing, almost as an aside.

Rock medicines are both male and female because they began with the marriage of the male rock and the female tobacco plant. Sometimes we place a male rock medicine with a female one and do not disturb them for a year. By that time a little rock will have come into the medicine bundle.[9]

Some stones are given to people in visions and ceremonies. We have accounts of people dreaming, and when they awake, the stone that appeared in their dream is there with them. Stones can be given or loaned to people, although it seems that they are always subject to recall by their original owner. And it is not unusual for medicine men to have several stones, each apparently specializing in one or two particular powers. My great-grandfather Saswe had a stone that would cause rain. All that needed to happen was for the stone to get wet, and severe thunderstorms would follow quickly.

There are so many stories about the stones that one comes to believe they form a separate spiritual universe in themselves and that a person with several stones must rank very high in the esteem of the spirits. We will look at a few typical narratives about the stones with the understanding that these stories do not represent the totality of the knowledge of them.

Repetition of similar stories, however, may not enhance our knowledge, nor inspire us to treat them with the reverence they deserve. In a discussion once with a prominent anthropologist, I was told that his museum had a number of stones from various medicine bundles and none of them did anything except sit on the shelf. He apparently believed that the stones would perform tasks for anyone who owned them, the same way cars and stereos operate whenever the proper buttons are pushed. He failed to understand that there was a personal relationship between the medicine man and the stone, and that not even a full-blood Indian could get the stone to do anything if he were not the right person.

HEALINGS WITH STONES— FRANCES DENSMORE'S SUMMARY

Densmore talked with four elders, including Old Buffalo and Used-as-a-Shield, who lived at Standing Rock, about the manner in which the men possessing them performed healings. While her summary is hypothetical, it does give us a general intellectual framework and a healing scenario that will help us understand the importance of these objects in the life of the people.

When a man skillful in the use of the sacred stones was called to attend a sick person he was expected to give a demonstration of his supernatural power. Many were invited to witness this exhibition, and it is said that harm would come to those who did not "believe in the sacred stones." The sick person filled a pipe, which he gave to the medicine man. After smoking it the man was rightly bound with things, even his fingers and toes being interlaced with sinews like those of which bowstrings are made, after which he was firmly tied in a hide.

The tent was dark and the medicine-man sang songs addressed to the sacred stones; he sang also his own dream songs. Strange sounds were heard in the darkness, and objects were felt to be flying through the air. Voices of animals were speaking. One said, "My grandchild, you are very sick, but I will cure you." Frequently a buffalo came, and those who did not believe in the sacred stones were kicked by the buffalo or struck by a flying stone or bundle of clothing. At last the medicine-man called, "Hasten, make a light!" Dry grass, which was ready, was placed on the fire. In its light the man was seen wedged between the poles near the top of the tipi, with all the restraining cords cast from him.[10]

CALLING THE BUFFALO

One of the powers possessed by the sacred stones was the ability to produce buffalo when called upon. We have two stories that illustrate this talent, both witnessed by reliable observers. The first story involved the fossil stone of the Cheyennes.

LISTENING TO THE GROUND'S FOSSIL STONE

A person had come to Listening to the Ground and had put down the stone horn before him. He afterwards said that this was some spirit who had taken pity on him and his family. The spirit told him to take the horn back to his people, and showed him what to do to call the buffalo, and taught him what songs he should sing.

Listening to the Ground's daughter died in 1875 at the age of about seventy. The first ceremony of calling the buffalo by Listening to the Ground was performed by placing the horn on the ground with the point to the east and telling everybody to watch. He said he would sing three times and that when he sang the third time all should look at his little daughter to see if her right ear moved as the buffalo calves' ears moved. They watched as directed, and saw the little girl's right ear move. Then he sang again, and her left ear moved. Then Listening to the Ground said, "Watch the stone," and the fourth time he sang, as the girl moved her left ear, the stone horn rolled over very slowly toward the north with its point still to the east. The next morning a watcher was selected to go to the top of a nearby hill and while ascending he saw a herd of buffalo coming toward camp. A hunt followed and the tongues were brought to Listening to the Ground, and boiled for a feast. The buffalo were called in a similar way for a second time; but in calling them a third time, while making the ceremony Listening to the Ground told the people that he had made a mistake, and fell back and died before being able to impart his secret.[11]

GOOSE CALLS A BUFFALO

Goose performed an amazing feat when a fur trader challenged his powers. Densmore visited Standing Rock around 1914, and the story she was told was still fresh in people's memories.

Goose, a prominent medicine-man, also dreamed of the sacred stones. He said that he had two of these stones in his possession some time before he tested his power over them. One day a fur trader ridiculed the medicine-man in his hearing. This white man said that all the medicine-men did was by sleight of hand, and that he would have to see an instance of their power before he would believe it. Goose entered into conversation with the trader on the subject, who offered him 10 articles, including cloth and blankets, if he would call a buffalo to the spot where they were standing. Goose sent both the sacred stones to summon a buffalo. The trader brought his field glasses and looked across the prairie, saying in derision, "Where is the buffalo you were to summon?" Suddenly the trader saw a moving object, far away. It came nearer until they could see it without the aid of the glasses. It was a buffalo, and it came so near that they shot it from the spot where they stood.[12]

The buffalo in western South Dakota were almost all killed off by the summer of 1883. With the exception of a small herd owned by Scotty Phillips, the man who saved the buffalo, there were no animals to be found in the region. How then did Goose's stones produce one? If one came from the Phillips herd, it had to travel a great distance very quickly. The medicine men insist that not only did buffalo winter in the Black Hills and come and go through Buffalo Gap, but many buffalo went into caves along the Missouri River. Could one of them have appeared? The incident was well known—and without explanation.

CROOKED FOOT FINDS THE BUFFALO

Crooked Foot was asked to ascertain by means of the sacred stones where buffalo could be found. The stone that he used was egg-shaped, and he was said to have found it on top of the highest butte near his home. When giving this performance, Crooked Foot had the stone encased in a bag. He said, "The stone has now gone to look for the buffalo, but when it comes back you will see it." The people then prepared a place on which it was expected that the stone would appear. This was done by pulverizing the earth for a space about a foot square and covering this place with buffalo hide or with part of a red blanket. All watched this place, and after a time, the stone appeared upon it. Crooked Foot questioned the stone concerning the location of the buffalo, and the tribe, acting on his advice, found the herd as he had indicated.[13]

POWERFUL PLACES

Sacred sites play an integral role in the creation of medicine men and the development of their powers and provide a communal shrine as their power is recognized. We know that each tribe has a number of locations particularly sacred to them, such as the Blue Lake at Taos Pueblo and Bear Butte in South Dakota. But a question that is rarely addressed is how Indians discerned the sacredness of the site in the first place. For a location such as the Pipestone Quarry in Minnesota, it is evident that the red stone for the pipes immediately registered on the people as a place that had to be treated with respect.

Fortunately, we have a description of how the Comanches discovered that the Medicine Mounds in Texas were a sacred location. We also have a report by Densmore of the discovery of a Sun Dance site many years after the dance was held and the subsequent condition of the land. Each sacred location has both a history extending far back in time and legends that explain why the location was sacred. While vision quests can be done in a variety of isolated locations, it is these special places that gave mature and experienced medicine men the ability to serve the people.

THE COMANCHES DISCOVERED A SACRED SITE

A Comanche medicine man first discovered its great power when once his band came to hunt in the vicinity of the mounds. He had a young and beautiful daughter who was ill of fever and was growing weaker day by day. Her father had sucked worms and evil spirits out of many a brave and many a squaw, had chanted away the pains of many a girl, and had smoked the weakness of many a boy, but he could not cure his own daughter. He had rattled his gourd all night long while he prayed and chanted. From his medicine bundle he had prepared cures, while the moon was dark and when it was full. He had mixed and tried his formulae in every way he knew. He had consulted other medicine men. But all without results.

One morning he came out of his tipi and in despair was gazing silently into the distance when suddenly his eyes came to rest on the rock-capped peak of the largest mound. Here was a powerful spirit that could help him he thought. So without touching water or food he went apart to pray and fast until the spirit should send him a revelation. At length it came. He was instructed to take his medicines to the high rock and there mix them so that the power of the good spirit should enter into them. He prepared the medicine as directed by the vision, gave it to his daughter, and then went out and prayed to the mound spirit—prayed with the patience of those who live under the sun, and watch shadows, and note day by day the greening and the browning of the grass. At length he heard the voice of his daughter. He bounded into the tipi. Her eye was bright, her color almost healthy. She had slept deeply, she said. From that hour she mended steadily and soon was able to return to her work.

Thereafter this medicine man made regular visits to the mound, made offerings to the mound spirit, and performed his cures through its aid. The fame of the spirit mound spread. Other medicine men came. From the gypsum water of a spring at the base of the mounds, the ailing Comanches came to drink. The spirit came to be a protector for the Comanche bands.[14]

THE PIPESTONE QUARRY

The French explorer Jean N. Nicolet reported one of my favorite stories about the change of weather when he was doing a survey of the Couteau de Prairie for the federal government in 1841. Many previous explorers had heard stories of the famous Pipestone Quarry, where the people of many tribes obtained the stone for their pipes. The quarry was regarded as a sanctuary, and there was a general agreement among the tribes that no one would be molested if they were visiting the area for that purpose. Apparently, parties coming to harvest the stone had to pause and receive the approval of the spirits before they could proceed down into the valley. Nicolet explained his understanding of the situation:

The idea of the young Indians, who are very fond of the marvelous, is that it [the Quarry] has been opened by the Great
Spirit; and that, whenever it is visited by them, they are saluted
by lightning and thunder. We may cite, as a coincident, our
own experience in confirmation of this tradition. Short of half
a mile from the valley, we were met by a severe thunder-storm,
during which the wind blew with so much force as to
threaten the overturning of Mr. Renville's wagon; and we
were obliged to stop for a few minutes during the short
descent into the valley.[15]

Notice the immediate response by Nicolet that the thunderstorm can be explained as a mere coincidence, and that the belief of
the Indians is merely a superstition. If I were in that party, I would
pay a little more attention to what the Indians were saying. If the
storm came close to overturning a wagon, it must have been sufficient warning to heed.

THE ISLAND SACRED ROCK

There is an episode reported by Sir George Simpson, an English
explorer, of an incident he experienced on the Columbia River.
Simpson and his party had visited an Indian fishing camp where the
Indians were busy catching, smoking, and drying salmon. Every so
often, one of the Indians would take some salmon and approach a
large rock and lay an offering in front of it, apparently a sharing of
the harvest with the spirit of the island. One of Simpson's men, when
everyone was asleep, went to the rock and scattered the food offerings
at its base. According to his report: "The Island contains, in its interior, a block of black basalt rudely chiseled by the Indians of ancient
days into a column of four or five feet in height and three in diameter." The natives believed, as did the early settlers, that if touched,
the stone would bring rain. Sir Simpson told how one of his men
once tried to move the stone, and that evening, a violent storm
descended on the area, thus vindicating the legend.[16]

The story gives us sufficient particularity so that we can appreciate the power of the spirits who lived in or near the rock. The Indians knew full well what would happen should the stone's integrity be violated and had told Simpson's party the tradition regarding the stone—that disrespect would bring catastrophe. Apparently, the early settlers also believed that dire results would follow if the stone were treated disrespectfully. I fail to see the difference between the Indian prediction of disaster and the warnings we are given about electrical appliances, household cleaners, and other commercial products. The principle is always the same: people with a specialized knowledge are in a better position than we are to know the consequences of certain actions, whether the result be a violation of a spiritual site or the misuse of utensils.

THE STANDING ROCK SUN DANCE SITE

Some medicine men say that sites where sun dances are held are marked forever as locations where sacred things happened. Some of the people at Standing Rock have told me that traces of a sun dance done by Sitting Bull when he was in Canada still remain after nearly 125 years. They say the holes where the poles were set in the ground, as well as the location of the altar, can be plainly seen because nothing has grown there during the intervening time. This experience, narrated by Densmore, puzzled her, but reaffirmed the faith of the Indians who took her to examine the site of the last sun dance on that reservation.

> On the afternoon of that day the entire party drove across the prairie to the place, about a mile and a half from the Standing Rock Agency, where the last Sun dance of these bands was held in 1882.
>
> A majority of the Indians who went to the site of the Sun dance with the writer were men who took part in the Sun dance of 1882 and had not visited the place since that time. When nearing the place they scanned the horizon, measuring the distance to the Missouri River and the buttes. At last they gave a signal for the wagons to stop, and, springing to the

ground, began to search the prairie: In a short time they found the "exact spot where the ceremony was held." The scars were still on the prairie as they were on their own bodies. A depression about 2 inches in depth still square in outline and not fully overgrown with grass showed where the earth had been exposed for the owap'ka waka' ("sacred place"). Only 3 or 4 feet away lay a broken buffalo skull. Eagerly the Indians lifted it and saw traces of red paint upon it—could it be other than the skull used in that ceremony. They looked if perchance they might find a trace of the location of the pole. It should be about 15 feet east of the "sacred place." There it was—a spot of hard, bare ground 18 inches in diameter.

One said, "Here you can see where the shade-house stood." This shade-house, or shelter of boughs, was built entirely around the Sun-dance circle except for a wide entrance at the east. It was possible to trace part of it, the outline being particularly clear on the west of the circle; to the east the position of the posts at the entrance was also recognized. The two sunken places (where the posts had stood) were about 15 feet apart, and the center of the space between them was directly in line with the site of the pole and the center of the "sacred place" at the west of it. More than 29 years had passed since the ceremony. It is strange that the wind had not sewn seeds on those spots of earth."[17]

Surely, there must be an explanation for this phenomenon, and yet if the Indian response is not believed, there is no way of understanding what the site represents.

CHAPTER SEVEN

Unusual Exploits of Medicine Men

* * * * * * * * * * * * * * *

We often think that ceremonies limited the scope of spiritual powers by these holy men because the most common ceremonies have been well covered by scholars. Thus we anticipate that apart from predicting the future, finding lost articles, and healing, and perhaps gaining some protection in battle, we have exhausted the scope of powers available. These next selections cover some of the unique and perhaps once-in-a-lifetime events that unbiased observers have reported. Although many people saw medicine men do similar feats, and the observers expressed frank puzzlement at what they had seen, there is no doubt that what they saw actually happened.

Early Colonial Observations

In 1632, Thomas Morton wrote one of the first books published in the United States, entitled *New English Canaan; or New Canaan, Containing an Abstract of New England*, a rather lengthy and misleading title. In the book, Morton mentioned the gifts that the Indian medicine men had and the demonstrations they could make to prove their powers. This selection, although similar in content to other exploits we have examined, needs to be considered since we have so few accounts from the early days and New England.

In the heat of the summer to make Ice appear in a bowle of faire water, first having the water set before him hee hath begunne his incantation according to their usuall accustome and before the same has bin ended a thick Clowde has darkened the aire and on a sodance thunder clap hath bin heard that has amazed the natives, in an instant hath he [displayed] a firme peece of Ice to flot in the middest of the bowle in the presence of vulgar people, which doubtless was done by the agility of Satan his consort.[1]

Two years later, in 1634, another colonial writer, William Wood, published *New England's Prospect*, in which he recited the feats of a medicine man named Passaconaway of Pawtucket.

If we may believe the Indians who report of one Passaconaway that he can make the water burn, the rocks move, the trees dance, matemorphise himself into a flaming man … in the winter, when there is no green leaves to be got, he will burn an old one to ashes, and putting those into water produce a new green leaf … and make of a dead snake's skin a living snake.[2]

It is rare to have information that covers what people attending the event experienced and what the medicine man himself remembered. The incident occurred at a Northern Cheyenne camp in southern Montana in 1867 and has been mentioned in several books citing a number of credible eyewitness accounts. Ice was a particularly powerful spiritual leader. It was he who made Roman Nose's famous warbonnet, and there are many stories about him that testify to his spiritual powers. The first selection deals with the exploit as the people of the community experienced it; the second selection is Ice's own testimony as to what happened during this performance.

FEAT OF ICE OR WHITE BULL AT BUSBY IN 1867

He had some men dig a hole first, deep enough for him to sit in, and carry the dirt away; you can still see it piled up there. And they put a tepee over it, and brought two rocks from the hills, so big and heavy that it took a number of men to carry them. Then Ice ordered the military society members to stand around the outside, while he and some others performed ceremonies inside the tepee. After that he got down into the hole and they put the rocks over it and covered it completely.

"Go on outside now," he ordered them, "and I will sing and then give a signal for you to come back and lift the rocks off."

So they did this, the men came in and removed the rocks, and Ice was gone. They all searched for him, and some dug and looked around in the hole to see that he was not hiding. When they had given up they put the rocks back on as he had told them to, and shortly they heard the signal and took them off again, and there was Ice.[3]

Now let us see how Ice remembered the experience.

ICE'S ACCOUNT

I sat in the hole under the rock, my hands were tied behind my back by the wrists, and my fingers were tied together with a bow-string. The rope from my wrists ran over my shoulders and tied my feet together at the ankles. My upper arms were tied tightly together to my thigh bones.

All the ropes were tied tight—by people who did not believe that I could do this thing. I sat there, with my face toward the rising sun (east). For a little while, after I was put in the hole, I seemed to know nothing that was happening. Then I heard something moving at my side, and I looked, and there was the little man. He patted me on the back and sides, and said to me, "Why have they got you here?"

I answered him, "The people think they are going to be in trouble, and they want help."

The little man said, "Shut your eyes," I did so, and the little man slapped me on the sole of my right foot, and then on the sole of my left foot, and took me by the hair and seemed to pull me up a little. Then the little man said, "Open your eyes." I did so, and found myself standing on the ground in front of the big lodge. Standing just in front of me was a woman, who at that very moment called out to the people in the lodge. "Why do you not hurry and sing a medicine song before he gets smothered under that big rock?"

"Who is to be smothered?" I said to her, and she looked back at me and was astonished to see me.

"Let them finish their song," I said, "and then ask them to make a light, and let us have something to eat, for I am hungry." Soon the news got about outside that I was there, and at length those in the lodge heard of it—they could hardly believe it. Someone said, "Look in the hole." My wife was the first one to push her head into the sweat-house. She called out: "The rock is moved off the hole. He is not there." The rocks were found piled up on one side of the hole, the robe on top of them, and the ropes and strings, with which I had been tied, on the robe.[4]

Surely, this is a spectacular achievement. The little man, leaving no trace of his presence, rescued Ice from the hole. When they first opened the hole, he was not there. Then they put the rocks back, and, at that point, he must have returned to the hole so that he was there when the people removed the rocks a second time. His wife saw the robes were already neatly stacked and the ropes coiled and in place. Ice did not reveal the messages the people wanted after the ritual was completed.

A rather clever story dealing with the same kind of phenomenon can be found in the Ojibwa tradition. The ability to materialize and then move to another location and return is not difficult to accept if our world is a variation on the hologram, as it appears to be. Since this power was only possessed by a few people in each generation of a small tribe or community, it was not possible for people to experience this event as observers in any except unusual circumstances. Frederick Starr, an adventurer in the Old West as the nineteenth century came to a close, reported this event in his book about his Western travels: "Ojibwa medicine men have often been tested by white men who doubted their powers. Thus an old medicine man had two little houses built at some distance apart. He was shut up in one, and the whites built a ring of fire around it. Then, no one could tell how, he appeared unharmed walking out of the other house."[5]

THE AOUTAENHROBI FIRE RITUAL

The Jesuit Father Paul LeJeune recorded one of the few references to the fire dance in 1637. Although this dance was a healing ritual, the Jesuit felt it was a work of the devil, even while admitting that he was reporting accurately. Some other tribes had medicine men who could handle hot coals, not in this particular format, but as easily as these Indians did. Considering the fire walkers in other parts of the world—indeed, some in the United States—the feat does not sound as spectacular as it might otherwise. Nevertheless, it is within the purview of what the old people could do.

> A number of stones were brought and to make them red-hot, a fire was prepared, hot enough to burn down the cabin. Twenty four persons were chosen to sing and to perform all the ceremonies. ... I was waiting all the time to see what they would do with these stones that they were heating, making red-hot with so much care. You may believe me—since I speak of a thing that I saw with my awn eyes—they separated the brands, drew them (the stones) from the midst of the fire, and holding their hands behind their backs, took them between their teeth, carried them to the patient, and remained some time without loosening their hold, blowing upon them and growling in their ears. I am keeping one of

the stones expressly to show you. ... The stone is about the size of a goose egg. Yet I saw a savage put it in his mouth, so that there was more of it inside than out. He carried it some distance, and after that it was still so hot that when he threw it on the ground sparks of fire issued from it.

One of our Frenchmen had the curiosity to see if, in reality, all this was done without anyone being burnt. He spoke to this Indian who had filled his mouth with live coals. He had him open his mouth and found it unhurt and whole, without any appearance of having been burnt. And not only these persons, but even the sick people were not burned when they let their bodies be rubbed with glowing cinders without appearing in the least affected.[6]

Some time later, in 1642, LeJeune appeared to have lost a con-vert who had originally joined in this dance and then was converted to Christianity. But then he returned to his old religion, and:

At the end of some time he had a dream, in which he saw himself present at one of these dances or festivals, and han-dling fire like the others, and he heard at the same time a song, which he was astonished to know perfectly on awaking. At the first feast of this kind which was made, he began to sing his song, and behold, by degrees he felt himself becoming frenzied,—he took the burning embers and the hot stones with his hands and with his teeth from the midst of the live coals, he plunged his bare arm to the bottom of the boiling kettles, and all without any injury or pain, in a word, he was master of his trade. And since then for the space of twenty years, it has befallen him sometimes to be present at three or four festivals or dances of this kind in one day, for the healing of the sick.

He assured us that, far from being burned then, one felt on the contrary, a coolness of the hands and mouth; but that all must be done following and depending upon the song that has been learned in the dream; that otherwise nothing extraordinary takes place.

He told us, besides, that then from time to time he saw himself in dreams present at these feasts, and that then something was given or lent him that he should wear about his person during the ceremony. This was a warning to him that he must not undertake it the next time unless he had about him that which he had seen in his dream; for this reason, at the next dance, he declared his wish, and immediately there was thrown him that which he had declared to be necessary to him, in order that he might dance.[7]

HOLDING THE JAR WITH FEATHERS

William E. Curtis quoted a story told him by Frank Cushing concerning the ability of the Zuni priests to lift a full water jar using two feathers. Cushing admitted to Curtis: "Of course there is some trick about it, but I was never able to discover it." It might, then, simply be a form of power that could not be rationally explained. According to Cushing, then, the Zuni priests:

sit themselves in a circle on the clay floor around a jar that will hold, perhaps a gallon, an ancient and sacred earthen vessel which is filled with water. The chief priest carries in his [hands] two ordinary eagle feathers, which are tied together at the quill ends so that they may make a fork. Behind the circle of priests are other members of the tribe, and the musicians with their drums and gourds, who join in the chants with as much emotion as is shown the attendants of a Negro camp meeting. The incantations continue for several hours, and when the participants and spectators are wrought up to a proper pitch of excitement the priest dips the feather tips in the water, lifts the jar with them, and holds it suspended for a minute or two at a height level with his face or breast. Then he lowers it slowly to the ground. This feat is repeated several times during the performance. Apparently there is nothing in the hand of the priest but the feathers, and they appear to be inserted into the mouth of the jar only two or three inches.[8]

CALLING UP OF THE WATERS

Curtis also quoted Cushing's account of a similar ritual performed at Zuni that was supposed to encourage the waters to come during the year instead of remaining away from the Zuni country. Again, Cushing admitted that he could not explain the phenomenon: "I do not attempt to explain it, except as an optical illusion or an example of hypnotism, but I am sure I saw that jar filled with water by some invisible agency. There could be no underground pipes, for such a thing would be impossible in Zuni, nor could anybody have poured in water unseen by me."

So every January, the Zuni priests would gather in a kiva and bring a very old, beautifully decorated jar completely lacking water.

> The jar is placed in the center of a circle and similar incantations take place. The words of the song describe the powers of the elements and offer them praise. When, in the course of the chant, the god of water is named, the two guardian priests pour a little water—perhaps a teacupful—into the jar, with certain fetiches. This is known as the "water seed". Then, as the incantations continue, the water rises in the jar until it reaches the rim and overflows in a little rivulet, running toward the altar upon which the image of the god of water stands. Then the high priest dips a sacred shell into the jar and allows each member of the tribe present to drink. After the last one has drained the shell the water slowly subsides and the incantation dies away.[9]

INVULNERABILITY TO ARROWS AND BULLETS

One of the most frequent reports was that of medicine men making themselves or persons they designated invulnerable to bullets and arrows fired at them to test their powers. These accounts are too numerous to pass off as superstition, but they do leave some serious questions in their wake. If medicine men could make people invulnerable, why didn't they ensure that everyone in a war party would be immune to firearms and arrows? Even more critical, why did not the shirts worn by the ghost dancers guaranteed to make the warriors safe from the white man's bullets work their magic? It appears that this power was not transferable to a large group of people but remained an individual power. When we examine the variety of ways that this feat was experienced, we can see the complexity of the problem.

BEAR CLAWS'S POWER

The boy was standing outside the door. He circled about the tipi around the south to the north, and passing through the door, he did the same thing inside. Dressed only in his breech-clout, he assumed a stooping posture, facing northward, from his position just south of the door. Bear Claws sang a bear medicine song. Then he blew across the room four times. Now he was ready to tell his arrow assistant to make his shot. He had worked up his power and sent it over to the neophyte. Using his knee to bend the bow, the archer took three practice pulls; on the fourth he let the arrow fly at the medicine seeker. The steel pointed arrow struck the boy. The point was bent, and the arrow flew up toward the top of the tipi.

The spearman's turn was next. He ran up to the neophyte, took three practice jabs, and thrust with all his force on the fourth. The spear point was bent, but the candidate was not fazed.

During all this action, the boy was grunting like a bear. It was proven that the power of this medicine was very strong.[10]

BRAVE BUFFALO'S FEAT

The Sioux elder Brave Buffalo has similar powers, according to Frances Densmore. "Brave Buffalo said that on waking from his dream, he went home and thought the matter over seriously. After qualifying himself for the ordeal, he requested his relatives to erect a very large tent of buffalo hide in which he would give his demonstration and challenge anyone to shoot him with arrows. He clothed himself in an entire buffalo hide with the head and horns. The whole tribe came to see whether anyone could not penetrate his skin. Several years later the test was repeated with guns, and Brave Buffalo stated that they were not able to injure him."[11]

The Pawnees had a time each year when they demonstrated their powers. George Bird Grinnell wrote of many of the feats performed by these spiritual leaders that today may seem impossible to us, but served to dazzle the community and reassure it that they were maintaining their relationships with the spirits. Rather than reproduce the many exploits he was able to record, we will look at only one instance where the powers displayed certainly boggle the imagination.

> Several men, representing elk, came into the ring; and trotted about, so as to be seen by everyone, imitating the movements of those animals. To their heads were tied branches to represent horns, and each wore an elk skin thrown over its back. A doctor came into the ring and handed to the spectators his arrows, which he examined and found to be ordinary arrows with the usual sheet-iron points. On receiving back the arrows from those who had examined them, the doctor pretended to hunt the elk, and at length shot at them, striking them in the sides or on the legs.
>
> The arrows, instead of penetrating the flesh, bound back, some of them flying fifteen or twenty feet in the air. They appeared to be shot with the full force of the bow, and when picked up and handed to the onlookers, the sheet-iron points were found to be doubled back as if they had been shot

against a plate of iron, and the shafts of some of them were split. The elk trotted away and out of the ring without injury.[12]

We can suppose that this demonstration, when performed at the proper time, along with the manifestations of power from the other doctors, was more to display the powers of healing rather than invulnerability. However, the bending of the arrowheads suggests that some kind of spiritual shield protected the elk dancers.

Some medicine men had powers of a different sort. Instead of being invulnerable to the bullets and arrows fired directly at them, they appear to have been able to confuse their enemies so that they were unable to hit them, either because the enemies' aim was bad, or they were able to distort the target they must have presented to their opponents. Apparently, this talent for deflecting missiles was one of Geronimo's spiritual powers. Considering the many battles in which he fought without receiving any serious injury, an old man's recollection of Geronimo's power should be taken seriously.

OLD MAN S.

One of Geronimo's Warriors Old Man S. was with Geronimo's bunch all through the war. ... He had power from the gun, they say. They say he used to get out on the bank; all the soldiers shot at him and couldn't hit him. One who went to shoot him might fall down or stop his gun; then S. would kill him instead. Another man told me he knows a gun ceremony. He, too, went through all the wars safely. Geronimo is said to have known this ceremony. He never got hurt either. Something always happens to your gun when you try to shoot at such a fellow. Your gun jams, for instance. The one who knows this ceremony can fix it for someone else so that, when he is shot at, he will be missed.[13]

BOX ELDER'S EXPLOIT

John Stands in Timber recited a story about the bravery of two old men when Dull Knife's village on the Powder River was attacked and destroyed in 1876. The first "old man" was Box Elder, the most venerated holy man among the Northern Cheyennes. He was the keeper of one of the four sacred wheel lances and had many powers. He could throw a blanket of invisibility over people, as he did the warriors who recaptured the Cheyennes' horse herd after Reynold's attack in March of 1876. He could also talk with wolves and foresaw the defeat and annihilation of General George Custer's command. This incident may have been one of the most important demonstrations of his power.

> The Cheyenne had all taken cover behind rocks or hills, when one old man came out in a high open place in front of the enemy and sat down, with a pipe. He had showed the rest of them that it was not lit by pushing his thumb down in it. Then he held it up and lit it from the sun. And he started to smoke, though the soldiers were shooting at him and the bullets were whistling past. Then Spotted Black Bird walked out there and sat down and smoked with him. He said he could feel the bullets almost touching him, but he took four puffs before he got up and walked out of sight.[14]

THE POWERS OF CRAZY MULE

Thomas B. Marquis, an old Cheyenne who remains anonymous, in talking about the powers of medicine men in the old days, spoke admirably of the powers of Crazy Mule.

> The spirits worked for him more than any other Indian I ever knew. Bullets might hit him, but they would not go into his body. I saw a test made upon him when our tribal camp was far up the Tongue River. I was then twenty-nine years old. He dressed his body with only a muslin shirt, this painted with his

special medicine colors, and on his feet he wore a pair of moccasins beaded in a certain way, according to his medicine plan. Twenty-seven Cheyennes who had rifles were chosen to take a position a short distance in front of him. They rested their rifles in upright forked sticks and fired at the painted muslin shirt. As soon as the shots had been fired, Crazy Mule reached down and pulled off his moccasins. From them he emptied out the twenty-seven bullets.[15]

This feat may be regarded as impossible, and skeptics will immediately complain that Crazy Mule must have hidden the bullets in his moccasins. But there is a problem with that accusation. Without a bullet in some twenty-seven guns, several of the rifles would have emitted a different kind of smoke, and perhaps shot out some cloth wrapping that would have taken the place of lead bullets. Almost every Plains and mountain tribe had people who could accomplish this feat.

What would be the principle behind this kind of power? We must recall that Roman Nose was warned that if he ate any food that had been touched by metal, the metal would remain in his body and attract the soldiers' bullets. And we have seen that indeed, this event did occur. Is it not possible then that Crazy Mule had been told the reverse in his vision? As long as he strictly followed the instructions given in his vision, no bullets of any kind could ever injure him. Metal, which was so revered as a sparse commodity by the Indians, seemed to have a power all its own.

POWERS OF ANIMATION

One reasonably commonplace practice was that of animating, for a very brief time, perhaps, something that was otherwise inert. Modern magicians have all manner of sleight-of-hand tricks, and critics of Indian spiritual powers may compare this particular gift with what we can see on television. There are, to be sure, some similarities. However, these stories have a ring of truth in them in that usually the medicine man was demonstrating his power in a very restricted place, an earth lodge or a tipi where the audience can see his every move. Additionally, the audience was made up of exceptionally alert people who would be looking for trickery. The first selection is taken from the Choctaws and is clearly in a setting where the medicine man is expected to prove his powers. Hence, there must have been a bit of show business also.

THE CHOCTAW MEDICINE MAN

> He took his tobacco-pouch which was an otter skin in which he kept his pipe and tobacco, which he threw into the middle of an open place where the people were assembled to judge of his skill: after he had uttered a number of obscurely articulated words and thrown himself repeatedly into the fire, from which he came out in a perspiration, and without being burned, this skin was seen to swell out, fill with flesh, and come to life, and to run between the legs of the Frenchmen, some of whom in the company having caressed it, and felt of it, found that it was like a true otter. When each one was satisfied it returned to the same place where it had come to life and was seen to diminish in size and return to the form which it before.[16]

FEAT OF ELK LEFT BEHIND

Grinnell reported on a demonstration of the power to animate given by a Pawnee doctor performed at one of the special times when the doctors displayed their powers. While we hear of magicians pulling rabbits from hats, secreting a living fawn in one's clothing to trick an audience would be pushing the art of concealment a little too far.

> In one of the doctor's dances he had the skin of a fawn in his hands. He called out to the people, "Now, you people, watch me; look close and see what I shall do, and you will find out what my bravery is, and that it all comes from this that you

see." In our presence he shook this fawn skin, and the fawn slipped out of his hand and then stood before him, a living fawn looking at him. "That is what I mean," he said. "If the enemies surround me, that is the way I come out of it. The fawn can run so fast that it can never be caught, nor can it ever be shot."[17]

THE ARICKARA BEAR MEDICINE SOCIETY BUFFALO HUNT

Perhaps most unique of all the accounts of medicine powers is the animation of inert objects performed by the Arickara medicine men. Fortunately, our eyewitness to this event was D. D. Mitchell, one of the most famous frontiersmen and the Indian agent and chief organizer of the famous Fort Laramie Treaty of 1851. Mitchell's credibility cannot be questioned, since he was the primary federal representative to the tribes of the northern Plains for many years. While the exploit begs credibility, nevertheless, it was an event that left its observers quite puzzled and subdued.

In 1831, Mitchell was leading an expedition up the Missouri, and on approaching the Arickara village, they lost their horses. Fearing more depredations, and on the advice of an old Canadian hunter, they decided to test the hospitality of the tribe by asking for, and receiving, an earth lodge in which to stay while they were visiting the village. Once accepted by the people, they were then invited to a demonstration of powers by the Bear Medicine Men Society.

> We were received in the village with much more politeness than we expected; a lodge was appropriated to our use, and provisions were brought to us in abundance. After we were completely refreshed, a young man came to our lodge and informed us that a band of bears, (as he expressed it) or medicine men, were making preparations to exhibit their skill, and that if we felt disposed we could witness the ceremony. We were much gratified at the invitation, as we had all heard marvelous stories of the wonderful feats performed by the Indian

medicine men or jugglers. We accordingly followed our guide
to the medicine lodge, where we found six men dressed in bear
skins, and seated in a circle in the middle of the apartment.
The spectators were standing around, and so arranged as to
give each individual a view of the performers. They civilly
made way for our party, and placed us so near the circle that
we had ample opportunity of detecting the imposture, if any
imposition should be practiced.

The actors (if I may so call them) were all painted in the
most grotesque manner imaginable, blending so completely
the ludicrous and frightful in their appearance that the spectator might be said to be somewhat undecided whether to
laugh or to shudder. After sitting for some time in a land of
mournful silence one of the jugglers desired a youth, who was
near him, to bring some stiff clay from a certain place, which
he named, on the river bank. This we understood, through an
old Canadian, named Garrow, (well known on the Missouri)
who was present and acted as our interpreter. The young man
soon returned with the clay, and each of these human bears
immediately commenced the process of moulding a number
of little images exactly resembling buffaloes, men and horses,
bows, arrows, &c. When they had completed nine of each
variety, the miniature buffaloes were all placed together in a
line, and the little clay hunters mounted on their horses, and
holding their bows and arrows in their hands, were stationed
about three feet from them in a parallel line. I must confess
that at this part of the ceremony I felt very much inclined to
be merry, especially when I observed what appeared to me the
ludicrous solemnity with which it was performed. But my
ridicule was changed into astonishment, and even into awe, by
what speedily followed.

When the buffaloes and horsemen were properly
arranged, one of the jugglers thus addressed the little clay
men, or hunters: "My children, I know you are hungry; it has
been a long time since you have been out hunting. Exert

yourselves today. Try and kill as many as you can. Here are white people present who will laugh at you if you don't kill. Go! Don't you see that the buffaloes have already got the scent of you and have started?" Conceive, if possible, our amazement when the speaker's last words escaped his lips, at seeing the little images start off at full speed, followed by the Lilliputian horsemen, who with their bows of clay and arrows of straw, actually pierced the sides of the flying buffaloes at the distance of three feet.

Several of the little animals soon fell, apparently dead—but two of them ran round the circumference of the circles (a distance of fifteen or twenty feet,) and before they finally fell, one had three and the other five arrows transfixed in his side. When the buffaloes were all dead, the man who first addressed the hunters spoke to them again, and ordered them to ride into the fire, (a small one having been previously kindled in the center of the apartment) and on receiving this cruel order, the gallant horsemen, without exhibiting the least symptoms of fear or reluctance, rode forward at a brisk trot until they had reached the fire. The horses were stopped and drew back, when the Indian cried in an angry tone, "why don't you ride in?"

The riders now commenced beating their horses with their blows, and soon succeeded in urging them into the flames, where horses and riders both tumbled down, and for a time lay baking on the coals. The medicine men gathered up the dead buffaloes and laid them also on the fire, and when all were completely dried they were taken out and pounded into dust. After a long speech from one of the party, (of which our interpreter could make nothing,) the dust was carried to the top of the lodge, and scattered to the winds.

I paid the strictest attention during the whole ceremony, in order to discover, if possible, the mode by which this extraordinary deception was practiced but all my vigilance was of no avail. The jugglers themselves sat motionless during the performance, and the nearest was not within six feet. I

failed altogether to detect the mysterious agency by which
inanimate images of clay were, to all appearance, suddenly
endowed with the action, energy and feeling of living beings.[18]

Three other stories illustrate the breadth of the power of animation. While not as spectacular as the Arickara clay hunter, they
nevertheless hint at the same kind of resuscitating power. One incident occurred when a party of Assiniboines sought guidance from
the buffalo on a journey that was characterized by great rivalry
between the leaders of the expedition. "White Dog made preparations to receive a vision. … As soon as two songs were finished, the
[buffalo] skull suddenly disappeared and in its place, furiously pawing the snow, stood a large buffalo bull, which made ready as if to
attack the men. Just as quickly the buffalo disappeared and the men
saw that the skull was back in it place."[19]

Grinnell reported on the Blackfoot practice that seems unlikely,
yet also explains some of the success of the Blackfoot in warfare:
"Often, in going to war, a man would get a raven's skin and stuff the
head and neck, and tie it to the hair of the head behind. If a man
wearing such a skin got near the enemy without knowing it, the skin
would give him warning by tapping him on the back of the head
with its bill. Then he would know that the enemy was near, and
would hide."[20]

EAGLE FEATHERS DANCING

Curtis included a story about how the Pueblo medicine men made
eagle feathers dance. Since this is a common occurrence in many
tribes, although not written up in any detail, this account is the only
one I could find to illustrate this phenomenon.

The members of the tribe gather in a circle around a fire in
the center of the floor of the estufa or underground temple,
and after preliminary incantations, accompanied by strange
chants which recite the glories of the tribe and the abilities of
the priests, when the emotions of the audience have been

worked up to a sufficient degree, the high priest, or cacique, takes from his bosom a bunch of eagle feathers and sticks the quill ends into the clay floor so that they stand upright.

Then with their eyes fastened upon them and with many gyrations the priests dance, sing and clap their hands until all at once the feathers begin to move and dance about upon the floor for five or 10 minutes or even longer, moved by invisible power, changing places, circling around one another and acting like puppets: but there is no connection between the hands of the priests and the feathers, at least no one has ever been able to detect such a thing.

Curtis noted that "This [ceremony] has frequently been seen by outsiders—army officers, traders, missionaries and visiting scientists—but nobody has ever been able to explain how it is done."[21]

THE POWER OF INVISIBILITY

People from many tribes report on the powers of their medicine men to become invisible. This skill was very much needed when going to war against another tribe so that the war party could enter camps and locate horses or hide themselves when the project failed and they needed the edge over their pursuing enemies. Since we have testimony from a variety of tribes, it would seem that this talent was rather widespread. To be noted in this practice is that none of our references give credit to any animal helper in performing the feat. The Sioux used a pipe to deflect the Chippewa advantage, but otherwise we are not told whether the medicine man had assistance from other creatures or somehow had achieved this power from higher spirits than birds and animals.

Karl L. Schlesier recorded that the Cheyenne medicine men performed the feat in a spirit lodge ritual, but it was part of a general demonstration of powers by various medicine men. He observed: "Some shamans, during a spirit lodge ritual or at other occasions, were able, with the aid of maiyun helpers, to dissolve physical form temporarily, thus making themselves invisible."[22] It is unclear if we are talking about dissolution of the physical body or simply changing the physical form enough to become invisible to the audience. If there was actual change of the physical, that tells us a great deal about the flexibility of the universe.

THE SHAWNEE'S POWER

John R. Swanton records a story from the southeastern tribes that is more typical of the exercise of this power. In this case, the exploit was performed by a Shawnee, not a member of their tribe, and therefore with powers that were not restricted to the Alabama traditions. It was, as we shall see, a useful power to possess.

> Some Alabama were once traveling along with this doctor. One night they heard what sounded like the whinnying of horses. The Shawnee told them, however, that it was produced by some Comanche Indians, and when day came they discovered four of these Indians in a tree. By his medicine he caused these persons to fall asleep and then tumble to the ground without waking up. In a river bend near by was a great crowd of Comanche, but the Shawnee rendered himself and his companions invisible so that the Comanche did not see them, and they passed safely on.[23]

THE APACHE INVISIBILITY TACTIC

Since Morris Opler did his research about the Chiricahua Apaches, we can assume that members of Geronimo's band exercised this power, since the incident was told to Opler while he was discussing Geronimo. The power was therefore present and being used in 1885, which makes it reasonably contemporary.

> One time they all saw the enemy coming, and the enemy saw them. The shaman said to the people, "I am going to make them disappear, and we shall disappear from their view also." Then he told the people to go behind a hill so they couldn't

see the enemy. He alone stood on top of the hill. After about twenty minutes the shaman told them all to come up again. When they came up, there were only cattle grazing where the enemy had been. The shaman told the men to herd the cattle, drive them to the river, and shoot them and eat them there.[24]

A good example of the spiritual conflict that ensued when two parties with varying degrees of power met in battle is recorded in this story. Here the Sioux and Chippewa use their powers to give them an advantage over the other. As it turned out, the Sioux won this contest because of their quick action that prevented the Chippewa from using their powers to their advantage.

HIDING FROM THE FLYING MAN

All the old Indians know about the flying man. He was a very powerful Mide 'a who could cause a feather to come to him out of the air. This feather would come toward him and enter into his body. Then the man could rise up and fly like a bird. The Chippewa depended upon him in the wars with the Sioux, for he could fly through the air and spy out the enemy. Once the Chippewa suspected that the Sioux were near and they sent this flying man to look over the country. As the Sioux were sitting in their camp they saw the flying man coming toward them in the air, and the leader of the Sioux said to his men: "Fill up the pipe as fast as you can," so they filled the pipe and lighted it.

They held the stem of the pipe up toward the flying man. They pointed it at him and he could not see the crowd of Sioux. He did not see them at all. So he returned to his friends and said that he did not see the Sioux anywhere. Then the Chippewa marched across an open field. The Sioux were watching, but they let them pass. Then the Sioux shot and killed them all, even the flying man.[25]

THE INVISIBLE WOMAN

This story has a much less bloody ending, and here it is not the individual with power who saves the day. Rather, a spirit intervenes on behalf of a woman who is hiding from the soldiers and the story has a strange twist that leaves us wondering how to explain the incident.

> When the Sioux were fighting the white men a party of them were closely pursued and one woman, unable to keep up with the warriors, hid in a pond. There she stayed four days, submerged in the shallow water at the edge of the pond, with a lily-leaf over her face. At the end of four days she heard a voice say, "The people who have been killing your friends are about to eat; come and share their food." The woman was afraid to leave her hiding place. Soon she heard the voice again, saying "Come, I am calling you to come." At last she believed the voice and came from the water. The voice said "Keep right on this path and I will see you after awhile." The next the woman knew she was among the soldiers and eating with them. She could see them, but they could not see her. After eating she started in the direction her people had taken. Then she saw the person whose voice she had heard. He was a manido' and appeared in the form of a white man.[26]

LAME MEDICINE MAN CAUSES BLINDNESS

Could the power to cause invisibility be described in other terms? The Cheyennes felt it was a power to make their enemies blind to their presence. In the summer of 1831, a Cheyenne party headed to Crow country to steal horses suddenly found themselves in the path of a much larger party of Crows headed south with the same intent. High Back Wolf, leader of the expedition, asked Lame Medicine Man to make the Crows blind so there would be no battle. The Cheyennes were lying flat on the ground hoping to avoid notice by the Crows.

Suddenly Lame Medicine Man rose and carrying Oxohtsemo (the sacred wheel lance) with him, crept out a short distance ahead of his men. There he thrust the point of the Sacred Wheel Lance into the ground, so that Oxohtsemo's stood firmly planted in Mother Earth. Then the holy man rose to his feet and, standing there in plain view of the enemies, began singing Oxohtsemo's sacred blinding song. The Crows kept right on riding toward them, passing close to them, then splashing their horses on across the stream that flowed below them. The People's men could hear them laughing and talking as they rode by. Lame Medicine Man paid no attention to the enemies. He continued his singing, repeating the blinding song over and over, until finally all the Crows had ridden on by them. Afterward, his men told the People that the Crows never looked toward the place where they were lying.[27]

PRODUCING THE ANOMALOUS THINGS

Highly unusual and exceedingly rare was the ability of certain medicine men to produce anomalous events that certainly beg explanation. Earlier, in discussing the ability to change weather patterns, we saw that the Cheyenne medicine men could cause snow to stop blowing and plants to begin growing during the winter when such things do not happen. We have also seen that medicine men could make plants and bushes grow at an incredible rate, and a kernel of corn could be made to grow in little more than a day's time. These next stories are halfway between these two powers, at least as the medicine men were able to produce anomalous things.

Robert H. Lowie commented that "Plenty-fingers, a contemporary of Medicinecrow's father, loomed in memory not because he claimed a bear revelation, but because he worked miracles by it. In midwinter he would produce turnips and sarvis-berries; he could transform bark into dry meat; bullet-proof he merely spat on his hands when shot, and immediately recovered."[28] Lowie also reported that "Gray-Bull believed in Wants-to-live [*a fellow medicine man*] because of ocular demonstration. One night the two wanted to smoke but lacked the wherewithal, but Wants-to-live asked for some bark, shook it in the air and produced some tobacco, which Gray-bull smoked. On another occasion, the same wonder-worker rolled mud into four balls, which turned into beads for Gray-bull to wear in his necklace."[29]

BUFFALO LUMP'S BULLETS

Two Leggings, the Crow warrior, described a feat of producing the anomalous thing performed by Buffalo Lump. In this instance, bullets were produced under circumstances that seem very suspicious and could easily be challenged. "We laid down several [robes] and crowded around as he walked up to the bearskin, rubbed his face against it, and returned to the robes. As he leaned forward a stream of bullets rolled out of his mouth, many more than any man could hold. He told us who liked hunting to take one, and four men did. Buffalo Lump said that was enough and picked up the rest, swallowing one after another. He asked for water and after drinking some poured a little on his head."[30]

A UNIFIED SMOKE

Frank Speck, writing on the Catawba Indians of South Carolina, reported a highly unusual practice. I have never heard a hint of this kind of phenomenon and, consequently, have included it here because it seems to me that the original idea must have come from a medicine man—but when? The ritual may go back thousands of years. The Catawba were still using it to reach decisions in 1938, when Speck visited them, and he does not report how they adopted this practice.

> Divination through interpretation of the movements of clouds of smoke rising from the "council pipe" passed around during the sessions of the tribal governing body is described in my rendering of the words of Chief Sam Blue (1938) when discussing the procedures of chief and council as he had heard

of them from his predecessors in office.

"The chief smokes the pipe, blowing clouds of smoke up in the air (from his mouth). Then he passes the pipe to the assistant chief sitting on his left side, thence it is passed from hand to hand around in the same direction to the councilmen in turn. If a big cloud of smoke forms in a single mass and hovers above them it is a sign that they come together in unity of mind and harmony of spirit to discuss the affairs before them. If the smoke separates into clots and does not combine into a mass it signifies that they are hot in unison of thought."[31]

CHAPTER EIGHT

THE SPIRITUAL UNIVERSE

* * * * * * * * * * * * *

We have examined a wide variety of stories relating the exercise of extraordinary powers possessed by Indian medicine men. Many of the stories are reported by reputable and ordinary eyewitnesses who, while they experienced these unusual happenings, were at a loss to explain them, at least in terms familiar to the non-Indian world. Some of these accounts derive from the early days of contact between Indians and non-Indians and may possibly be overstated or inadequately summarized, giving but a hint of the actual powers being demonstrated. With the exception of the spirit lodge that is still performed in eastern Canada, we do not, as a rule, have people who can perform feats that command our attention, as do these stories from the old days. The Arickaras do not conduct miniature buffalo hunts anymore.

The chief explanation offered by non-Indian skeptics, then and now, is that in some way, the medicine man was able to hypnotize the observers and that what they experienced was simply a delusion or fantasy. This explanation/accusation overlooks the fact that some of these demonstrations of powers occurred in front of a large crowd of people who would often have delighted in seeing the practitioner discredited. We know that the medicine man could feel any disbelief, disrespect, or negative attitude among the observers and participants. Paul Kane could not sneak up on the proceedings in the woods. Thus, while we cannot ourselves evaluate these powers from the viewpoint of an intimate experience, we can rely on these accounts as equal to reports by scientists on their experiments.

For many of the non-Indian religious observers, be they Protestant or Catholic, everything the medicine men did was the work of the devil, even though they often healed serious illness, warned people of danger, made accurate predictions, and retrieved lost objects. While the electoral process today seeks to demonize candidates, characterizing an unusual positive event as the devil's doings is hardly an acceptable interpretation of phenomena. I have not dwelled on witchcraft that is a perversion of powers granted to people who proved to be a negative force in the community because it is a low-level activity generally taking place on a personal basis when two families or individuals could not get along and sought to express revenge or jealousy.

Our expectations in life are that events will occur in a cause-and-effect universe in which it is relatively simple to trace the beginnings and end of any natural phenomenon. When we experience an event or feeling out of the ordinary, we tend to dismiss it as unreal, a fantasy that somehow broke into our consciousness. We cannot explain what we have experienced because we have only this narrow, materialistic framework in which to evaluate what has happened. In a practical sense, the Newtonian billiard balls that clang together creating events and guaranteeing uniformity are sufficient for us. But what if we learned to have other expectations? Suppose we were of such a nature that we could discern the life force in everything and were thus assured that as we made our way through life, unusual things could happen. What if these events gave testimony that the physical world we know was but a manifestation of a larger cosmos that was beyond our powers to discern and was also part of our lives. We would then begin to attribute the cause of some unusual events as the intervention or intersection of unseen yet powerful forces that played a role in our experience, even if we could not see them. In theory, but not in daily practice, we do live in such a world.

Judging the exploits of medicine men by reference to the physical

Newtonian universe is completely irrelevant today with the advances in knowledge of the universe achieved by quantum physics and microbiology. If we were to measure the medicine men's powers by the criteria and beliefs advanced by these two sciences, we would discover that every story in this collection is well within the probable boundaries of a new and emerging vision of the universe. Time, space, and substance are not ultimate entities in the quantum universe, but merely handy concepts that apply when we investigate nature from our point of view. They vanish or dissolve into each other at subatomic levels of activity. In the same way, time, space, and substance do not have ultimate values in a ceremony. They appear as a function of the ceremony, not as a border or boundary beyond which it is not possible to go.

How much do the experiences of Indian medicine men coincide with or illustrate the same values and results as those found in modem science? Beginning with the idea of substance, the ultimate constituent of the physical universe that has been the mainstay of Western science since the early Greek philosophers, let us see what useful parallels can be drawn between these two radically different approaches to gaining a better understanding of the physical world. We will examine substance, space, and time and try to understand a people who lived and experienced life in a world in which everything was alive and related.

SUBSTANCE

There seems to be a reasonable number of Western scientists and thinkers who subscribe to the idea that the ultimate constituent of the universe is mind, or mind-stuff. Fred Alan Wolf, a physicist writing popular interpretative books on the new understanding of the universe, said: "Today our position is close to the one discovered by basic tribal peoples. The concept of universal energy in our language might be called the 'universal quantum wave function' or 'matter wave' or 'probability wave of quantum physics.' This 'wave' pervades everything, and like the universal energy, it resists objective discovery. It appears as a guiding influence in all that we observe.

"Perhaps it is the same thing as the 'clear light'—the all pervading consciousness without an object of Buddhist thought."[1]

David Foster, the English philosopher, agrees: "When physics is explored to its depths, one comes across a world of mathematics rather than a world of 'things.' Similarly, in modern biology we have seen that beyond biochemistry we come to a world of information and literary logic in the DNA, and if one wishes to enquire 'what is behind the DNA?' there is little choice but to propose a similar LOGOS. It would seem that the developments in biology are even more suggestive than those from physics in confirming that 'the stuff of the world is mind-stuff' for while only some of us can grasp a basic mathematical reality, we can all understand the nature of language."[2]

F. David Peat, another English philosopher, elaborates somewhat in echoing Wolf's and Foster's understanding of the mental/spiritual universe: The "fundamental symmetries and their structures have their origin in something that *is close to a pure intelligence which springs from an unknown creative source.* The ground out of which matter emerges is also the source for consciousness, and indeed, since these two orders are essentially indivisible, it may be expected that 'fundamental symmetries' play a role in the structure of consciousness as well."[3] (Emphasis added)

Werner Heisenberg earlier suggested: "I think that on this point modern physics has definitely decided for Plato. For the smallest units of matter are in fact not physical objects in the ordinary sense of the word; they are forms, structures or—in Plato's sense—Ideas, which can be unambiguously spoken of only in the language of mathematics."[4]

Carl Gustav Jung once admitted: "The mana theory maintains that there is something like a widely distributed power in the external world that produces all those extraordinary effects. Everything that exists acts, otherwise it would not be. It can be only by virtue of its inherent energy. Being is a field of force. The primitive idea of mana, as you can see, has in it the beginning of a crude theory of energy."[5] Even scholars working with near death experiences find themselves aligning with the quantum universe. Filippo Liverziani, an Italian scholar, said: "The spiritual dimension of the other side appears to be a world constituted solely by thought. Thought creates it, directly, without any instrumental mediation; and it is also thought that knows it, experiences it, directly, and without any mediation of bodily senses."[6]

The above thinkers, and many others not quoted here, are of the opinion that the world we think of as solidly physical is, in fact, a strange, indescribable "mind stuff" that provides the foundation for everything. Jeffrey Iverson, writing on the near death experience, speculates: "The universe might be composed of thought, which could explain how an observer might appear to interact with his experiment. If matter is a "frozen thought" in a universe composed of "mind-stuff" then almost anything is possible—including the paranormal."[7] The idea that matter is frozen mind stuff should be sufficiently clear to enable us to speculate further.

The conclusions reached by contemporary physicists, biologists, and near death scholars are a result of a long, tedious path from the Greek atomists and philosophers, through the European struggles with the false mind/body dichotomy, to the achievements in physics during the twentieth century. As increasingly sophisticated instruments became available to scientists, enabling them to pierce into the depths of the atom and then to wave/particle conceptions, the intellectual movement has been away from a hard physical universe to the descriptions cited above. Present conceptions of the universe therefore reach a conclusion that seems to represent the cumulative wisdom of Western science.

We have already seen that tribal peoples observed the world around them and quickly concluded that it represented an energetic mind undergirding the physical world, its motions, and provided energy and life in everything that existed. This belief, as we have seen, is the starting point, not the conclusion. Assuming or intuiting mind as the dominant entity, would not the tribal peoples' questions vary substantially from the questions asked by the Western philosophers? Would they not seek to know more about the mind behind everything they saw, felt, and dreamed? A significant number of American Indian tribes did adopt the idea that the world was mind, and we should examine their beliefs in this respect.

John R. Swanton, the great anthropologist, writing about the Muskogee Indians, summarized their beliefs regarding the nature of the world:

> The world and all that it contained were the products of mind and bore everywhere the marks of mind. Matter was not something which had given birth to mind, but something which had formerly been mind, something from which mind had withdrawn, was quiescent, and out of which it might again be roused. This mind was visibly manifested in the so-called "living things," as plants, and still more, animals. Nevertheless, latent within inorganic substance no less than in plants and animals, was mind in its highest form, i.e. human mind. This might come to the surface at any time but it did so particularly at the fasting warrior, the "knower," and the doctor. Indeed, the importance of these two last lay in their ability to penetrate to the human life within the mineral, plant, and animal value in ordering the lives of their fellow beings. Not that mind was attributed to one individuality, but that it was recognized as everywhere of the same nature.[8]

The Omaha understanding is similar and provides an articulate summary of the beliefs and practices of many tribes:

> An invisible and continuous life was believed to permeate all things, seen and unseen. This life manifests itself in two ways: First, by causing to move—all motion, all actions of mind and body are because of this invisible life; second, *by causing permancy of structure and form, as in the rock; the physical features of the landscape mountains, plains, streams, rivers, lakes, the animal and man.* This invisible life was also conceived of as being similar to the will power of which man is conscious within himself— a power by which things are brought to pass. Through this mysterious life and power all things are related to one

another, and to man, the seen to the unseen, the dead to the living, a fragment of anything in its entirety. This invisible life and power was called Wakonda.[9] (Emphasis added)

The Sioux, according to A. McG. Beede, "believed (with no thought of gainsay) in Spirit (Woniya), which is the author and source of 'force and energy' in all things, or rather persons, for the entire world, to them, consisted of persons. So fully did the Western Sioux conceive all things as actually being, fundamentally mind, intelligence, reason, spirit."[10] And the Hopis, according to Frank Waters, begin their creation story: "first, they say, there was only the Creator, Taiowa. All else was endless space. There was no beginning and no end, no time, no shape, no life. Just an immeasurable void that had its beginning and end, time, shape, and life in the mind of Taiowa, the Creative. Then he, the infinite, conceived the finite."[11]

Scientists may well quarrel with the tribal terminology and say that the Indians were simple creationists, and, in a rigid sense, that was true. However, they did not draw the same conclusions as did the Middle Eastern peoples. With no scriptures to limit their inquiry or narrow their conceptual universe, the tribal elders had the belief that "the peculiar gift of an animate or inanimate form can be transferred to man. The means by which this transference takes place is mysterious and pertains to Wakonda but is not the Wakonda."[12] We know from the discussion of how medicine men came to be that this mysterious energy generally summoned them through the offices or intercession of other forms of life, and then, through dreams and visions, they obtained powers that were shared with other forms of life.

The Indians developed as comprehensive analysis of the nature of the world as has Western science, but the goals have been very different. Western science is based on Roger Bacon's command to pry nature's secrets from her, by torture, if nothing else. The medicine men sought additional alliances with other entities and, according to some tribes, accumulated both spiritual powers and cumulative knowledge over several lifetimes. The Muskogees thought that much knowledge had been given at the beginning of the world, and this governed each kind of entity and its activities. "While these things [other entities] did, indeed, have certain characteristic appearances and activities which were 'Natural'—that is, the things normally expected from them—they owed these to a certain impression made upon them in the beginning of things, or at least at some time in the distant past, and it was not to be assumed that they were all the powers which such beings and objects—or, assuming the Indian point of view, we might say simple beings possessed."[13]

Delving further into the Muskogee understanding, they discovered, as did all tribes, that "The power could be invoked by the use of charms and the repetition of certain formulae. 'By a word' wonderful things could be accomplished; 'by a word' the entire world could be compressed into such a small space that the medicine man who was master of the word could encircle it in four steps. It was power of this kind which was imparted to medicines, yet the source of this power was after all the anthropomorphic powers, which, at the very beginning of things, declared what diseases were to be and also appointed the remedies to be employed in curing them."[14]

If we live in a world of spirit and the landscape and entities around us are really frozen thoughts, then, in a reverse fashion, from creation or manifestation as a physical being, spiritual gifts can easily change, enhance, or contract the actors and events in the physical universe. We have seen sometimes there was diagnosis of an illness and recommendations that a certain medicine man could heal the disease, and other times when the healer simply did one or two things and the healing took place. The physical did not and could not withstand the attention directed toward it by spiritual powers.

There were two ways the medicine men used that established and maintained the link between the spiritual and physical worlds. When they offered and burned tobacco, sweetgrass, and sage, the spiritual world opened itself up to them. Equally powerful were the songs that the spirits gave them. I know of no story that did not have sacred songs as an essential element in invoking the spirits. Indeed, songs were to the medicine men what instruments are to Western scientists searching for a deeper knowledge of the world. As we have seen, sacred songs appear to be more powerful and are much faster in their application and effect. Smudging seems to be the preamble to what thereafter follows.

The compatibility of tribal beliefs and Platonic philosophy is astounding. Black Elk remembered, "Crazy Horse dreamed and went into the world where there is nothing but the spirit of all things. That is the real world that is behind this one, and everything we see here is something like a shadow from that world."[15] Identifying the substance of the universe, then, as the function of mind, Black Elk felt that whatever we do of a spiritual nature enhances the physical and increases our appreciation of it. Recalling his vision experience, he said: "When I looked into the cloud, only [the] grandfathers were beholding me and I could see the flaming rainbow there and the tipi and the whole vision I could see again. I looked at what I was doing and saw that I was making just exactly what I saw in the cloud. This on earth was like a shadow of that in the cloud."[16]

The substance of the universe is relationships, the symmetries and their structure, as Peat expressed it. Indians say, "We are all relatives." Modern physics seeks to uncover the final piece of the puzzle in its pursuit of Higgs boson, believing that in finding this elusive particle, they can completely describe the universe. Even if successful, they will have only completed the logical circle and described the physical universe which is, after all, merely a frozen thought. In their ceremonies, medicine men are able to change the world and present it with new paths to follow. By healing, predicting, and locating lost objects, they cancel out the determinism of the physical and create different worlds that are consonant with the activities and direction of the world behind appearances.

SPACE

Time and space were the defining concepts of the Western philosophical tradition from the Greek atomists until the mid-twentieth century, when we were able to split the atom and show that the Einstein formula $E = MC^2$ described the substance of the universe. These concepts were believed to represent absolute entities in the composition of the universe. In Newtonian terms, they represented a structured universe and were dependable in that they always formed the context within which everything else happened. With the discoveries in subatomic physics, we learned that they merged together and became useless when describing miniscule atomic events. Today, they are regarded as flexible concepts, useful in a human-sized world but increasingly mysterious at macro and micro levels of inquiry.

Space is found in most tribal traditions, hidden within ceremonies, but certainly occupying a critical place in helping to orient us to our sensory world. The Plains Indians, in beginning a ceremony, always point their pipes to the six directions: up, down, north, south, east, and west. This ritual pays respect to the powers of the universe and recognizes that they appear to us as a group of powers and center our emotional universe for the purpose of communing with the spirits. The sweat lodge is built in the shape of a sphere and reproduces, as closely as possible, the cosmos as a whole. The sand paintings also represent the universe, and to avoid being trapped within the powers that the paintings summon, the work is never finished and a little lapse in the continuity of the drawings is left. The spirit lodge has a unique feature in that it is an elongated version of the cosmos and provides a forum within which we can communicate with the spirits.

The power of space is one of relationships, and since the entire cosmos cannot be contained in our daily lives, we learn that sacred places represent the power by showing us that we can become a part of a preexisting set of relationships. Each tribe has its own center and its own boundaries marked out by reference to existing landscape features. Thus some Plains tribes say that Pikes Peak in Colorado is the center of the universe, but Rainy Mountain or Harney Peak are the center of their particular universes. When people accommodate themselves to a landscape, they learn the parameters of their spiritual existence, although sometimes these boundaries change according to the needs of the people. Thus a good number of tribes saw the Pipestone Quarry or the Bear's Lodge (Devils Tower) as part of their universe, even though they were not centrally located. One might, indeed, draw a map with inconsistent and overlapping boundaries to illustrate the economic, political, social, and religious worlds of each tribe.

With space so flexible and places reminding us of the power of space, it was natural that Indians would find a way to incorporate this flexibility into their ceremonies and learn how to use the space in startling ways. Charles Lummis reported two feats of Navajo medicine men that seem blatantly impossible, but to which he nevertheless gave credence.

This exploit was apparently commonplace in the Southwest when Lummis was writing his books on New Mexico and Arizona. Lummis was puzzled as to why the Navajos could perform this feat, but the Pueblos couldn't—or didn't. If sand paintings and the *sipapu* are but miniatures of the universe, and if smoking the pipe to the six directions acknowledges the power of the universe, then the creation of a tiny universe would certainly be within the range of possibilities. We cannot say no to the possibility of spiritual powers manifesting themselves in unusual ways.

NAVAJOS MOVING THE SUN

Lummis frankly admitted: "One of their manifestations, which I have never found among the Pueblos, is the 'moving of the sun.' This takes place in the medicine lodge at night—the time of all official acts of the medicine-men. At the appointed time a sun rises on the east (inside the room) and slowly describes an arched course until at last it sets in the west side of the room, and darkness reigns again. During the whole performance a sacred chant is kept up, and once started dare not be interrupted until the sun has finished its course."[17] The continuity demanded in this performance raises some questions— what would happen if the singing stopped with the tiny sun midway across the sky? Unfortunately, Lummis didn't gather enough data or give an adequate explanation of the feat so that we can learn much about the universe and the particular power that enabled these men to do this thing.

A NAVAJO THUNDERSTORM

Perhaps as unusual, and certainly involving audience participation, was the ability of the Navajo medicine men to create a thunderstorm inside a hogan. Again, Lummis expressed his utter bewilderment at the process whereby they did this. In his own words:

> Another equally startling trick is performed when the room has been darkened by extinguishing the countless candles which gave abundant light on the other ceremonies. The awed audience sits awhile in the gloom in hushed expectancy. Then they hear the low growl of distant thunder, which keeps rolling nearer and nearer. Suddenly a binding flash of lightning shoots across the room from side to side, and another and another, while the room trembles to the roar of the thunder, and the flashes show terrified women clinging to their husbands and brothers. Outside the sky may be twinkling with a million stars, but in that dark room a fearful storm seems to be raging. ... These artificial storms last but a few moments, and when they are over the room is lighted up again for the other ceremonies. How these effects are produced I am Utterly unable to explain, but they are startlingly real.[18]

The Navajo practitioners were able to create a small world and one of its primary elements—the thunderstorm—with song and prayers. Imagine, if you will, standing outside the medicine lodge where the atmosphere is calm and looking in the door where a very intense thunderstorm is taking place. You are at the intersection of two real, similar, yet distinct manifestations of the flexibility of space. Thus it is that many medicine men will say that the bowl of the pipe contains worlds we have never dreamt existed.

One final example might be how space changes to accommodate the spiritual energy that can be mustered in a ceremony. We have no examples of this phenomenon, but only the undocumented statements of medicine men as to their experiences. The Lakota tradition says that there is another world beneath the Bear's Lodge with trees, lakes, and prairies. It can be entered only by certain people who have this power. The popular name for these locations is the portal between worlds. In the Cheyenne tradition, Bear Butte is such a spot. It is where Sweet Medicine received his revelation and the sacred arrows that guided the people for thousands of years. There is no cave at Bear Butte—except for the one into which the medicine men can enter.

The Pawnees have identified a number of buttes in Nebraska that are, in fact, animal lodges where the animals and spirits of animals reside. We have already seen the immense powers of the men of this tribe, and one power reported—but not in written sources—is that of transforming themselves into their animal spirits. Walter Echohawk, a prominent Pawnee elder, said that when Quahnah Parker came to visit his tribe and sought permission to speak to the doctors in the sacred lodge, they greeted him in their animal form.

William K. Powers discussed the practice of the Sioux in calling upon all the powers of the universe. In this procedure, sacred space is created. "When an Oglala wants to call upon all the types of sicun in the universe he must prepare one tobacco offering for each of them. Each tobacco offering, called canli wapahte 'tobacco bundle,' is made from a one-inch square of cotton cloth into which a minute pinch of tobacco has been placed; the cloth is shaped into a small ball and tied to one string. During certain rituals such as the vision quest and Yuqipi, all 405 tobacco offerings are tied to one string that is used to delineate a sacred area metaphorically called the hocoka. Hocoka is an old word that refers to the inner part of a camp circle, but as used ritually it means a sacred space, the center of the universe, within which a sacred person or suppliant prays, sings, or otherwise communicates with spirits."[19]

In summary, then, space is critical to the Indian perception of the world, but primarily because it can be created by the holy people, and energies and information can be transported from the larger cosmos to the particular location where humans need help and sustenance. If other religious traditions have a similar idea of space, their beliefs have not been articulated or communicated.

TIME

There should be no question that, like space, time is an unusually flexible experience. But it is difficult to pin down examples, because our own perceptions of time vary so significantly. It seems an hour listening to a boring lecture, but only a few minutes when engaged in enjoyable recreation. Dreams sometimes are experienced as several days long, while the actual chronological time is very short. Black Elk was comatose for twelve days, and yet if we attempt to determine the duration of his vision, it does not take long at all for him to experience what he reported.

The growing of corn and other plants provides us with an empirical example when, through songs, the Zunis and Pawnees were able to increase the rate of growth of plants so that they matured in a very short time. Here we have an intersection between the two worlds, physical and spiritual. We also have the intervention of the sacred changing the nature and experience of the plants. How then do we gauge the kind of time with which we are involved? We have already seen how Geronimo could make his people invisible. There is another story where he made the night last longer than usual.

GERONIMO'S POWER

An unusual twist in the manner we understand time can be illustrated by a story an Apache elder told Morris Opler. He was one of Geronimo's warriors and therefore provides an eyewitness testimony. It seems, considering the exploits of the famous Chiricahua warrior, that he must have had immense medicine powers since it took three-quarters of the standing American army to chase him, and he arranged a surrender that, had the United States kept its word, would have been better terms than General Lee received from General Grant at Appomattox. "When he was on the warpath, Geronimo fixed it so that morning wouldn't come too soon. He did it by singing. Once we were going to a certain place, and Gerommo didn't want it to become light before he reached it. He saw the enemy while they were in a level place, and he didn't want them to spy on us. He wanted morning to break after we had climbed over a mountain, so that the enemy couldn't see us. So Geronimo sang, and the night remained for two or three hours longer. I saw this myself."[20]

THE LENGTH OF A LIFETIME

Very interesting is the apparent knowledge of the future of the chronological time that is given to people having a dream or vision. They are sometimes shown or told about the length of their lives, including a sketch of their accomplishments or talents, and how they will look when they are old—a guarantee perhaps of old age. We might suppose that this aspect of the vision provides them with a sense of invulnerability in the face of future events, at least until the conditions surrounding their deaths appear. Here we refer back to the Jesuit story of the vision, in which the person was told he would survive to old age, have four children, become sexually dysfunctional with his wife, and enjoy great success as a hunter.

BRAVE BUFFALO'S EXPECTATIONS

Sometimes, the promise of longevity carries with it a certain kind of power. Brave Buffalo reported the promise of a long life given to him during his dream of the buffalo. "The buffalo in my dream told me that I would live to be 102 years old. Then they said: 'If you are to show people the great value of the buffalo one proof which you must give them is a demonstration of your endurance. After properly qualifying yourself you will be able to show that weapons can not harm you and you may challenge anyone to shoot you with arrows and a gun.'"[21] He reported that several times, he had allowed people to shoot at him with arrows and guns and always proved invulnerable to them.

Two famous Plains medicine men learned in their early visions that they would grow to a very old age: Black Elk and Plenty Coups, the revered Crow elder. It is instructive to examine their accounts.

BLACK ELK'S EXPECTATION

Black Elk met and counseled with the powers of the universe and received instructions on how to use his powers and which powers were to be his, and, finally, his vision became intensely personal as he

listened to the Sixth Grandfather speak. "Now I knew the sixth
Grandfather was about to speak, he who was the Spirit of the Earth,
and I saw that he was very old, but more as men are old. His hair was
long and white, his face was all wrinkles and his eyes were deep and
dim. I stared at him, for it seemed I knew him somehow; and as I
stared, he slowly changed, for he was growing backwards into youth,
and when he had become a boy, I knew that he was myself with all
the years that would be mine at last."[22] This phenomenon of watching people's faces change as they seem to be moving backward in
time occurs with some frequency in Plains Indian dreams and
visions. For some people, it is a reassurance of a long life, and for others, encountering deceased relatives in dreams is an affirmation of the
continuing life in the spirit world where time does not exist.

PLENTY COUPS, CHIEF OF THE CROWS

He was given an extensive vision during which the man-person, his
spiritual guide, took him down into the earth, and together they visited many distant surface locations where the man-person explained
the road of life that lay ahead of him. Some of the predictions were
gloomy, and Plenty Crows realized his life task would be leading his
people through traumatic times. In the vision, he received some
assurance that he would bear the burdens lying ahead. Then they
came into a dark, thick forest area in the Crow homeland.

> I followed him [the helping spirit] back through the hole with-
> out seeing anything until we came out right over there
> [pointing] where we first entered the hole in the ground.
> Then I saw the spring down by those trees, this very house
> just as it is, these trees which comfort us today, and a very old
> man sitting in the shade alone. I felt pity for him because he
> was so old and feeble. "Look well upon this old man," said the
> Man-person. "Do you know him, Plenty Coups," he asked me.
>
> "No," I said, looking closely at the old man's face in the
> shade of this tree.
>
> "This old man is yourself, Plenty Coups," the Man-person

told me. And then I could see the Man-person no more. He was gone, and so too was the old man. Instead I saw only a dark forest.[23]

A CHIRICAHUA APACHE PREDICTION

Predictions of old age seem to be almost throwaway prophecies when they occur in a dream or vision. Opler reported on an old Chiricahua Apache who flatly stated: "When I was a young boy, I had this experience and I was told that I would live to be an old man. Old age was promised me, and I got it. The power told me 'you shall see your country again, but you shall be alone.' I have lost my family, all except two boys. The power told me, 'When you get old, you can tell about the ceremony.' That is why I tell you this."[24]

TWO LEGGINGS

In a dream, the major spiritual characters changed form. At least they appeared to Two Leggings to have aged somewhat. And the thought of old age came to him as he observed the change in countenance of his dream person: "After the hawk had shown me several directions it shut its eyes, folded its wings, and hung its head. My dream person had appeared young but now he seemed like an old man. This meant I would also grow old."[25] This prediction of old age seems to have some parallels with Black Elk's realization that his identification with the Sixth Grandfather meant he would live into old age.

THE BUFFALO AND HILLSIDE

This vision of old age comes as a result of an immediate contact with the buffalo soul. After a large buffalo bull was killed and skinned, Hillside took it upon himself to attach the skull to his back and drag it all day until he received a message. By evening, he was exhausted, and that's when he received his prediction.

I was about twenty years old, and among the Many Lodges band. Over at White Mountains a big buffalo was killed. Its head was cut off and its hide skinned, leaving the tail on. I had myself cut in two places on the back and dragged the skull outside the camp. The people all saw me. My brother, the same who had made the arrow for me, pierced my back.

I started early in the morning and traveled all day with the skull; when the sun was low I was too weak to drag it any longer. I went to the mountain with it, my brother cut it off and I slept on the skull for a pillow. It was raining hard. In my sleep I heard a man say: "Wait, poor fellow, you will eat now." He had the foot of a buffalo on him. On the Pryor side I saw a large crowd of people with this person in the lead. When I was asleep, a buffalo came up to me and licked me. His hair was gray; this showed that I was to live to be an old man.[26]

THE NIGHTHAWK CEREMONY PREDICTION

Another Apache prediction cited by Opler basically outlined the individual's future life similar to the prediction for Catherine Wabose in that many details were offered that could be verified as the person went through life. The prediction was made by two medicine men performing the Apache nighthawk ceremony.

All during their ceremony they learned many things about my future. They told me that in the future I was going to have land and own everything and have children too. They said that the first was to be a boy, and it was. And they said, "You are not only going to have this boy but girls too. In the spring you are going to plow. You will look up and see just one little cloud. And it will open and rain first on your place." And it all really came true. In the spring I was plowing back of East Mountain. It rained first on my place. It did this for several years.[27]

THE CIRCUMSTANCES OF DEATH

There is another aspect of time so peculiar that it cannot easily be understood. There were two great Indian warriors in the closing days of freedom of the Plains Indians: Crazy Horse of the Oglala Sioux and Roman Nose of the Cheyennes. In their visions, they were told not when they would die, but the circumstances in which their deaths might occur. No suggestions were made to ensure them of a long life. They were only told that, should certain circumstances arise, to avoid, if possible, things that could cause their deaths.

Crazy Horse was given certain ornaments to wear that made him invulnerable to the weapons of his enemies. He was promised that he would never be harmed in battle as long as he had these special protections. His war record proves beyond a doubt that his vision held true. But he was told that he would be killed by the treachery and connivance of his own people. His death occurred when certain chiefs, jealous of him, conspired with the soldiers to take him prisoner and hold him in a stockade until he could be sent to a prison camp in the south, probably Dry Tortugas. He, of course, resisted and, while his arms were held, was bayoneted in the side at Fort Robinson, Nebraska, and died a few hours later.

Roman Nose, or Hook Nose, was regarded as perhaps the bravest warrior among the Northern Cheyennes. He one day came to Ice, the great medicine man, and asked "Do you ever see anything?" Ice had had a vision a long time before of the warbonnet that the Thunder wore. Roman Nose had seen the same bonnet, and that was the reason he approached the medicine man. So Ice made the bonnet and used only natural materials, nothing manufactured and nothing metal. With the warbonnet came specific instructions: he was always to paint himself before he put on other clothing; he must not shake hands with anyone; and he could not eat any food that had been lifted from a dish with a metal implement. If he did, he would die.

Roman Nose became a spectacular war leader and once rode back and forth in close proximity to the soldiers in a battle in Wyoming to draw fire and overheat the soldiers' breech-loading rifles. At the Battle of Beecher's Island in Colorado in 1868, he was visiting a camp of Sioux nearby the Cheyenne village and was served bread that had been lifted from a skillet with an iron fork. Roman Nose did not know of this violation of his powers until Eight Horns, a Cheyenne Dog Soldier, noticed the woman using the iron fork. Roman Nose quietly said, "That breaks my medicine." It was too late to undergo purification ceremonies to restore the power. Knowing he would be killed, he nevertheless led the last charge of the afternoon, was hit by a bullet in the small of the back, and died at sunset.

Both of these men could have behaved differently and lived to a nice old age without anyone calling their courage into question. Knowing that the circumstances of their deaths had arisen, each remained faithful to themselves and triggered the inevitable fate they had been promised. What role did time play in their lives in that a particular set of circumstances, already forecast in their youths, could be brought to fruition any time during the lives resulting in their deaths? Did they not have some control over the length of their lives in that at any moment, they had the possibility of ending their lives through a simple exercise of their wills or a dreadful lapse in concentration? We cannot say that the length of their lives had already been determined, because those particular situations could have arisen at any time, yet only the pattern appears, not the inevitable remise.

Is the universe itself the subject of a sketch similar to the boundaries that Wakan tanka gives to each entity? Do certain sets of circumstances lie ahead of us wherein we change the world radically by the choices we make? The old medicine men were apparently instructed not to reveal the whole content of their visions, since that would render them secular knowledge and they would lose their powers. But certain men were told that if they gave away the whole vision, they would soon die since their purpose in life could no longer be accomplished.

SIYA'KA'S DEATH

Frances Densmore sadly recounted one of these instances. One of her major sources of knowledge was Siya'ka, and we have already discussed some of his experiences. Densmore kept pressuring him to tell her his whole vision. When he finally relented and told her his vision, she commented: "Siya'ka was deeply affected by the narration of his dreams. Some men fear that such an act will cause their death, but Siya'ka did not speak of this. He took the writer's hand, saying that he had given her his most cherished possession. In little more than a year, Siya'ka was laid to rest in the prairie he loved."[28] Surely, Densmore did not wish to contribute to Siya'ka's death. But just as surely, she knew that in revealing everything in his dream, the old man was bringing his life to a close, his task completed since the vision had become common property. Many times, the thoughtless scholar is the cause of great tragedy among Indians.

Do the actions of humans, when making decisions, radically change the manner in which the world proceeds? The passage of time, while it has certain homogeneity, also seems to have some quirks that are reminiscent of chaos theory. To understand the complexities of life as experienced in chronological time, then, we must be alert to the possibility that some things in the future are ordained, and humans can advance or inhibit the procession of sacred revelation and fulfillment that will require adjustment on the spiritual plane. Had either Roman Nose or Crazy Horse sought a safe life and avoided the circumstances that resulted in his death, Western history would have been dramatically different. They could have died much earlier in their careers or lived to be old men hardly able to walk. Perhaps the possibility of parallel worlds fulfilling the possibilities of a human choice can give us insight into the responsibilities we have in following our best thoughts and sentiments.

There is a form of predestination present in these stories of the length of a lifetime that suggest a continuity between the spiritual world and our physical world so that a commonly shared sense of time emerges. Does this time dimension hold for everyone or just for those chosen few who have an intimate relationship with the spirits? There are many stories of Indians anticipating their death or receiving a warning that they are about to depart the physical world. But these kinds of experiences are shared with people from many other traditions. Even warnings of possible death seem to suggest a scenario that has a high chance of being realized. The night before the Battle of the Little Big Horn, it is said that the colors carried by the 7th Cavalry kept falling over with no apparent breeze causing their collapse.

This supposition must inevitably lead us to an examination of the idea of reincarnation and the modern ideas that we are allowed to choose the circumstances of our next lives. Indians had their own ideas of this topic, and many tribes saw reincarnation as a guarantee that death was not to be feared. Indeed, the various near death experiences that people had suggested another life much better than the present one, giving credence to the idea that there was a happy hunting ground. These complex ideas must wait for another book. What is important here is that the Indian stories of the powers of medicine men, affirmed many times by objective reports of highly skeptical outside observers, are glimpses into a world dominated by spiritual energies and concerns.

It is my hope that Indians will read these stories and know that many powers are available through the ceremonies and rituals of the tribes and that the powers can be applied to our daily lives to enrich our well-being and enhance our understanding of life in the physical world. Unlike other religious traditions, which have an early revelation followed by millenia of critical examination of the premises and substance of the spiritual experience, Indians have access to these spiritual powers here and now. They can be applied in our lives, and, indeed, the validation of these powers must always be in a change in the conditions of the physical world. Indian spiritual powers manifest themselves immediately in healings and prophecies. We would do well to return to those roots.

ENDNOTES

* * * * * * * * * * * * * *

PROLOGUE

[1] Thomas Lewis, *The Medicine Men* (Lincoln: University of Nebraska Press, 1990), 96.

INTRODUCTION

[1] The Omahas and the Blackfeet, among other tribes, described the universe in almost identical terms. See Walter McClintock, *The Old North Trail: Life, Legends, and Religion of the Blackfeet Indian* (Lincoln: University of Nebraska Press, 1968), 167: "The Great Spirit or Great Mystery, or Good Power, is everywhere and in everything—mountains, plains, winds, waters, trees, birds and animals. Whether animals have mind and the reasoning faculty admits of no doubt with the Blackfeet. For they believe that all animals receive their endowment of power from the Sun, differing in degree, but the same in kind as that received by man and all things animate and inanimate." And see Alice Fletcher and Francis La Flesche, *The Omaha Tribe* (Lincoln: University of Nebraska Press, 1968), a reprint from a report from the Smithsonian Institution, Bureau of American Ethnology, no. 27 (Washington, D.C.: Government Printing Office, 1911):

> An invisible and continuous life was believed to permeate all things, seen and unseen. This life manifests itself in two ways: First, by causing to move—all motion, all actions of mind or body are because of this invisible life; second, by causing permanency of structure and form, as in the rock; the physical features

of the landscape, mountains, plains, streams, rivers, lakes, the animals and man. This invisible life was also conceived of as being similar to the will power of which man is conscious within himself—a power by which things are brought to pass. Through this mysterious life and power all things are related to one another, and to man, the seen to be unseen, the dead to the living, a fragment of anything to its entirety. This invisible life and power was called Wakonda.

[2] Frances Densmore, *Teton Sioux Music and Culture* (Lincoln: University of Nebraska Press, 1992), 207–208. Reprint from a report from the Smithsonian Institution, Bureau of American Ethnology, Government Printing Office.

[3] Ibid., 72–73.

[4] John (Fire) Lame Deer and Richard Erdoes, *Lame Deer, Seeker of Visions* (New York: Simon & Schuster, 1972), 162.

[5] Rupert Sheldrake, *The Rebirth of Nature: The Greening of Science and God* (New York: Bantam Books, 1991), 213.

[6] Luther Standing Bear, *Land of the Spotted Eagle* (Boston: Houghton Mifflin, 1933), 192.

[7] Ibid.

[8] Morris Opler, *An Apache Lifeway* (Lincoln: University of Nebraska Press, 1996), 206.

CHAPTER ONE

[1] Densmore, *Teton Sioux Music and Culture*, 266.

[2] Ibid., 177.

[3] Ibid., 178.

[4] John Neihardt, *Black Elk Speaks: Being the Life Story of a Holy Man of the Oglala Sioux* (Lincoln: University of Nebraska Press, 1979), 48–49.

[5] Ibid., 50.

[6] *George Schmidt's Vision Experience*, Boas Collection, American Philosophical Society #30 (x8a.4), 119–120.

[7] Standing Bear, *Land of the Spotted Eagle*, 72–73.

[8] Densmore, *Teton Sioux Music and Culture*, 251.

[9] Edward Goodbird, *Goodbird the Indian* (St. Paul: Minnesota Historical Society Press, 1985), 25–26.

[10] Robert Ruby, *The Oglala Sioux: Warriors in Transition* (New York: Vantage Press, 1955), 52.

[11] Lame Deer and Erdoes, *Lame Deer, Seeker of Visions*, 163.

[12] Lee Irwin, *The Dream Seekers: Native American Visionary Traditions of the Great Plains* (Norman: University of Oklahoma Press, 1994), 160.

[13] Lame Deer and Erdoes, *Lame Deer, Seeker of Visions*, 163.

[14] George Bird Grinnell, *The Cheyenne Indians: Their History and Ways of Life*, vol. 2 (Lincoln: University of Nebraska Press, 1961), 128–129.

[15] James R. Walker, *Lakota Belief and Ritual* (Lincoln: University of Nebraska Press, 1991), 79.

[16] Opler, *An Apache Lifeway*, 202.

[17] Densmore, *Teton Sioux Music and Culture*, 214.

[18] Ibid., 184.

[19] Lame Deer and Erdoes, *Lame Deer, Seeker of Visions*, 183.

[20] Ibid., 65.

[21] Ibid., 128.

[22] Father Paul LeJeune, *The Jesuit Relations and Allied Documents, 1642–1643*, vol. 23, 155, 157, 159.

[23] Frederick Johnson, "Notes on Micmac Shamanism," *Primitive Man*, vol. xvi, nos. 3 and 4, July and October 1943, 63.

[24] Densmore, *Teton Sioux Music and Culture*, 184–185.

[25] Peter Nabokov, *Two Leggings: The Making of a Crow Warrior* (Norman: University of Oklahoma Press, 1967), 146–147.

[26] William Wildschut, *Crow Indian Medicine Bundles*, vol. xvii (New York: Museum of the American Indian, 1960), 44–45.

[27] Elsie Clews Parsons, *North American Indian Life: Customs and Traditions of Twenty-Three Tribes* (New York: Dover Publications, 1992), 51–52.

[28] Francis Parkman, *The Oregon Trail* (Boston: Little, Brown & Co., 1925), 138–139.

[29] Henry R. Schoolcraft, *The Indian Tribes of the United States: Their History, Antiquities, Customs, Religion, Arts, Language, Traditions, Oral Legends, and Myths*, vol. 1, 391–393.

[30] Frank Linderman, *Pretty-Shield: Medicine Woman of the Crows* (Lincoln: University of Nebraska Press: 1972), 166.

[31] James R. Murie, *Ceremonies of the Pawnee*, ed. Douglas Parks, vols. 1 and 11 (Washington, D.C.: Smithsonian Press, 1981), 319.

[32] Ibid., 156.

[33] Ella E. Clark, *Indian Legends from the Northern Rockies* (Norman: University of Oklahoma Press, 1966), 119–121.

[34] James Mooney, *The Ghost-Dance Religion and Wounded Knee* (New York: Dover Publications, 1991), 752. Originally published by the Bureau of American Ethnology, Smithsonian Institution, 14, part ii (Washington, D.C.:

Government Printing Office, 1896).

[35] Goodbird, *Goodbird the Indian*, 28.

CHAPTER TWO

[1] Standing Bear, *Land of the Spotted Eagle*, 52.

[2] Paul Radin, *The Road of Life and Death: A Ritual Drama of the American Indians* (New York: Pantheon, 1945), 3–4.

[3] Leland C. Wyman, "Navajo Diagnosticians," *American Anthropologist*, vol. xxxviii, 1936, 237–238.

[4] Franc Newcomb, "The Navajo Listening Rite," *El Palacio*, vol. xlv, 1938, 46.

[5] Ibid.

[6] Wyman, "Navajo Diagnosticians," 240.

[7] Ibid., 245.

[8] Ibid.

[9] Morris Opler, "Notes on Chiricahua Apache Culture," *Primitive Man*, vol. xx, nos. i and ii, 1947, 9.

[10] Gladys Tantaquidgeon, *Manuscript Field Notes*, 1928.

[11] Ibid.

[12] Grinnell, *The Cheyenne Indians*, 138.

[13] Standing Bear, *Land of the Spotted Eagle*, 207–208.

[14] Captain M. J. Healy, "Black Arts Adept," Humeston, Iowa: *New Era*, 9 September 1896.

[15] Ake Hultkranz, *Shamanic Healing and Ritual Drama: Health and Medicine in Native North American Religious Traditions* (New York: Crossroads Publishing Company, 1992), 35.

[16] Ibid., 92–93.

[17] Raymond J. DeMallie, *The Sixth Grandfather: Black Elk's Teachings Given to John G. Neihardt* (Lincoln: University of Nebraska Press, 1984), 179.

[18] Densmore, *Teton Sioux Music and Culture*, 254.

[19] Francis La Flesche, "Omaha Buffalo Medicine Men," *Journal of American Folklore*, vol. 3, 1890, 216–221.

[20] Hultkranz, *Shamanic Healing and Ritual Drama*, 151.

[21] Ibid., 67.

[22] Charles Lummis, *Some Strange Corners of Our Country: The Wonderland of the Southwest* (Tucson: University of Arizon Press, 1989), 79.

[23] George Bird Grinnell, *Pawnee Hero Stories and Folk-Tales: With Notes on the Origins, Customs, and Character of the Pawnee People* (Lincoln: University of Nebraska Press, 1961), 378–379.

[24] Ibid., 379.

25 Grinnell, *The Cheyenne Indians*, 126–127.

26 John Stands in Timber and Margot Liberty, *Cheyenne Memories* (Lincoln: University of Nebraska Press, 1972), 112.

27 Robert H. Lowie, *The Assiniboines*, Anthropological Papers of the American Museum of Natural History, vol. iv, part i (Washington, D.C.: Government Printing Office, 1909), 44–45.

28 Densmore, *Teton Sioux Music and Culture*, 210.

29 Ibid., 235.

30 Ibid.

31 Ibid., 238.

32 Ibid., 218.

33 Stands in Timber and Liberty, *Cheyenne Memories*, 104.

34 June Collins, "John Fornsby: The Personal Document of a Salish Coast Indian," in *Indians of the Urban Northwest*, ed. Marian W. Smith (New York: Columbia University Press, 1949), 328–329.

35 Frances Densmore, "Songs for the Treatment of Sick in British Columbia," Anthropological Papers, nos. 27–32, Smithsonian Institution, Bureau of American Ethnology (Washington, D.C.: Government Printing Office, 1943), 19.

36 John R. Swanton, *Source Material for Social and Ceremonial Life of the Choctaws*, Anthropological Papers, no. 103, Smithsonian Institution, Bureau of American Ethnology (Washington, D.C.: Government Printing Office, 1931), 229.

37 William H. Keating, *Narrative of an Expedition to the Source of St. Peter's River* (Minneapolis: Ross and Haines, 1959), 424.

38 Jonathon Carver, *Travels through the Interior Parts of North America in the Years 1766, 1767, and 1768* (Minneapolis: Ross and Haines, Inc., 1956), 126–129.

39 John Mason Brown, "Indian Medicine," *Atlantic Monthly*, vol. 18, issue 105, July 1886, 117–118.

CHAPTER THREE

1 William K. Powers, *Sacred Language* (Norman: University of Oklahoma Press, 1983), 96.

2 Ibid., 102.

3 Gideon H. Pond, *Dakota Superstitions* (St. Paul: Collections of the Minnesota Historical Society, 1867), 56–57.

4 Stephen E. Feraca, *Wakinyan: Contemporary Teton Dakota Religion (Studies in Plains Anthropology and History)*, (Browning, Mont.: Museum of the Plains

Indian, 1963), 36.

5 Father Paul LeJeune, *The Jesuit Relations, 1643*. See also Vincent H. Gaddis, *American Indian Myths and Mysteries* (New York: Dorset Press, 1988), and Richard Stanton Lambert, *Exploring the Supernatural: The Ghosts in Canadian Folklore* (Toronto: McClelland and Steward, Ltd., 1955).

6 Andrew J. Blackbird, *History of the Ottawa and Chippewa Indians of Michigan* (Ypsilanti, Mich.: Ypsilanti Job Printing, 1887), 83.

7 Schoolcraft, *The Indian Tribes of the United States*, 389.

8 Paul Kane, *Wanderings of an Artist among the Indians of North America* (Edmonton: Hurtig Publishers, 1968), 311.

9 Regina Flannery, "The Gros Ventre Shaking Tent," *Primitive Man*, vol. xvii, nos. 3 and 4, July and October 1944, 56.

10 A. Irving Hallowell, *The Role of Conjuring in Saulteaux Society* (New York: Octagon Books, 1971), 80–81. Originally published by the Philadelphia Anthropological Society, vol. ii.

11 Schoolcraft, *The Indian Tribes of the United States*, 390.

12 James W. Schultz, *My Life as an Indian* (New York: Duell Sloan & Pearce, 1935), 102.

13 Gaddis, *American Indian Myths and Mysteries*, 132–133. See also Francis Dickie, "Mystery of the Shaking Tents" in *Real West*, vol. 37, September 18–19, 1964.

14 Stephan Schwartz, *The Secret Vaults of Time: Pyschic Archaeology and the Quest for Man's Beginning* (Charlottesville, Va.: Hampton Roads Publishing Company, Inc., 2005), 207.

15 J. G. Kohl, *Kitchi-Gami, Wanderings Round Lake Superior* (Minneapolis: Ross and Haines, Inc., 1956), 35–36.

16 Hallowell *The Role of Conjuring in Saulteaux Society*, 74.

17 Ibid., 78.

18 John R. Swanton, *Religious Beliefs and Medical Practices of the Creek Indians*, Smithsonian Institution, Bureau of American Ethnology, no. 42 (Washington, D.C.: Government Printing Office, 1924–1925), 616.

19 Father Peter Powell kindly read an early draft of the manuscript and corrected my most glaring errors of research and interpretation. Any errors with regard to the interpretation of the Cheyenne ceremonies are due to extensive reordering of the manuscript just prior to publication.

20 Grinnell, *The Cheyenne Indians*, 113–114.

21 Sister Bernard Coleman, *Ojibwa Myths and Legends* (Minneapolis: Ross and Haines, 1962), Inc., 108–109.

22 Donald Collier, "Conjuring among the Kiowas," *Primitive Man*, vol. xvii, nos. 3 and 4, July and October, 1944, 46–47.

CHAPTER FOUR

[1] Karl L. Schlesier, *The Wolves of Heaven: Cheyenne Shamanism, Ceremonies, and Prehistoric Origins* (Norman: University of Oklahoma Press, 1993), 12.

[2] Luther Standing Bear, *My Indian Boyhood* (Lincoln: University of Nebraska Press, 1959), 70.

[3] Melvin R. Gilmore, *Prairie Smoke* (New York: Columbia University Press, 1929), 161.

[4] Charles Eastman, *Indian Boyhood* (New York: Dover Publications, 1971), 7.

[5] Luther Standing Bear, *My People, the Sioux* (Lincoln: University of Nebraska Press, 1975), 39.

[6] Lame Deer and Erdoes, *Lame Deer, Seeker of Visions*, 135.

[7] Opler, *An Apache Lifeway*, 250.

[8] Neihardt, *Black Elk Speaks*, 151.

[9] Carl Gustav Jung, *The Visions Seminar* (Princeton, N.J.: Princeton University Press, 1997), 3.

[10] Ian Wilson, *The After Death Experience: The Physics of the Non-Physical* (New York: William Morrow & Co., 1989), 186.

[11] Stanley Vestal, *Warpath C: The Full Story of the Fighting Sioux Told in a Biography of Chief White Bull* (Lincoln: University of Nebraska Press, 1984), 109–110.

[12] Grinnell, *The Cheyenne Indians*, 106.

[13] Stanley Vestal, *Jim Bridger, Mountain Man* (Lincoln: University of Nebraska Press, 1972), 237–238.

[14] Brown, "Indian Medicine," 119.

[15] Grinnell, *The Cheyenne Indians*, 106.

[16] Standing Bear, *My Indian Boyhood*, 56–57.

[17] James W. Schultz, *Blackfeet and Buffalo: Memories of Life among the Indians* (Norman: University of Oklahoma Press, 1962), 89.

[18] Charles Cooper, *The Gros Ventres of Montana: Part II, Religion and Ritual* (Washington, D.C.: The Catholic University of America Press, 1957), 415.

[19] Schultz, *Blackfeet and Buffalo*, 317.

[20] Schultz, *My Life as an Indian*, 18–19.

[21] Ibid., 50–51.

CHAPTER FIVE

[1] John C. Cremony, *Life among the Apaches* (Lincoln: University of Nebraska Press, 1983), 296.

[2] Grinnell, *Pawnee Hero Stories and Folk-Tales*, 379–380.

[3] Ibid., 380–381.

[4] Ibid., 382–383.

[5] Robert H. Lowie, *The Religion of the Crow Indians* (New York: Hold, Rinehart & Winston, 1956), 351.

[6] Lummis, *Some Strange Corners of Our Country*, 89.

[7] Ibid., 85.

[8] William E. Curtis, "Indian Jugglers," Boise, Idaho: *Boise Daily Statesman*, 10 August 1899.

[9] "Extraordinary Feat of Zuni Priests," *The New York Times*, 1 December 1922.

[10] Opler, *An Apache Lifeway*, 216.

[11] Herbert Lehmann, *Nine Years among the Indians, 1870–1879: The Story of the Captivity and Life of a Texan among the Indians*, ed. J. Marvin Hunter (Albuquerque: University of New Mexico Press, 1933), 81.

[12] Swanton, *Religious Beliefs and Medical Practices of the Creek Indians*, 616.

[13] Ibid.

[14] Wooden Leg, *Wooden Leg*, trans. Thomas B. Marquis (Lincoln: University of Nebraska Press, 1972), 146–147.

[15] Standing Bear, *Land of the Spotted Eagle*, 207.

[16] McClintock, *The Old North Trail*, 320–321.

[17] Ernest Wallace and E. Adamson Hoebel, *The Comanches: Lords of the South Plains* (Lincoln: University of Nebraska Press, 1987), 172.

[18] George Bird Grinnell, *Blackfoot Lodge Tales: The Story of a Prairie People* (Lincoln: University of Nebraska Press, 1962), 260.

[19] John Cooper, "The Shaking Tent Rite among Plains and Forest Algonquians," *Primitive Man*, vol. xxvii, 1944.

[20] Opler, *An Apache Lifeway*, 216.

[21] Frances Densmore, *Chippewa Customs* (St. Paul: Minnesota Historical Society Press, 1979), 81. Originally published as Anthropological Papers, no. 86, Smithsonian Institution, Bureau of American Ethnology (Washington, D.C.: 1929).

[22] Vestal, *Warpath C*, 15.

CHAPTER SIX

[1] DeMallie, *The Sixth Grandfather*, 376.

[2] Ibid., 198.

[3] A. McG. Beede, *Western Sioux Cosmology* (Bismarck: North Dakota State Historical Society, 1919), 13.

[4] Clark, *Indian Legends from the Northern Rockies*, 273–275.

[5] Lame Deer and Erdoes, *Lame Deer, Seeker of Visions*, 194–195.

[6] Standing Bear, *Land of the Spotted Eagle*, 208.

[7] Grinnell, *Blackfoot Lodge Tales*, 125.

[8] Robert H. Lowie, *The Crow Indians* (New York: Hold, Rinehart & Winston, 1956), 261–262.

[9] Nabokov, *Two Leggings*, 27.

[10] Densmore, *Teton Sioux Music and Culture*, 247.

[11] Museum of the American Indian, *Indian Notes*, vol. iv, no. ii, April 1927, 152–153.

[12] Densmore, *Teton Sioux Music and Culture*, 210.

[13] Ibid., 229.

[14] Wallace and Hoebel, *The Comanches*, 204–205.

[15] Jean N. Nicolet, "A Map of the Hydrographical Basis of the Upper Mississippi," 15. *Senate Journal* 237, 26th Cong., 2nd sess., 16 February, 184.

[16] Emory M. Strong, *Stone Age on the Columbia River* (Portland, Ore.: Binford and Mort, 1982), 22–23.

[17] Densmore, *Teton Sioux Music and Culture*, 93.

CHAPTER SEVEN

[1] Thomas Morton, *New English Canaan; or New Canaan, Containing an Abstract of New England, 1632*, reprint (New York: Thomas Smith, 1947), 25–26.

[2] William Wood, *New England's Prospect (1634)*, reprint (Amherst: University of Massachusetts Press, 1977), 61.

[3] Stands in Timber and Liberty, *Cheyenne Memories*, 104–105.

[4] Grinnell, *The Cheyenne Indians*, 116–117.

[5] Frederick Starr, *American Indians* (New York: D. C. Heath & Co., 1898), 84.

[6] LeJeune, *The Jesuit Relations, 1641–1642*, 163–167.

[7] Ibid., 151, 153.

[8] Curtis, "Indian Jugglers."

[9] Ibid.

[10] Wallace and Hoebel, *The Comanches*, 161–162.

[11] Densmore, *Teton Sioux Music and Culture*, 175.

[12] Grinnell, *Pawnee Hero Stories and Folk-Tales*, 377.

[13] Opler, *An Apache Lifeway*, 310–311.

[14] Stands in Timber and Liberty, *Cheyenne Memories*, 104.

[15] Thomas B. Marquis, *Cheyenne and Sioux: The Reminiscences of Four Indians and a White Soldier* (Honolulu: Pacific Center for Western Historical Studies, 1973), 34.

[16] Swanton, *Source Material for Social and Ceremonial Life of the Choctaws*, 228–229.

[17] Grinnell, *Pawnee Hero Stories and Folk-Tales*, 383–384.

[18] D. D. Mitchell, "Extraordinary Indian Feats of Legerdemain," *Southern Literary Messenger*, vol. 1, no. 12, August 1835, 657–658.

[19] David Rodnick, "An Assiniboine Horse-Raiding Expedition," *American Anthropologist*, vol. 41, 613.

[20] Grinnell, *Blackfoot Lodge Tales*, 261.

[21] Curtis, "Indian Jugglers."

[22] Schlesier, *The Wolves of Heaven*, 61.

[23] Swanton, *Religious Beliefs and Medical Practices of the Creek Indians*, 627.

[24] Opler, *An Apache Lifeway*, 215.

[25] Frances Densmore, *Chippewa Music*, Smithsonian Institution, Bureau of American Ethnology (Washington, D.C.: Government Printing Office, 1910) 45.

[26] Ibid., 144.

[27] Peter John Powell, *People of the Sacred Mountains: A History of the Northern Cheyenne Chiefs and Warrior Societies, 1830–1879* (San Francisco: Harper & Row, 1979), 20.

[28] Lowie, *The Crow Indians*, 238–239.

[29] Ibid., 239.

[30] Nabokov, *Two Leggings*, 97.

[31] Frank Speck, "Catawba Religious Beliefs, Mortuary Customs and Dances," *Primitive Man*, vol. xxii, no. ii, April 1939, 35.

CHAPTER EIGHT

[1] Fred Alan Wolf, *The Dreaming Universe: A Mind-Expanding Journey into the Realm Where Psyche and Physics Meet* (New York: Simon & Schuster, 1994), 206.

[2] David Foster, *The Philosophical Scientists* (New York: Dorest Press, 1985), 169.

[3] F. David Peat, *Synchronicity: The Bridge Between Matter and Mind* (New York: Bantam Books, 1987), 196.

[4] Werner Heisenberg, *Across the Frontiers* (New York: Harper & Row, 1974), 116.

[5] Carl Gustav Jung, *Civilization in Transition* (Princeton, N.J.: Princeton University Press, 1975), 69.

[6] Filippo Liverziani, *Life, Death and Consciousness: Experiences Near and After Death* (England: Prism Press, 1991), 151.

[7] Jeffrey Iverson, *In Search of the Dead: A Scientific Investigation of Evidence for Life after Death* (San Francisco: HarperCollins, 1992), ix.

[8] John R. Swanton, "Tokuli of Tulsa, in Parsons," *American Indian Life*, ed. Elsie Clews (Lincoln: University of Nebraska Press, 1922), 142.

[9] Fletcher and La Flesche, *The Omaha Tribe*, 134.

[10] Beede, *Western Sioux Cosmology*, 2.

[11] Frank Waters, *Book of the Hopi: The First Revelation of the Hopi's Historical and*

Religious Worldview of Life (New York: Viking Press, 1963), 3.

[12] Irwin, *The Dream Seekers*, 70.

[13] John R. Swanton, *Social Organization and Social Usages of the Indians of the Creek Confederacy*, Smithsonian Institution, Bureau of American Ethnology (Washington, D.C.: Government Printing Office: 1928), 489.

[14] Swanton, "Tokuli of Tulsa, in Parsons," 143

[15] Neihardt, *Black Elk Speaks*, 85.

[16] DeMallie, *The Sixth Grandfather*, 215.

[17] Lummis, *Some Strange Corners of Our Country*, 86.

[18] Ibid., 80, 83.

[19] William K. Powers, *Vision and Experience in Oglala Ritual* (Lincoln: University of Nebraska Press, 1984), 29.

[20] Opler, *An Apache Lifeway*, 216.

[21] Densmore, *Teton Sioux Music and Culture*, 175.

[22] Neihardt, *Black Elk Speaks*, 39.

[23] Frank B. Linderman, *Plenty-Coups: Chief of the Crows* (New York: John Day, 1930), 65.

[24] Opler, *An Apache Lifeway*, 219.

[25] Nabokov, *Two Leggings*, 102

[26] Lowie, *The Religion of the Crow Indians*, 339.

[27] Opler, *An Apache Lifeway*, 301.

[28] Frances Densmore, *Music in its Relation to the Religious Thought of the Teton Sioux*, Smithsonian Institution, Bureau of American Ethnology (Washington, D.C.: Government Printing Office, 1916), 71.

BIBLIOGRAPHY

* * * * * * * * * * * * *

Amiotte, Arthur. "Our Other Selves," in *I Become a Part of It*. New York: Parabola Books, 1989.

Austin, Mary. "Can Prayers Be Answered?" New York, 1934, quoted in "Notes on the Indians' Belief in the Friendliness of Nature," Frances Densmore, *Southwestern Journal of Anthropology*, vol. 4, no. 3, Spring 1948.

Beede, A. McG. *Western Sioux Cosmology*. Bismarck: North Dakota State Historical Society, 1919.

Black, A. K. "Shaking the Wigwam." *The Beaver*, December 1934.

Blackbird, Andrew J. *History of the Ottawa and Chippewa Indians of Michigan*. Ypsilanti, Michigan: Ypsilanti Job Printing, 1887.

Brown, John Mason. "Indian Medicine." *Atlantic Monthly*, vol. 18, issue 105, July 1886.

Carver, Jonathon. *Travels through the Interior Parts of North America in the Years 1766, 1767, and 1768*. Minneapolis: Ross and Haines, 1956.

Clark, Ella E. *Indian Legends from the Northern Rockies*. Norman: University of Oklahoma Press, 1966.

————. *Indian Legends of the Pacific Northwest.* Berkeley: University of California Press, 1953.

Coleman, Sister Bernard. *Ojibwa Myths and Legends.* Minneapolis: Ross and Haines, Inc., 1962.

Collier, Donald. "Conjuring among the Kiowas," *Primitive Man.* vol. xvii, nos. 3 and 4, July and October 1944.

Collins, June. "John Fornsby: The Personal Document of a Salish Coast Indian," in *Indians of the Urban Northwest*, ed. Marian W. Smith. New York: Columbia University Press, 1949.

Cooper, Charles. *The Gros Ventres of Montana: Part II, Religion and Ritual.* Washington, D.C.: The Catholic University of America Press, 1957.

Cooper, John. "The Shaking Tent Rite among Plains and Forest Algonquians," *Primitive Man*, vol. xxvii, July and October 1944.

Cremony, John C. *Life among the Apaches.* Lincoln: University of Nebraska Press, 1983.

Curtis, Edward. *The North American Indian*, vol. 5. Cambridge: The University Press, 1930.

Curtis, William E. "Indian Jugglers." Boise, Idaho: *Boise Daily Statesman*, 10 August 1899.

Cusick, David. *The Iroquois Trail.* Fayetteville, N.Y.: H. C. Beauchamp, 1892.

Deloria, Ella. *Standing Bull's Vision.* American Philosophical Society Library, x 8a.4(.2)

DeMallie, Raymond. *The Sixth Grandfather: Black Elk's Teachings Given to John G. Neihardt.* Lincoln: University of Nebraska Press, 1984.

Densmore, Frances. Anthropological Papers, no. 19, Smithsonian Institution, Bureau of American Ethnology. Washington, D.C.: Government Printing Office, 1929.

———. "Songs for the Treatment of Sick in British Columbia." Anthropological Papers, nos. 27–32. Smithsonian Institution, Bureau of American Ethnology. Washington, D.C.: Government Printing Office, 1943.

———. *Chippewa Customs*. St. Paul: Minnesota Historical Society Press, 1979, 81. Originally published as Anthropological Papers, no. 86, Smithsonian Institution, Bureau of American Ethnology. Washington, D.C.: 1929.

———. *Chippewa Music*. Smithsonian Institution, Bureau of American Ethnology. Washington, D.C.: Government Printing Office, 1910.

———. *Music in its Relation to the Religious Thought of the Teton*. Smithsonian Institution, Bureau of American Ethnology. Washington, D.C.: Government Printing Office, 1916.

———. "Notes on the Indians' Belief in the Friendliness of Nature." *Southwestern Journal of Anthropology*, vol. 4, no. 3, Spring 1948.

———. *Teton Sioux Music and Culture*. Lincoln: University of Nebraska Press, 1992. Reprint from a report from the Smithsonian Institution, Bureau of American Ethnology, no. 61. Washington D. C.: Government Printing Office, 1918.

Dickie, Francis. "Mystery of the Shaking Tents," *Real West*, vol. 37, September 18–19 1964.

Eastman, Charles. *Indian Boyhood*. New York: Dover Publications, 1971.

"Extraordinary Feat of Zuni Priests." *New York Times*, 1 December 1901, SM5.

Feraca, Stephen. *Wakinyan*. Browning, Mont.: Museum of the Plains Indian, 1963.

Flannery, Regina. "The Gros Ventre Shaking Tent." *Primitive Man*, vol. xvii, July and October, nos. 3 and 4, 1944.

Fletcher, Alice and Francis La Flesche. *The Omaha Tribe*. Lincoln: University of Nebraska Press, 1968. Reprint from a report from the Smithsonian Institution, Bureau of American Ethnology, no. 27, Annual Report Reprint. Washington, D. C.: Government Printing Office, 1911.

Fortune, R. F. *Omaha Secret Societies*. New York: Columbia University Press, 1932.

Foster, David. *The Philosophical Scientists*. New York: Dorest Press, 1985.

Gaddis, Vincent H. *American Indian Myths and Mysteries*. New York: Dorset Press, 1988.

Gilmore, Melvin R. *Prairie Smoke*. New York: Columbia University Press, 1929.

Goodbird, Edward. *Goodbird the Indian*. St. Paul: Minnesota Historical Society Press, 1985.

Grinnell, George Bird. *Blackfoot Lodge Tales: The Story of a Prairie People*. Lincoln: University of Nebraska Press, 1962.

———. *The Cheyenne Indians: Their History and Ways of Life*, vol. 2. Lincoln: University of Nebraska Press, 1961.

———. *Pawnee Hero Stories and Folk-Tales: With Notes on the Origins, Customs, and Character of the Pawnee People*. Lincoln: University of Nebraska Press, 1961.

Healy, Captain M. J. "Black Arts Adept." Humeston, Iowa: *New Era*. 9 September 1896.

Heisenberg, Werner. *Across the Frontiers*. New York: Harper & Row, 1974.

Hallowell, A. Irving. *The Role of Conjuring in Saulteaux Society*. New York: Octagon Books, 1971. Originally published by the Philadelphia Anthropological Society, vol. ii.

Hultkranz, Ake. *Shamanic Healing and Ritual Drama: Health and Medicine in Native North American Religious Traditions*. New York: Crossroads Publishing Company, 1992.

Iverson, Jeffrey. *In Search of the Dead: A Scientific Investigation of Evidence for Life after Death*. San Francisco: Harper Collins, 1992.

Irwin, Lee. *The Dream Seekers: Native American Visionary Traditions of the Great Plains*. Norman: University of Oklahoma Press, 1994.

Johnson, Frederick. "Notes on Micmac Shamanism." *Primitive Man*, vol. xvi, nos. 3 and 4, July and October 1943.

Jones, David. *Sanapia, Comanche Medicine Woman*. Prospect Heights, Ill.: Waveland Press, 1984.

Jung, Carl Gustav. *Civilization in Transition*, Princeton: Princeton University Press, 1975.

———. *The Visions Seminar*. Princeton: Princeton University Press, 1997.

Kane, Paul. *Wanderings of an Artist among the Indians of North America*. Edmonton: Hurtig Publishers, 1968.

Keating, William H. *Narrative of an Expedition to the Source of St. Peter's River*. Minneapolis: Ross and Haines, Inc., 1959.

Kendall, Edward Augustus. *Travels through the Northern Parts of the United States in the Years 1807 and 1808*. New York: L. Riley, 1809.

Kohl, J. G. *Kitchi-Gami, Wanderings Round Lake Superior*. Minneapolis: Ross and Haines, Inc., 1956.

La Flesche, Frances. "Omaha Buffalo Medicine Men." *Journal of American Folklore*, vol. 3, 1890.

Lambert, Richard Stanton. *Exploring the Supernatural: The Ghosts in Canadian Folklore*. Toronto: McClelland and Stewart, Ltd., 1955.

Lame Deer, John (Fire) and Richard Erdoes. *Lame Deer, Seeker of Visions*. New York: Simon & Schuster, 1972.

Lehmann, Herbert. *Nine Years among the Indians, 1870–1879: The Story of the Captivity and Life of a Texan among the Indians*, ed. J. Marvin Hunter. Albuquerque: University of New Mexico Press, 1933.

LeJeune, Father Paul. *The Jesuit Relations and Allied Documents, 1642–1643*, vol. 23.

Lewis, Thomas. *The Medicine Men*. Lincoln: University of Nebraska Press, 1990.

Linderman, Frank. *Plenty Coups*. New York: John Day, 1930.

————. *Pretty-Shield: Medicine Woman of the Crows*. Lincoln: University of Nebraska, 1972.

Liverziani, Filippo. *Life, Death and Consciousness: Experiences Near and After Death*. England: Prism Press, 1991.

Lowie, Robert H. *The Assiniboines*. Anthropological Papers of the American Museum of Natural History, vol. iv, part i. Washington, D.C.: Government Printing Office, 1909.

————. *The Crow Indians*. New York: Hold, Rinehart & Winston, 1956.

————. *The Religion of the Crow Indians*. New York: Holt, Rinehart & Winston, 1956.

Lummis, Charles. *Some Strange Corners of Our Country: The Wonderland of the Southwest*. Tucson: University of Arizona Press, 1989.

Marquis, Thomas B. *Cheyenne and Sioux: The Reminiscences of Four Indians and a White Soldier*. Honolulu: Pacific Center for Western Historical Studies, 1973.

McClintock, Walter. *The Old North Trail: Life, Legends, and Religion of the Blackfeet Indian*. Lincoln: University of Nebraska Press, 1968.

McFarling, Lloyd. *Exploring the Northern Plains, 1804–1976*. Caxton, Idaho: The Caxton Printers, 1955.

Mitchell, D. D. "Extraordinary Indian Feats of Legerdemain." *Southern Literary Messenger*, vol. 1, no. 12, August 1835.

Mooney, James. *The Ghost-Dance Religion and Wounded Knee*. New York: Dover Publications, 1991. Originally published by the Bureau of American Ethnology 14, part ii. Washington, D.C.: Government Printing Office, 1896.

Morton, Thomas. *New English Canaan; or New Canaan, Containing an Abstract of New England, 1632*, reprint. New York: Thomas Smith, 1947.

Murie, James R. *Ceremonies of the Pawnee*, ed. Douglas Parks, vols. i and ii. Washington, D.C.: Smithsonian Press, 1981.

Museum of the American Indian. *Indian Notes*, vol. iv, no. ii, April 1927, 152–153.

Nabokov, Peter. *Two Leggings: The Making of a Crow Warrior*. Norman: University of Oklahoma Press, 1967.

Native American Theological Association, Black Hills III. Redwood Falls, Minn: Prescott Printing Services, 1981.

Neihardt, John. *Black Elk Speaks*. Lincoln: University of Nebraska Press, 1979.

Newcomb, Franc J. "The Navajo Listening Rite." *El Palacio*, vol. xlv, 1938.

Nicolet, Jean N. "A Map of the Hydrographical Basis of the Upper Mississippi," 15. *Senate Journal* 237, 26th Cong., 2nd sess., 16 February.

Olden, Sarah. *The People of Tipi Sapa*. Milwaukee: Morehouse Publishing, 1918.

Opler, Morris. *An Apache Lifeway*. Lincoln: University of Nebraska Press, 1996.

———. "Notes on Chiricahua Apache Culture." *Primitive Man*, vol. xx, nos. i and ii, 1947.

Parkman, Francis. *The Oregon Trail*. Boston: Little, Brown & Co., 1925.

Parsons, Elsie Clews. *North American Indian Life: Customs and Traditions of Twenty-Three Tribes*. New York: Dover Publications, 1992.

Peat, F. David. *Synchronicity: The Bridge between Matter and Mind*. New York: Bantam Books, 1987.

Pond, Gideon H. *Dakota Superstitions*. St. Paul: Collections of the Minnesota Historical Society, 1867.

Powell, Peter John. *People of the Sacred Mountains: History of the Northern Cheyenne Chiefs and Warrior Societies, 1830–1879*. San Francisco: Harper & Row, 1979.

Powers, William K. *Sacred Language*. Norman: University of Oklahoma Press, 1983.

———. *Yuwipi: Vision and Experience in Oglala Ritual*. Lincoln: University of Nebraska Press, 1984.

Radin, Paul. "The Reincarnations of Thunder Cloud, a Winnebago Indian." *American Indian Rebirth*, eds. Antonia Mills and Richard Slobodin. Toronto: University of Toronto Press, 1994.

———. *The Road of Life and Death: A Ritual Drama of the American Indians*. New York: Pantheon, 1945.

Riggs, S. J. *Dakota Grammar and Ethnology*. Washington, D.C.: Department of the Interior, 1893.

Rodnick, David. "An Assiniboine Horse-Raiding Expedition." *American Anthropologist*, vol. xli.

Ruby, Robert. *The Oglala Sioux: Warriors in Transition*. New York: Vantage Press, 1955.

Schleiser, Karl L. *The Wolves of Heaven: Cheyenne Shamanism, Ceremonies, and Prehistoric Origins*. Norman: University of Oklahoma Press, 1993.

Schoolcraft, Henry R. *The Indian Tribes of the United States: Their History, Antiquities, Customs, Religion, Arts, Language, Traditions, Oral Legends, and Myths*, vol. 1, 391–393.

Schultz, James W. *Blackfeet and Buffalo: Memories of Life among the Indians*. Norman: University of Oklahoma Press, 1962.

———. *My Life as an Indian*. New York: Duell Sloan and Pearce, 1935.

Schwartz, Stephan. *The Secret Vaults of Time: Pyschic Archaeology and the Quest for Man's Beginning*. Charlottesville, Va.: Hampton Roads Publishing Company, Inc., 2005.

Scott, William Berryman. *Some Memories of a Paleontologist*. New York: Arno Press, 1980.

Sheldrake, Rupert. *The Rebirth of Nature: The Greening of Science and God*. New York: Bantam Books, 1991.

Simmons, Leo W. *Sun Chief*. New Haven: Yale University Press, 1942.

Simmons, William S. *Spirit of New England Tribes*. Hanover: University Press of New England, 1986.

Speck, Frank. "Catawba Religious Beliefs, Mortuary Customs and Dances." *Primitive Man*, vol. xii, no. ii, April 1939.

Standing Bear, Luther. *Land of the Spotted Eagle*. Boston: Houghton Mifflin, 1933.

———. *My Indian Boyhood*. Lincoln: University of Nebraska Press, 1959.

———. *My People, the Sioux*. Lincoln: University of Nebraska Press, 1975.

Stands in Timber, John and Margot Liberty. *Cheyenne Memories*. Lincoln: University of Nebraska Press, 1972.

Starr, Frederick. *American Indians*. New York: D. C. Heath & Co., 1898.

Strong, Emory. *Stone Age on the Columbia River*. Portland, Ore.: Binford & Mort, 1982.

Swanton, John R. *Religious Beliefs and Medical Practices of the Creek Indians*. Smithsonian Institution, Bureau of American Ethnology, no. 42. Washington, D.C.: Government Printing Office, 1924–1925.

———. *Social Organization and Social Usages of the Indians of the Creek Confederacy*. Smithsonian Institution, Bureau of American Ethnology. Washington, D.C.: Government Printing Office: 1928.

———. *Source Material for Social and Ceremonial Life of the Choctaws*. Anthropological Papers, no. 103. Smithsonian Institution, Bureau of American Ethnology. Washington, D.C.: Government Printing Office, 1931.

————. "Tokuli of Tulsa, in Parsons," *American Indian Life*, ed. Elsie Clews. Lincoln: University of Nebraska Press, 1922.

Tantaquidgeon, Gladys. *Manuscript Field Notes*, 1928.

Vestal, Stanley. *Jim Bridger, Mountain Man*. Lincoln: University of Nebraska Press, 1972.

————. *Warpath C: The Full Story of the Fighting Sioux Told in a Biography of Chief White Bull*. Lincoln: University of Nebraska Press, 1984.

Walker, James R. *Lakota Belief and Ritual*. Lincoln: University of Nebraska Press, 1991.

Wallace, Ernest and E. Adamson Hoebel. *The Comanches: Lords of the South Plains*. Norman: University of Oklahoma Press, 1987.

Wallis, W. L. *The Canadian Dakota*. Anthropological Papers of the American Museum of Natural History, vol. 41,1. Washington, D.C.: Government Printing Office, 1947.

Waters, Frank. *Book of the Hopi: The First Revelation of the Hopi's Historical and Religious Worldview of Life*. New York: Viking Press, 1963.

Wildschut, William. *Crow Indian Medicine Bundles*, vol. xvii. New York: Museum of the American Indian, 1960.

Wilson, Ian. *The After Death Experience: Physics of the Non-Physical*. New York: William Morrow & Co., 1987.

Woiche, Istel, Annikadel. *The History of the Universe*, rec. and ed. C. H. Meriam. Tucson: University of Arizona Press, 1992.

Wolf, Fred Alan. *The Dreaming Universe: A Mind-Expanding Journey into the Realm Where Psyche and Physics Meet*. New York: Simon & Schuster, 1994.

Wood, William. *New England's Prospect (1634)*, reprint. Amherst: University of Massachusetts Press, 1977.

Wooden Leg. *Wooden Leg*, trans. Thomas B. Marquis. Lincoln: University of Nebraska Press, 1972.

Wyman, Leland C. "Navajo Diagnosticians." *American Anthropologist*, vol. xxxviii, 1936.

More Books by Vine Deloria Jr.

* * * * * * * * * * * * * * * * *

God Is Red
A Native View of Religion
30TH ANNIVERSARY EDITION
Vine Deloria Jr.
New forewords by
Leslie Marmon Silko
and George E. Tinker
6 x 9 • 344 pages • PB $21.95
ISBN 1-55591-498-5

In a special thirtieth-anniversary edition that celebrates three decades of publication, the classic bestseller reminds us to learn "that we are a part of nature, not a transcendent species with no responsibilities to the natural world."

"As accurate and prophetic as it was thirty years ago ... "
—from the new foreword by Leslie Marmon Silko, author of Ceremony

Evolution, Creationism, and Other Modern Myths
A Critical Inquiry
Vine Deloria Jr.
6¼ x 9¼ • 320 pages • HC $24.95
6 x 9 • 320 pages • PB $18.95
ISBN 1-55591-159-5 (HC)
ISBN 1-55591-458-6 (PB)

Deloria takes Western science and religion to task in this witty and erudite assault on the current state of evolutionary theory, science, and religion. Incorporating non-Western and Native American ideas, Deloria provides us with a framework to better understand our beginnings.

"Certain to be controversial, likely to outrage the faithful of both camps, and a stunning good read."
—BookList

Red Earth, White Lies
Native Americans and
the Myth of Scientific Fact
Vine Deloria Jr.
6 x 9 • 288 pages • PB $18.95
ISBN 1-55591-388-1

Claiming that science has created a largely fictional scenario for American Indians in prehistoric North America, Deloria offers an alternative view of the continent's history.

"Vine Deloria at his very best— challenging, taunting, acerbic— and powerful."
—Alvin M. Josephy Jr., author of Now That the Buffalo's Gone